Praise for *The*

W9-BRF-677

"Fascinating and delightful."   —*The Times Literary Supplement* (UK)

"Copies should be made available at every border crossing. . . . A fascinating, even valuable book, full of surprises."   —*Daily Mail* (UK)

"A lively and informative description of the country's cultural habits and social codes. First-time travelers to France will find useful tips, and for most North Americans this is a good introduction to the long history and complex culture of the country."

—*The Globe and Mail* (Canada)

"A riveting study . . . French conversation can be terrifying, and now I know why."   —*Irish Independent*

"Engaging and often funny, filled with examples drawn from the authors' experiences, this is a guide to the most essential of French arts: conversation."

—Ann Mah, author of *Mastering the Art of French Eating*

"Whether 'bonjour' is the beginning or the end of your French vocabulary, you'll find something fascinating, surprising, or just plain *fou* on nearly every page. Before reading this invaluable codebook to French language and culture, I feared that I'd somehow insulted every French waiter, shopkeeper, and clerk between Paris and Nice. Now I *know* I did, but at least I know why!"

—William Alexander, author of *Flirting with French*

"You will find yourself devouring this book and shouting ah!"

—*Montreal Review of Books*

"A highly entertaining look at France and the French as they are now . . . fundamentally a guide to human behavior—ours as well as theirs."

—*The Tuam Herald* (Ireland)

"I love this book!"   —Michael Patrick Shiels, *Michigan's Big Show*

"Very funny."   —*Rudy Maxa's World with the Careys*

"This book confirms what the English have suspected for many years, that French is not so much a language as a dance, a ritual, a code to be cracked. *The Bonjour Effect* cracks it."   —David Boyle

"If you follow Barlow and Nadeau's formulas for conversation . . . you will come away from your trip with a very positive feeling f' the French language culture."   —*4-T*

"No matter your level of proficiency with the French la' will read, and enjoy, and be reminded of why you wil' immediately to the City of Light."   —thesimp'

Also by Julie Barlow and Jean-Benoît Nadeau

Sixty Million Frenchmen Can't Be Wrong

The Story of French

The Story of Spanish

The Bonjour Effect

The Secret Codes
of French Conversation Revealed

Julie Barlow and
Jean-Benoît Nadeau

ST. MARTIN'S GRIFFIN
New York

www.stmartins.com

THE LIBRARY OF CONGRESS HAS CATALOGED THE HARDCOVER EDITION AS FOLLOWS:

Names: Barlow, Julie, 1968– author. | Nadeau, Jean-Benoît, author.
Title: The Bonjour effect : the secret codes of French conversation revealed / Julie Barlow and Jean-Benoît Nadeau.
Description: First edition. | New York : St. Martin's Press, [2016] | Includes bibliographical references and index.
Identifiers: LCCN 2015042739| ISBN 9781250051851 (hardcover) | ISBN 9781250102447 (e-book)
Subjects: LCSH: National characteristics, French. | France—Social life and customs. | French language—Social aspects. | Oral communication—France. | Language and culture—France. | BISAC: LANGUAGE ARTS & DISCIPLINES Translating & Interpreting. | SOCIAL SCIENCE / Anthropology / Cultural. | TRAVEL / Europe / France.
Classification: LCC DC34 .B275 2016 | DDC 944—dc23
LC record available at http://lccn.loc.gov/2015042739

ISBN 978-1-250-13027-3 (trade paperback)

Our books may be purchased in bulk for promotional, educational, or business use. Please contact your local bookseller or the Macmillan Corporate and Premium Sales Department at 1-800-221-7945, extension 5442, or by e-mail at MacmillanSpecialMarkets@macmillan.com.

First St. Martin's Griffin Edition: May 2017

10 9 8 7 6 5 4 3 2 1

To our daughters,

for taking us places we never expected

Contents

❧

Introduction

❦

What kind of people say no when they mean yes, refuse to admit they "don't know" even when they obviously don't, and systematically claim to hate their jobs even when they love them? That would be the French.

What kind of people think arguing is a good way to start a conversation and think you are smiling because you have something to hide? That's also the French.

With 84 million visitors per year, France remains the world's top tourist destination. France has been so successful in disseminating its culture that visitors arrive with high expectations. And that's where the problems start. Travelers mistake familiarity for understanding. When they attempt to communicate with the French, they end up frustrated, confused, and sometimes even hurt. Communication between French and foreigners is rarely effortless and often unpleasant.

What many fail to realize is that language is not the real obstacle. We have met a number of native and fluent French speakers—Americans, Canadians, Belgians, Senegalese, Algerians, and more—who find conversation with the French perfectly bewildering. We have also met people who barely speak French but get by very well. The difference? The latter understand that speaking French grammatically is not the same as "talking French" culturally. Even for people like us, who live in Montreal and communicate in French daily, cultural differences with the French can be daunting.

This book is not an advanced French conversation guide, or a book on how to speak French. There are lots of excellent books out there for that. The objective of *The Bonjour Effect* is to take readers beyond what the French say to explain what they mean. France is a culture that turned verbal expression into an art form. But like an iceberg, you can only grasp the totality of what the French say if you know what's under the surface. In the case of the French, it's a complex set of rules, codes, conventions, and taboos.

For starters, the French don't communicate. They *converse*. Conversation defines the French, even more than cuisine or fashion—they did invent salon culture and the idea of the *intellectuel,* after all. But French conversation is not about "connecting" to others, or even showing interest in them. The objective of conversation is to show *you are interesting*. French conversation also has its own rather complex set of rules and taboos. Asking for someone's name or what that person does for a living will get you nowhere at best. In France, it can actually drive people away. The subject of money leaves the French cold, while language can be the fodder for feverish impromptu debates between strangers. Confrontation is almost always more appealing to the French than consensus.

We are convinced that the most universal stereotypes of the French—that they are arrogant and rude—come from the fact that foreigners miss the most basic of French codes. As we'll discuss, you won't get anywhere with the French if you don't say *bonjour* first. We would not even hazard a figure of the number of journalists, diplomats, and businesspeople who have been victims of this blind spot. And *bonjour* is only the most obvious example.

The Bonjour Effect was based on our experience living in France for a year with our twin daughters, but the actual gestation period of the book lasted fifteen years. We spent two years in France, from 1999 to 2001. That resulted in a first book, *Sixty Million Frenchmen Can't Be Wrong,* which explains some of the fundamental reasons the French think and organize themselves the way they do. After living in Paris, we spent a year traveling in the French-speaking world for a book about the French language, then changed tack and moved to the United States to write another book, this time about Spanish. We became parents in the interim. On the drive home from our six-month stay in Arizona, somewhere between Idaho and Illinois, we realized we weren't done with the French. So three years after that, we packed the family up again and moved to Paris.

We were aware of the danger of trying to re-create our old life in Paris and looked for ways to avoid walking the same path, like choosing an apartment on the other side of town. But we didn't have to look hard. We came to Paris as a family this time, not as a childless couple, and family life revealed many things that had escaped us the first time we lived in France. We saw the French education system from the inside, through our daughters' eyes, and discovered that it is nothing less than a gigantic machine designed to teach children how to talk, and to think, in very specific ways.

There are other reasons this book is vastly different from *Sixty Million Frenchmen Can't Be Wrong.* We did not live in France this time as fellows of the Institute of Current World Affairs, the amazing little American foundation that underwrote our first stay in France. Back then, we joked about having a "rich American uncle" who paid our bills while we roamed France observing the natives to our hearts' content. There was no uncle this time. We paid the bills ourselves by working as freelance writers in Paris. Though definitely less comfortable, the formula had the advantage of bringing us closer to experiencing the daily grind of French people—or at least as close as freelance writers ever do anyway.

The other difference was that unlike in 1999, we knew France quite well when we arrived. When we were researching *Sixty Million Frenchmen Can't Be Wrong,* we were authentic newcomers to France. In the years after we published it, we returned to France frequently to promote our books, to write magazine articles, and to spend holidays. We had a pretty good idea of the questions we wanted to answer in *The Bonjour Effect* from the outset. We landed in our six-hundred-square-foot apartment in the Latin Quarter with our eight pieces of luggage and our twin daughters on the first Wednesday of September 2013 at eleven thirty in the morning and, at noon, recognized the wailing of the alarm sirens that resonate in France every first Wednesday of the month. We almost felt at home.

One thing that did not change was our method. We described it in our first book as "more anthropological than journalistic." Once again, we did interviews and met key figures but also lived regular lives and kept detailed personal journals about our interactions. As in our very first encounters with the French, we tried to soak up the culture, recording impressions no matter how superficial. Another thing that didn't change was that we worked together as a team. During the launch period of our first book on the French, we had lunch with an editor at *The New York Times* who had lived in Paris a number of years. He was surprised that after only two and a half years in France we had been able to identify and explain some of the fundamental differences between the French and North Americans. We told him the "rich uncle" factor helped—we had had lots of free time to visit the country and mull things over. But the fact that we had worked as a team was also key, as it is today. We can do twice as much work in the same time and can use each other as sounding boards for ideas anytime, day or night. We also have a native foot in two linguistic universes, French and English. Among other things, that advantage helps us see through cultural prejudices surrounding the French and single out the real cultural differences.

Writing is solitary work, but grappling with cultural differences by oneself can leave a writer unbalanced, to put it mildly. So there is still something magical about having a partner who can provide constant feedback almost around the clock. Ideas sometimes hit us late at night, when we were watching French TV in our living room (which, this being Paris, was also our dining room, family room, and office). Having a partner also means we can do a certain amount of processing on the spot. We have someone to inform us that The Great Idea is not that great, or that This Weird Hunch is the one worth pursuing. This built-in peer-review system means that, though written with four hands, our books have one voice and one point of view. (The perspective now includes that of our daughters, ten years old at the time, who were excellent sounding boards, too, going way beyond the call of duty to help us. We wholeheartedly thank them for that, and for just being themselves through the whole French experience.)

The main challenge any writer on cultural difference faces is, of course, the risk of overgeneralizing. It's easy to jump to the wrong conclusions. The most obvious problem is deciding if our sample is valid. Can a particular experience be generalized to an entire population? Was a French person we encountered representative of the French, or just some isolated oddball who happened to be on the scene when something noteworthy happened? There are no easy answers, but mingling with the French in different situations for the last fifteen years has helped us define what is "baseline" French.

There's also a fine line between overgeneralizing and overrelativizing. We realized this one morning in March when we were having brunch with a friend, Capucine, a young executive on the rise and a graduate of Sciences Po, France's famous social sciences university. We were talking about the book, which was still in the early stages, when Capucine stopped us short to ask what methodology we were using. The fact that we were writing a book with a combined journalistic and anthropological approach (which sounds haphazard to most academics) did not trouble her as much as the possibility that we might be overgeneralizing. Capucine is from the Savoy region in the French Alps, and she still nurtures deep roots there. "The Savoyards [inhabitants of Savoy] don't talk like Parisians," she told us. "They are a lot less interested in big ideas and more interested in practical questions."

Indeed, the French are not cookies from a factory. We recognize, as a matter of principle, that few French people would have every cultural reflex we describe in this book. But all of them have been subjected to a specific type of French "formatting," through education and the transmission of a particular set of values that are practically universal across the country and even in France's overseas territories. The closer the French get to centers of power, the more they fit the specific framework for which they have been trained. If they want to climb the ladder, they don't really have a choice. So a Savoyard like Capucine, who is working toward a high-level career, will figure out how to fit into the mold. Her preoccupation with our methodology, for that matter, was a *pure* product of French higher education.

The other trap in generalizing about French culture is listening exclusively to the "noise." As in any culture, there is a big difference between what the French say out loud in public and what they say in private. The French often resent discussing money or even economics with people they don't know, but that doesn't mean that they don't care about money: they did not end up creating one of the world's main economic engines by sheer luck. This is one problem with trying to understand the French (or any culture for that matter) through the news. The news is mainly based on "official" comments or staged noise (other news, protests, rumors). We were careful to listen closely for the silences and the taboos, and to what people other than talking heads were saying. Richard Nixon popularized the notion of "the silent majority" in a speech in 1969. The year we were in France, we watched the silent majority gain its voice. France's political elite had long assumed silence meant approval. How wrong they were. The French were rebelling against their leadership in ways no one had expected, and no one in the French elite—with the exception of far-right leader Marine Le Pen—knew what to do about it (which of course doesn't mean we are giving Le Pen any credit).

We had a great many choices to make in order to turn this book into more than a collection of short essays. As our research advanced, we decided to give the book a simple structure. The book is divided in two sections: Form and Content. The first seven chapters are about the reflexes that make up the operating system, or architecture, that shapes what the French say, and don't: what is taboo, what is proper, how they define what is private versus public, how schools and families teach kids to express themselves. The next eleven chapters focus on what the French talk about, or don't: general culture, negativism, the French language, the incursion of English, food, the world outside France, their jobs, politics, money, and identity. Some divisions were tricky. Consider two almost universal French reflexes: the habit of starting verbal exchanges with the word "no" and the general negative posture the French adopt in verbal exchanges. They seem like two faces of the same coin, but on reflection, we realized they were actually separate phenomena that each deserved its own chapter.

The Bonjour Effect is a reflection on the French. We didn't write a conversation guide, but we did want the book to be practical for readers. There are useful tips, a few "dos and don'ts" along the way (summarized in the epilogue), and the chapters can be read in any order, depending on what a reader wants to understand. That said, each section starts from the fundamentals and then moves into more complex or specialized topics. For instance, no matter where you are in France and no matter whom you are addressing, *bonjour* and *non* will be part of the exchange. They are universal stepping-stones (though *non* can seem more like a stone wall) in any interaction with the French. We leave the topic of conversation until the end of the section because you need to know a certain amount before you can jump into it successfully, or come out of it satisfied. Besides, important as conversation is to all French, not all of them excel in it.

The same logic applies to the section on content: general culture, geography, history, and food are almost universal subjects of conversation in France. The subject of English is more complex and specialized, not to mention full of paradoxes, as is the topic of gender relations. Politics and identity, the closing chapters, are fascinating ground for discussions, but need to be broached carefully because they are so divisive—and sometimes lethal.

Throughout our year in France, which corresponded roughly to the school year 2013–2014, we had the impression we were sitting on a volcano. When terrorists slaughtered seventeen people at the *Charlie Hebdo* magazine and the Hyper Cacher grocery store in Paris in January 2015, and then, only ten months later, when terrorists in Paris slaughtered 130 innocent people, we could still feel ourselves in Paris's streets, particularly in the eleventh arrondissement, a neighborhood we often walked in. Like many French, we were stunned and angry after the killings, but like most of our French friends, we couldn't say we were surprised. What the French say—and don't say—about the killings is fascinating, sometimes harrowing. We discuss this in chapter 18.

There was a reason we wrapped the book up with newsy topics like politics, race relations, and gender relations. *The Bonjour Effect* is not about current affairs, strange as this might sound coming from two journalists. It's much easier to understand how the French talk about these topics when you understand basic features of how the French communicate. We're pretty sure our observations about, and analyses of, the French will apply to many news stories for many years to come—after all, the roots of some of the characteristics we describe go back hundreds of years.

This is not to say that we think the French have some kind of immutable essence or nature. On the contrary, having adopted twin daughters from Haiti, we believe human beings are the products of their circumstances. Circumstances change constantly and so do cultures. France is a multilayered society that has always been in flux, with different layers evolving at different speeds.

Over the span of the fifteen years that was the gestation period of this book, we saw things in the French that hardly changed—like the fear of making mistakes or the importance they place on diplomas—

but also witnessed momentous shifts, like the disappearance of anti-Americanism, the newfound interest in economics, the development of a completely paradoxical stance toward the English language, the savage rejection of political and managerial elites, and a new relish in the idea that France is in the middle of an irremediable decline. And the tragic events of 2015 will also have their effects. Some are already obvious, like the open demonstrations of patriotism, a gesture previously associated with France's far right that is now becoming acceptable in mainstream French society.

Some of these changes sound dramatic, maybe even alarming to outsiders. Maybe they are; maybe they aren't. The fact of the matter is, you can't really be a good judge of what's going on in France until you understand how the French talk, and why they say some of the things they say. When you learn to "talk French," we discovered, everything about France and the French looks different. When you understand the real meanings behind their words and gestures, and know how to answer them, French waiters become friendly, French store clerks helpful, and the French, on the whole, approachable and good-humored.

Part One

Form

1

I Greet, Therefore I Am

There are many situations in Paris that call for good etiquette. Boarding a city bus, it turns out, is one of them.

It was a fresh Sunday morning in April and the four of us clambered onto Bus 91 to catch a train to Paris's Gare de Lyon. We were heading out of the city for a hike. With our walking sticks and knapsacks we were a bit noisy and cumbersome, but that wasn't the problem.

The girls and Julie pushed their tickets into the rackety green validating machine standard on all French city buses and headed to the back. Jean-Benoît, last aboard, heard the bus driver grumble "*mal élévé.*" Jean-Benoît was mystified. In France, "*mal élévé*" (badly brought up) is about as damning as "raised in a barn." He validated his ticket and said "*merci,*" still confused.

"You can't even say *bonjour?*" the bus driver spat back at him.

We were all stunned. After eight months in France, we thought we had the French greeting ritual down pat. Did we really need to say *bonjour* when we were getting on city buses? Bus 91, in particular, is a busy route that links three train stations, six hospitals, and connects to ten subway lines. On a regular day, this bus driver would open his door for an average of twenty-eight thousand passengers (we checked). Surely he didn't expect them all to greet him with a heartfelt *bonjour?*

But of course he did. Saying *bonjour* is so automatic the French hardly notice when you say it. But they notice when you don't.

There are no exceptions to the compulsory *bonjour.* Being handicapped—and in a pinch—doesn't even get you off the hook. In early October, Julie spent a week wheeling Paul, a Canadian friend, through the city for an article she was writing about visiting Paris in a wheelchair. Paul had visited the city a decade earlier and confirmed that things had improved. As he said, "Last time I came here, I thought the city had rounded up all the handicapped people and put them in a warehouse somewhere." Since his last visit, Paris had equipped its buses with ramps and reserved zones for wheelchairs, and attitudes in the city, according to Paul, had improved considerably. Bus passengers were generally courteous. Some Parisians even helped Paul and Julie haul the wheelchair up stairs; others graciously moved aside to make room in cramped cafés. One metro passenger even tunneled through a crowd inside a car to make room for the wheelchair.

Then, on one of their outings, Julie found herself struggling to get Paul's wheelchair through the gates of the Censier-Daubenton metro station near our apartment in the Latin Quarter. After a fruitless glance around the station entrance, she approached the metro agent sitting at the information counter for help, thinking the problem was pretty obvious: she was pushing a man in a wheelchair and couldn't figure out how to get him through the turnstile.

"*Excusez-moi, monsieur,*" she began. "Could you tell me how to get this wheelchair through the gate?" In the heat of the moment, Julie forgot the magic word. "*Bonjooourrr*" the agent replied, drawing the word out sarcastically. Julie had to start again. "*Bonjour, monsieur . . .*"

Just what is it about the word *bonjour* that makes it the exclusive key to human communication in France, even when there are extenuating circumstances? To begin with, France is a country of codes. The French are raised to use certain buzzwords and gestures to initiate interactions, whether social or professional. No matter with whom you wish to speak in France, and no matter in what circumstances you find yourself, you have to pass through a certain number of communication gates first.

Bonjour is the first and most important one.

If we added up the time we've spent in France over the last two decades, for work and holidays, it would amount to about four years. Strangely, saying *bonjour* has never become a reflex for us. Though it's a reflex for the French, *bonjour* is always an effort for North Americans, even the ones, like us, who are perfectly aware that the well-articulated *bonjour* has to be voiced for any kind of interaction with the French to take place. At best, four years of practice have made us able to pull it off without sounding too forced.

But why does everyone in France say *bonjour* all the time? Or more important, why does everyone *have to* say it?

Bonjour is not actually a word. It belongs to the linguistic category of "phatics." It was a British anthropologist, Bronislaw Malinowski, who first coined the expression in 1923: phatic comes from the Greek word *phanein,* meaning "to show oneself." In the 1960s, the Russian linguist Roman Jakobson theorized about the concept as one of the six "functions of language." The phatic function, he wrote, was what opened communication channels. In other words, phatic expressions do not convey information. They send a message: that a social connection of some sort is being established.

Bonjour is the king of phatic expressions in France, but there are others that come in handy, like *je vous en prie, au revoir,* and *bon appétit,* or any expression of a wish that starts with *bon,* like *bon courage, bonne soirée,* or *bonne journée.*

Je vous en prie translates literally as "I beg you" but is usually used as a polite way to respond after someone has thanked you for something. It's a tricky expression. Unlike *bonjour,* it doesn't really translate. It means something like "it's my pleasure" though not necessarily in response to anything in particular. *Je vous en prie* can seem a little too ceremonious to English speakers. That's one reason Julie struggled to use it for over a decade. Every time she said it she felt like she was immodestly drawing attention to her own good deeds. She would have preferred the French equivalent of "no problem" but the closest equivalent, *pas de souci,* just sounds too offhand in France.

Then one day Julie was leaving a translators' office on the Champs-Élysées when the reflex finally "took." As she entered a closet-size elevator on the eighth floor, an elegant elderly lady, dressed in a hat and white gloves, approached the door. Julie threw out her arm to hold the door open, after which the lady delivered a heartfelt, *"Merci, madame."* Maybe it was her age, or the white gloves, but suddenly, Julie felt a little formality was called for. *"Je vous en prie, madame,"* she replied.

Bon appétit is not just what you say to wish someone a good appetite. It's also a phatic. The French also say it to declare that eating is about to take place—eating being highly ritualized in France. The French don't snack much and still tend to eat at fixed times and in a fixed order or in courses. Even when someone eats in a nonsocial way, for instance, while walking or even standing, onlookers occasionally say *bon appétit* to re-create the sense of ritual eating carries for them (and sometimes they say it pointedly to underline the fact that you are not respecting the rules of proper eating).

Another fascinating French phatic is *râlâlâ* (pronounced rah-lah-lah, or even roh-loh-loh for emphasis). It's not, properly speaking, even a word. It's an interjection, a phatic signal to announce that one is about to *râler* (to moan). English speakers sometimes mistake this for *Oh là là!* and think it's an expression of enthusiasm, or even admiration. *Oh là là* means "oh my" or "oh dear" or even "oh no" and is much milder than *râlâlâ*. It's what the French say to announce they are disappointed or annoyed, as in "Oh no, I forgot the tickets."

Why exactly do the French need to announce they are about to moan before they do it? The French are quite comfortable with expressing bad humor in public, and there's nothing wrong with open confrontation. But there are rituals to follow, and this is one of them. In fact, the phatic power of *râlâlâ* is so strong that sometimes just uttering it is enough to get a situation solved, no explanation required.

Phatic words and expressions are not meant to "say" anything. The *jour* is not necessarily *bon*. You will probably not *revoir* (see again) most of the people you say *au revoir* to. And you don't intend to beg people who have thanked you for something. The function of these words and expressions is strictly social, like saying "hello" when you pick up the phone, but even vaguer. Phatics are part of the communication protocol that establishes links, like the scratchy, squealing sound modems made back in the 1990s when people had to dial up the Internet.

France is of course not the only place in the world with phatic codes. It can be hard to function in the United States if you don't grasp the different meanings that "hey" or even "okay" take on, depending on the tone in which they are pronounced. In the same vein, it is hard to get good service in Britain, or in English Canada, without saying "I'm sorry, but . . ." (not to mention the fact that Canadians say sorry when they mean the exact opposite). North Americans in general begin verbal exchanges with "Excuse me" or even "How are you?" But it's not because they actually want to know how you are. It's their way of acknowledging that they are interrupting you, or that they want to ask you for something. In short, phatics don't translate, which is what makes it so essential to understand what they actually mean in their context. If you ask a French person, *Comment allez-vous?* (How do you do?), it's not a salutation. The person is actually going to tell you. And you'd better be ready to listen. When you say, *excusez-moi* to the French, they wonder what you are excusing yourself for—it sounds like you've done something wrong.

Curiously, the French say *au revoir* (see you again) not to terminate, but to perpetuate social contact. *Au revoir* means that you are glad to have seen someone and hope to see her again, as the literal translation (until we meet again) suggests. Even if the chances of seeing someone again are very slim, you say it out of respect. The French even pronounce *au revoir* with a rise at the end, like it's a question (see you again?).

Saying *au revoir* is really no more nor less logical than saying *bonjour*. But it can save a situation if you happened to have botched your first *bonjour*. And that was how Jean-Benoît repaired the faux pas we committed on Bus 91 when we failed to say *bonjour* to the driver. When we arrived at the Gare de Lyon train station, Jean-Benoît waited so he was the last one to leave the bus. He then locked eyes with the driver and pronounced a perfect Parisian *au revoir,* with the question mark. Even if it was clear that they would most certainly never *revoir* one another, the bus driver smiled before he closed the door.[1]

But of all France's phatic expressions, *bonjour* is by far the most important. It is a universal greeting and the key to any exchange, even interactions that call for other expressions from the phatic toolkit. You can never say too many *bonjours*. Our rule of thumb is to say *bonjour* in all contexts and all circumstances. When it seems like overkill, you are probably right on.

Though it translates as "good day," *bonjour* has several meanings, none of which have anything to do with the day. The most primary phatic function of *bonjour* is to announce, "I am here." In France, you don't really exist unless you say so. I greet therefore I am.[2] *Bonjour* even performs this magic for non-French speakers who never say another thing. (If you exist, no one can ignore you.)

The next thing French people mean when they say *bonjour* is "we're going to communicate," or "I am going to talk." This also might seem self-evident when you are already talking, but not to the French. Believe it or not, all conversation in France begins with a tacit mutual agreement between participants that they are going to talk. Even if the conversation never goes further than "*bonjour*," the French will instinctively feel slighted if you skip the preliminary greeting. In France, you can't just take for granted that you can communicate with someone without asking if it's okay first.

Once the *bonjour* circle is complete and the conversation is up and running, you can say practically anything you want in France. You can interrupt or contradict or behave like you really were raised in a barn. It's beside the point. Consensus and congeniality are not, generally speaking, things the French seek in conversation, nor do they expect them. On the contrary, they like going beyond chitchat as soon as possible, adding a bit of crunch, some contradiction, some new information, ideas, or a paradox if they can pull it off.

That, of course, begs the question: if the French just want to argue anyway, why do you need to say *bonjour* in the first place? Particularly in situations where there will clearly be no conversation—like walking in front of a bus driver you will probably never see again.

The answer lies in the third meaning of *bonjour,* which is "I'm entering your territory." Julie was equal parts perplexed and impressed one afternoon as she waited for our daughters to wrap up their badminton class at the local gym. She was sitting with one other mother in what we dubbed the Fish Bowl, a small, glassed-in mezzanine above the gym, which had obviously been designed to keep parents as far as possible from the game. Julie was flipping through a fresh copy of *Elle* magazine when a little girl, no older than eight, who was clearly running late, bustled through the mezzanine on her way to the gym, staring at her feet. As she passed Julie, the girl raised her head and reflexively said, *"Bonjour, mesdames,"* then looked down at her feet again and carried on.

Why this greeting to perfect strangers? For starters, French children are explicitly taught to respect adults. Most kids don't need a parent to prompt them to say *bonjour* to a grown-up. But Julie still wondered, why did the little girl take the time to greet her at this particular moment, when she was obviously in a hurry? It was because the little girl was crossing the Fish Bowl, and that was parents' territory. She knew she was supposed to acknowledge that. She did it automatically. Unlike our family with our hiking gear in the city bus, the little girl knew she was on someone else's turf, and she knew what was expected of her in that particular scenario.

(A week later, Julie was having an afternoon snack in the Luxembourg Gardens when two friends, mothers at our daughters' school, started bemoaning how French manners are going down the tubes. "People aren't teaching their kids to be respectful anymore," they claimed solemnly. Julie pointed out that few, if any, North American children would *ever* spontaneously greet an adult they didn't know. The two moms rubbed their chins thoughtfully.)

So, just how do you know you're venturing into someone else's territory in France? It can be pretty subtle. When we went on our evening walks through the winding streets of our Paris neighborhood, we obviously didn't say *bonjour* to each of the hundreds of individuals whose paths we happened to cross. Streets belong to everyone. But on one of our routes, we took a scenic shortcut down a long private passage that was essentially a stretched-out inner courtyard. We had to open gates on both ends to access it. Between the gates, we said *bonjour* to every soul we met (or they said *bonjour* to us, and we answered). It was just a polite way of acknowledging that we knew we were in their space and we were grateful they let us enjoy it. (It was also a bit of posturing, a way to pretend we had business there, which we didn't.)

In short, the more intimate the space—even if it's public, or semipublic—the more important it is to acknowledge to whoever "owns" it that you know you are on their turf. A few years earlier we spent a month in a hamlet in the Auvergne region. La Bastide had a permanent population of exactly five, which grew to nine in the summer. It was the ancestral village of Rudi, a close friend of ours who grew up in Quebec. Before we visited, Rudi gave us the rundown on the hamlet's genealogy and told us to make sure we said *bonjour* to everyone, every time we saw them, without exception.

It wasn't as if La Bastide's nine inhabitants were especially fussy about protocol. And they certainly were glad to have visitors: the entire village greeted us with a welcome banner when we arrived. Yet the previous summer, two of La Bastide's well-loved summer residents had rented their homes to a Nordic couple who spent a month there without uttering *bonjour* to anyone. Of course the village ignored them, pointedly, and it was a long summer for everyone.

Even though we were Rudi's friends, we followed his directions to the letter. Every day at around 3:00 P.M., we walked through the village and said *bonjour* to every person there. And every time, we said it like it was the first time. The results were simply enchanting. In France, before-dinner drinks, called *l'apéro,* usually start around 6:00 or 7:00 P.M. During our summer in La Bastide, bottles started popping open around 3:00 P.M., which was when we started our daily rounds. Our fridge quickly filled up with local specialties of sausage, cheese, and homemade jam.

Since our first stay in France, fifteen years earlier, we noticed that the number of situations that required a compulsory *bonjour* had increased. It used to be mandatory to say *bonjour* mainly in stores; now it's expected throughout the service industry and even in public services like buses and swimming pools. We're guessing the *bonjour* ritual is expanding because it underlines equality—a principle the French value much more than either liberty or fraternity. In France, there is a philosophy that members of the "upper classes" should not greet "servants" any differently than servants would greet them. By inference, bus passengers (who are the nobility of the bus) are expected to show proper deference to drivers (the laborers) by saying *bonjour.*

There's one other situation where it's absolutely essential to say *bonjour:* when you want something from someone. Like the territorial *bonjour,* the trick here is understanding when you are actually asking for something. When it comes to service, a persistent cultural misunderstanding plagues French-American relations to this day. North Americans think service is owed to them. Specifically, polite service is the payoff customers should get for giving someone their business—

even if it doesn't always work out that way in reality. Still, it's a question of expectations. When North Americans present merchants with a problem, they expect them to find a solution.

If you approach the French service industry with this attitude, you'll end up being disappointed at best, and, more likely, humiliated. When you enter a French store or a restaurant or even walk up to an information kiosk, the first thing you have to do in France is acknowledge that you are entering their turf. That's because you are asking for something from an employee who may have something more important to do. Whether or not that employee actually does have something better to do is not the point. You are interrupting him to ask for something. He does not owe you anything in exchange for you giving him your business. The French just don't think that way. When you address a merchant or a clerk or a hostess or even a waiter, *bonjour* is not a word. It's not a greeting or even a form of courtesy. *Bonjour* is code for "please allow me to indulge in your services."

Whether in restaurants or cafés, at ticket counters or museums, in the metro or in a taxi, in stores or even at an information desk, foreigners often get cold, even hostile treatment from the French if they don't know the password for good services and don't fully grasp the message their ignorance sends. If you don't greet a person behind the desk somewhat humbly, she will not help you, or if she does, she will definitely not do it with a smile.

Foreigners take this as a rebuff and are mystified. But in France, you are asking something from someone, so you have to be humble.

Having forgotten her place in the world of French retail, Julie got horrible service on her first few trips to our local Franprix grocery store on rue Mouffetard. The first time, she dashed in to buy eggs (easy to miss in a French grocery since they are never stacked in a fridge, but on regular shelves, generally with the sterilized milk—a detail Julie had forgotten). She simply marched to the back of the store and asked the young man stocking shelves there where the eggs were. He looked at her, bent over, pointed to his right and said, "*Dat* way," practically in a drawl, mouthing the words in English like he was speaking to a toddler. Since he was pointing to the entire south side of the store, Julie repeated the question.

What Julie really needed to do was work on her pitch. The shelf-stocker stomped over to the milk section, bent over even more—presumably to underline how childish Julie was behaving—and pointed to the shelf of eggs. "Look! Read it. *Œuf-fah,*" he said, pronouncing the French word for egg, *œuf,* in two syllables as if Julie needed it broken down for her.

Julie couldn't believe her ears, first, that he'd made fun of her ignorance, then that he'd mocked her mother tongue. She was halfway back to the apartment when she realized her mistake. In her rush, she had not only skipped the *bonjour.* She had also forgotten to excuse herself for interrupting him (easy to forget since the store wasn't particularly busy) before brazenly demanding service. You can't skip stages in communications in France, not even to buy eggs. If you treat a French store clerk in an off-handed manner, you will get exactly the kind of treatment the French believe you deserve in return. You cannot even ask for the time without saying *bonjour* in France. Jean-Benoît tried it once. "Excuse me sir, do you have the time?" The man answered, "Yes," and walked on.

It's like you have to knock before you can come in. This sort of officiousness drives North Americans crazy. We are shocked to discover that employees in France regularly treat us like underlings, like uninvited, unwelcome intruders interfering with the exercise of other more important duties. In France, employees rarely offer to help. You have to ask, and ask nicely.

One of the paradoxes of the *bonjour* ritual is that, though it's automatic, you still have to sound like you mean it. If you say *bonjour* in a clipped, offhand, or routine-sounding way, you might as well not say it at all. The more deliberate and drawn out you make it, the better. We've found it's even good to bow a little obsequiously, or even bend your head slightly to the side to look powerless, like you are putting yourself at a merchant's mercy.

But above all, don't rush it. Julie nicknamed the receptionist at our local post office the "Ice Queen," in reference to her curt, cold service. The first time Julie stepped inside the office, to carry out the deceptively simple task of mailing a letter back home, Julie looked at the automated stamp machine, blanched, and went straight to the Accueil (which incongruously translates as "welcome," even though in France customer-service counters often operate as fortresses). She then proceeded in what she felt was a courteous enough manner, greeting the receptionist with *bonjour,* and explaining the nature of her problem.

By the time Julie realized her mistake, it was too late. The last twist to the French *bonjour* ritual is that after you say *bonjour,* you have to wait for your collocutor to say *bonjour* back. Otherwise it doesn't count. Worse, barging forward too quickly after your *bonjour* makes it sound like you are issuing some kind of order—and who are customers to do that? By denying the receptionist at La Poste the several-second window she required to reciprocate the *bonjour,* Julie was basically foisting a problem on her without her consent.

In short, never try to carry out any kind of transaction—even the briefest—before completing the obligatory verbal transaction of "*bonjour.*" Sometimes there is no turning back. At the post office, the Ice Queen charged through the operation so quickly that Julie knew she'd have to come back for help again next time. Trying to salvage the situation, Julie apologized and wished the receptionist a good day, "*Je vous souhaite une bonne journée, madame.*" But it was hopeless. When Julie returned to the post office she got exactly the same cool reception she had gotten the first time. Post office errands became Jean-Benoît's responsibility. He had never had a problem with the Ice Queen.

Fortunately, the damage of a botched *bonjour* can sometimes be undone. We learned this in our first few weeks of French school life. Every school day started and ended with our principal, Madame Montoux, standing outside the school entrance saying *bonjour* and *au revoir* to some three hundred kids and one hundred parents, grandparents, and nannies. On the third week of school Julie approached Madame Montoux to see if she could volunteer or participate in school life somehow. On her first attempt, Julie took the direct approach—too direct, it turned out. "*Bonjour,* I was wondering if there was a way I could get involved or help out?" Madame Montoux just stared back. For a second, Julie wondered if her Quebec accent had startled the principal.

But that wasn't the problem. Julie had failed to wait for the reciprocal *bonjour.* Julie backtracked and reapproached with better pacing. Unlike the Ice Queen at the post office, our school principal was willing to forgive and forget. She directed Julie to a parent volunteer who happened to be on the sidewalk that morning, and ten minutes later, Julie was sitting in the corner café with members of the parents' association of our school. By the end of the meeting, she was running for a seat on the Conseil des parents—no small matter, since school elections are organized nationally in France, with competing parties and formal voting ballots.

In other words, Julie was literally running for political office three weeks after arriving in Paris. That's how far a well-delivered *bonjour* can get you in France.

~ 2 ~

Privacy Rules

While she was researching her story on services for handicapped tourists in Paris, Julie met the city's deputy mayor of Paris responsible for disability, Véronique Dubarry. Madame Dubarry took her activist role very seriously. She actually spent most of the interview criticizing Parisians' disdain for the disabled. According to what Julie had seen, things weren't too bad, but there were exceptions. Julie mentioned the fact that she had occasionally watched mothers push their strollers into the zones reserved for wheelchairs on city buses. Madame Dubarry nearly exploded—not at Julie's observation, which she agreed with, but at Julie's inadvertent sexism. "WHO pushes strollers? *People* push strollers, not *mothers!*"

Julie tried to salvage the situation by directing the conversation away from wheelchairs to the issue of *non-voyants* (visually impaired). She assumed the neutral terminology would appease Madame Dubarry. How wrong she was. "*Ils sont aveugles* (blind)!" Madame Dubarry shouted. If Julie had been interviewing someone in Madame Dubarry's shoes in North America, that person might have corrected her, but she would have taken care not to make it sound too much like a reproach. In France, it's perfectly acceptable to emphatically contradict a virtual stranger.

Simon Kuper, a reporter for the *Financial Times* based in Paris, wrote a bold column in 2013 that got straight to the heart of what stumps most foreigners in Paris: the damn codes. All societies have codes, Kuper argues, but Paris sets the bar too high. There are two kinds of codes in France. There are the signals the French use for communicating, specific things people say all the time, like *bonjour*. But then there are the unarticulated rules, which Kuper was referring to. "If you overlay an intellectual capital on an artistic and fashion capital in a former royal capital, all of it in the country that invented how to eat, there are so many codes governing so many behaviors that the demands of sophistication become all-encompassing."[1] As he put it, "In Paris, Big Brother (often in the form of oneself or one's spouse) is always watching to see if you commit a faux pas."

Those codes in France can seem like invisible road signs on a stormy night. But they're not. Many of the mysteries around French codes boil down to one issue: the French have vastly different notions of what constitutes public versus private behavior. For example, North Americans always find it a bit unsettling in casual conversation when the French decline to offer their names or state what they do for a living, sometimes after hours of talking. But that's because names and occupations are considered personal information in France. Asking for someone's name even after you have said *bonjour* is considered invasive and inappropriate, and comes across as an interrogation. Then, as Madame Dubarry reminded Julie, in France arguing is a perfectly acceptable, even desirable, thing to do with people you don't know and may never see again.

To grasp what's public and what's private in France, it's best to forget about the "damn codes" and to think about "bubbles" instead. It was the great anthropologist Edward T. Hall, in the 1960s, who introduced the concept, which he actually called "spatial dimensions." According to Hall, people in all cultures have imaginary rings that define the territory around them in slices, or in spheres. These territories represent the degree of control a person expects to have over whoever is inside them. At the core, very near the self, you have the *intimate* sphere, into which very few people are admitted. The next ring is the *personal* sphere, where several more people are welcome. Then, outside of that, there is the *social* bubble, which refers to anyone with whom a person is willing to interact. And then, on the outside of that, there is the *public* bubble, the largest ring, which consists of everyone you are vaguely aware of.

It's actually not that difficult to understand the French bubbles. Regardless of whether you are close or far, it's what's said—or not said—inside them that determines the nature of the relationship with an interlocutor. If there's no talk, there's no relationship. Merely smiling in France is not a signal anyone wants to be your friend. Someone has to say something first. As we've seen, you can't even be part of the bubble that constitutes the public sphere in France without opening your mouth.[2] If you don't say *bonjour,* you don't exist. For that matter, when you find yourself in a packed subway car in Paris, pushed physically against another passenger, even in quite intimate physical contact, the French mark the distance by *not* saying a word. They don't communicate in the least, not even by smiling—something North Americans find unsettling, because it's our preferred technique for sending the message "it's not personal."

Getting access to the different bubbles is mostly a matter of understanding what topics are broached inside them, and what aren't. If someone starts arguing with you, it might not signify anything more than the fact that the person acknowledges you, and maybe wants to interact with you. It is quite acceptable to voice critical opinions to a perfect stranger in France. And if you do it, people will not cut you off or tell you to quiet down (unless maybe you are in a theater). Correcting is also normal public behavior. The French remark rather freely on everything from others' language to their appearance. It's not always nice, but it's not impolite.

Julie had a hard time getting the knack of this the first time we moved to France. Like many North Americans, when a Parisian joked about her accent—or her ignorance—she took it personally. The problem was, as a North American, Julie instinctively felt that poking fun at someone is something you do in private. It took her a while to understand that for the French, ribbing someone is not only acceptable public behavior; it's actually quite flattering in its way. Occasionally, it is blatant bullying, but more often than not, it means someone wants to talk to you. After a year of smarting from what felt like head-on attacks by the merchants in our neighborhood, Julie had a breakthrough and realized it was best to think about French conversation as a recreational sport.

It also took us a while to get used to the fact that disagreement among couples is acceptable public behavior. It is, in fact, almost desirable, since it passes for a sign that a relationship is strong. This is the main reason French couples casually slip into spats, right in front of everyone. In France, arguing contradictory viewpoints as though your life depends on it is not gauche. Up to a certain point, it's considered good fun. We observed this over and over at different dinner parties with North American and French acquaintances. The North American couples, consciously or not, work together to project an image of harmony. They support each other's views, or if they do disagree, they do it gently, often packaging their views with an explanatory note that opens a social escape hatch for their partner ("my wife and I don't always agree on everything"). Meanwhile, over on the French side of the table, the couples are heartily sparring about politics, art, women's rights, or the president's latest fling. At dinner, French couples just do what they normally do, maybe even better. The French are actually suspicious about couples that seem too harmonious. They think they're hiding something.

So how do you move into the French personal sphere? In the most famous French novella of all time, Antoine de Saint-Exupéry's *The Little Prince,* one of the best-known anecdotes involves the little prince meeting a fox. When the prince tells the fox he wants to play with him, the fox answers that he can't, because the prince needs to "tame" him (*apprivoiser*) first. The prince then asks what that means, and the fox explains that it is about establishing ties. With his tale about the universal theme of friendship, Saint-Exupéry appealed to audiences far beyond the borders of France, but the topic struck a chord with the French in particular because it explores the things you have to do to be part of someone's private sphere. For the French, creating a bond with someone—entering someone's personal or private sphere and becoming friends—is akin to taming. There are a series of stages that must be followed.

Luckily, the process of becoming friends in France is quite straightforward once you know the key words. When the French want to have a more personal relationship, when they want to go from the social bubble to the personal or even the intimate, they send crystal-clear signals, far more obvious signs than North Americans do. In a nutshell, they talk about private topics, which for them are family, work, and money. They also use humor—the private version of wit, which they display in public.

Fifteen years ago, Jean-Benoît befriended Daniel in his hiking club, after mistaking him for a snob. Daniel is always impeccably dressed in well-cut jackets and well-waxed shoes (which he actually polishes with champagne). Jean-Benoît is Daniel's scruffy alter ego, but despite being aesthetically mismatched, the two connected instantly. That was personal chemistry. Friendship was a different matter. In retrospect, Jean-Benoît realized that Daniel was the first of our French *connaissances* to send a clear message he was opening the door to friendship. And he did that by broaching two topics the French only discuss with friends: his job and his family. The two became friends because Jean-Benoît reciprocated. It all unfolded spontaneously, and Julie was soon included in the circle.

When they are not at work, the French rarely talk about it with strangers, except in impersonal terms. They will not say they like their work, or discuss their true feelings regarding their peers and their superiors outside of general terms. If a French person tells you she likes her work, it's a sign she regards you as a friend. Likewise, the French won't mention family problems until they are ready to go all the way and welcome you into their inner circle.

In addition to talking about their families or their jobs, there's another sure sign a French person is inviting you into his or her personal sphere: humor and self-deprecation. In France, humor is definitely reserved for the private sphere. In public, the French practice *esprit,* a form of high-spirited wit that can be quite funny but that doesn't have the self-deprecating dimension of humor. The French love to show wit in public, essentially a spirited display of their intelligence and level of culture. Wit shows people you are smart and can communicate.

The French can be extremely funny in public, but it will rarely be humorous. Humor is almost always self-deprecating and puts you on the same level as everyone else. In North America, politicians prefer humor over wit, because with wit they run the risk of looking lofty or arrogant. Humor charms, and brings them down to a level ordinary people can relate to. But the French don't think there's anything funny about authority figures poking fun at themselves, particularly in public. Attempts at humor are yet another sign that the French want to establish a more personal relationship. If you try to be humorous with someone as a means of getting acquainted, he'll think you are making a fool of yourself. Of course France has hordes of great comedians and humorists. And they do laugh at themselves in public. It's their job description. French comedians do publicly what no one else would do, except in private.

Humor is one of the many problems of François Hollande, one of the most unpopular French presidents in French history. In Parisian press circles Hollande is reputed to be hilarious—in private. One of his many nicknames is *Monsieur petites blagues* (Mister small jokes). Because he's so funny, he wins people over in one-on-one meetings. That might explain how he worked his way up to being a presidential candidate for France's Socialist Party. But humor has no value in public. Hollande's advisers do everything they can to make him seem *less* funny, to keep him from making a fool of himself. The result can be summed up by yet another nickname, Flanby, the name of a bland, jiggly caramel custard.

The refreshing thing about the French is that once you grasp these basic codes, you pretty much know where you stand with people. When the French don't want a relationship or a friendship, they simply don't reciprocate. They won't engage in humor or talk shop or about family.

And if you refuse to broach those topics as well, they'll instantly understand that you are keeping them at bay. No explanation required.

Two months after our arrival, we were invited to an informal supper at the home of Mélanie and Antoine, the parents of one of our
daughters' school friends. Julie had met Mélanie at the café near our
daughters' school, where parents' association meetings took place. An
invitation to dinner soon followed. The evening was odd, even odder
than the mismatched meal of waffles and good burgundy wine. While
we ate, we learned that Mélanie was part of a group of parents who
were trying to get a teacher at our daughters' school fired. We tried
to keep an open mind, but we really liked the teacher, who was an immigrant himself and particularly welcoming to students from other
countries. Our reticence to engage with this couple probably shone
through in our reserve. We didn't really pry. Like almost all French
dinner parties, opinions flowed as fast as wine, so when we left, we
had a pretty clear idea of what Mélanie and Antoine thought about religion and the quality of France's school system. But we didn't have a
clue what either of them did for a living. And while we spent half the
evening listening to stories about Antoine's family wine business in
Burgundy, we didn't hear a peep about either Antoine's or Mélanie's
actual families beyond their involvement in the wine business. Jobs and
family are just not things you talk about with strangers, or even *connaissances,* and that's what we were, connaissances—and that's what
we remained. No questions asked.

French people who have lived for a while in North America, whether
in New York City, Los Angeles, or Montreal, all have the same trau-
matic story. They find themselves in a bar chatting with a perfect
stranger. They drink; they tell each other their personal story. The
French are convinced they have a friend for life. And then, when they

meet that person two days later and realize that person doesn't remember their name, they are lost. This situation happens because in North America, giving your name and talking about your personal life is something you do in public and it doesn't mean anything. In France, name exchanges amount to something of a commitment. (Strangely, outside of formal contexts, introductions almost never happen, and when they do, they come late—if at all. The logic is that if you know about a person, you're in and you don't need to be introduced.)[3]

The zone between friend and stranger is where things get tricky in France. Many people learning French assume that the choice of the personal pronoun *tu* versus the more formal *vous* is directly related to the degree of intimacy you share with a collocutor and can operate as signposts to tell you where you are with someone. If only it were that simple. *Tu* and *vous* are, indeed, codes. The French even make them into the verbs *tutoyer* ("to use tu") and vouvoyer ("to use vous") and nouns *tutoiement* ("tu-saying") and *vouvoiement* ("vous-saying"), to make it possible to talk about the rules that govern their use.[4] In whatever form, the terms can signify many things. The use of *vous* signals formality but also solemnity. *Vous* is used to address someone older; it's a mark of rank or perceived distance. Even someone who is introduced to you by first name should be addressed in the *vous* form to mark rank. A waiter, for instance, who uses *tu* with a customer is being condescending, even insulting. *Tu* is used, in some contexts, not to mark familiarity but common membership or allegiance. For instance, graduates of any *grande école* address each other with *tu* no matter what their differences in age or rank.

The French choose whether you use *tu* or *vous* to send specific signals. Even in a formal or relatively formal context, a stranger may address you as *tu* because of perceived or demonstrated equality. When the proper use is not clear, it's usually a good idea to use *vous* as a default. (It's never impolite.) The worst that can happen is that you end up sounding a bit insecure. But you're better safe than sorry. Especially if you are unsure about French proxemics and don't really know exactly what bubble you are in.[5]

When used properly, the *tu-vous* distinction can be a great tool for building relationships with the French. That's because acknowledging hierarchical positions is a good way to establish a foothold with anyone in France. We had brunch one afternoon with Armand Compte, the brother of a friend who had invited us. Armand, who was working on a Ph.D. in history, regaled us with stories of letter writing in the academic world, in particular, the strict codes—formulas, really— that scholars and students use to mark rank. If you are a professor writing to a student, he told us, you have to sign your letter "*Bien à vous*" (with best wishes) or "*Cordialement*" (cordially). But if you are a student responding to a professor, you have to write "*Respectueusement*" (respectfully). Likewise, if you are a professor writing to a superior, say, to a minister or to the principal of your university, you have to conclude your letter "*Respectueusement*." But then the principal will come back to you with *cordialement* or *bien à vous* (because he or she is your superior), unless a previous relationship allows for more familiarity. "If you deviate from these rules, you're sunk," Armand told us. (Armand was just dumbfounded by the almost universal habit in U.S. academic circles of signing exchanges with "Best." "Who is best?" he asked us. "Why are they best?")

Jean-Benoît did not know about this nuance—Quebeckers are more casual about such things. But when he consciously applied Armand's rules, he suddenly got more answers to his e-mail queries. The people he approached as a journalist did not feel slighted. That's what under-standing the codes can do for you.

One of the most remarkable cultural differences between the French and the Americans is that the French have few *amis,* friends. Despite what English-French dictionaries say, *ami* does not have the same mean-ing as the English "friend." The French have strict rules about what constitutes *un ami,* and the term can't be used casually to refer to some-one you like but don't know well. They refer to that category of ac-quaintances as a *connaissance. A connaissance* still has to travel quite a long road to become *un ami.*

When the French have a business or social connection with a *con-naissance,* that person becomes a relation. Interestingly, even *connaissances* have degrees. When the French speak of someone they know very well, they will qualify the *connaissance* as "old" rather than "good"—a *vieille connaissance* implies that you have known the person for a while, but it actually refers to someone you know well. The expression is curiously dispassionate: a *vieille connaissance* may or may not be someone you actually like. When this *connaissance* becomes more affectionate, the French speak of a *pote* (pronounced like "putt"), which is very collo-quial. A *pote* isn't exactly a friend either. It's a person with whom you share *les atomes crochus* (good chemistry). In today's French, *copain* im-plies a love relation. (Strangely, the French have no direct translation of "girlfriend" or "boyfriend." Quebeckers do. They call a girlfriend *une blonde* and a boyfriend, *un chum.*)

A true *ami,* also called *un intime,* is for the happy few and has the specific meaning of a "very good friend, almost family."[6] You have to beware of its use in certain contexts: when someone you hardly know speaks directly to you as *"mon ami,"* it's almost always condescending.

And you become *un ami* after you have gone through the obligatory stages of *connaissance, relation*, and *pote,* and have progressed from talking about ideas and arguing to discussing family and work and using humor. It is the French adult's version of the little prince taming his fox.

French authors and artists have written beautifully about friendship over the centuries, and it's a testament to the incredible value the French place on intense relationships. The French writer Michel de Montaigne (1533–1592) is probably most famous for summing up the essence of friendship when he wrote about his relationship with the French writer and philosopher Étienne de La Boétie (1530–1563). "*Parce que c'était lui, parce que c'était moi*" (Because he was he, and I was I). It might be the most beautiful pair of phrases ever written about a platonic relationship.

Second prize would go to the painter and sculptor Georges Braque (1882–1963), who wrote about his relationship with Pablo Picasso. The two artists, who jointly forged Cubism among other things, had a legendary, fusional friendship between 1907 and 1914, when they saw each other at least once a day and developed a totally new way of looking at physical reality and representing it. Much later, in a rare interview, Braque said: "In those years Picasso and I said things to each other that nobody will ever say again, that nobody could say anymore. . . . It was rather like a pair of climbers roped together."[7] (World War I separated the pair. Picasso, a Spaniard, was never called to arms. Braque, a lieutenant, was nearly blinded in combat and spent a year convalescing. By the time Braque recovered, he had moved on and the rope was cut, their *atomes* no longer *crochus*.)

The true dimension of *un ami* is something close to family and love, and it is a mutual and reciprocal feeling—this is the intimate circle. Although the process is codified, it doesn't necessarily take long to get through the stages to friendship. When we met our friends Anne and François in March 1999, things moved so quickly that Julie became the godmother of their daughter Ambre a year later.

To the French, having a lot of friends sounds like you take friendship lightly. Like love and like family, friendship comes with privileges, and with responsibilities. The main privilege is access. The responsibility is an unspoken promise to help whenever asked, no questions asked. During one of our first dinners with Anne and François, when we returned to France in 2013, we told them we had not brought our daughters' guitars to France because of luggage limitations. François stared at us for a second, then turned around, picked up the phone, and called his old friend, Alain Mazaud, a guitar maker in the Normandy village of Fresney-le-Puceux. "*Salut,* Alain, it's me. . . . Look, I have a friend here, Jean-Benoît. . . . Yes, him. He has these twin daughters who play guitar. But they left their guitars back in Montreal. So, listen, I need that old guitar of yours. You know the one . . . yes. They are here for the year. . . . Bring it with you when you come next weekend. And don't forget the case. Bye."

François didn't even specifically ask his friend Alain to help us. He told him he needed a guitar, thanked him, and hung up. Alain probably remembered meeting us a decade earlier, but it didn't matter. Alain and François were friends. And François was our friend. In France, friends don't explain why they are asking favors (or in our case, receiving favors). That's one big reason the French may have lots of *relations,* but very few friends. Who could possibly manage more than a few?

~ 3 ~

Finding the Yes in Non

All cultures have distinct ways of saying no. Not all of them include actually saying no. The British and Americans pad refusals with expressions like "I hear you" or "I understand what you are saying." The Japanese never say the word "no" when they are speaking to a superior or to a client; instead, they hem and haw until their collocutor picks up the cue and provides them with a way out.

The French just say no. They say it everywhere, all the time, with no *états d'âmes,* no compunction. They say no when they mean yes. And they say no when they want you to think they might eventually say yes. The trick is in understanding the many things "no" can actually mean.

In situations that require politeness or deference, "no" can be dressed up in perplexing phrases like "*Ça ne va pas être possible*" (That will not be possible), or sometimes even "*C'est la France*" (That's France for you). In other situations, the French can turn a no into a categorical refusal with expressions like "*Pas question*" (It's out of the question), or our favorite, "*Ça n'existe pas*" (It doesn't exist). The most polite form of "no" is "*je suis désolée*" (I'm very sorry).

Whatever its form, *non* is a foundational concept in French culture. It's actually something of a republican reflex: the French Revolution was about the irrevocable right of all citizens to refuse, and *non* has a quality of *revanche des petits contre les grands* (revenge of the underclasses) that seems to satisfy the inner peasant or proletarian in every French person, of any class.

But the *non* reflex is more than revolutionary romanticism. *Non* is how the French express and emphasize authority, whether at home or at work. French children are raised in the belief that what has not been explicitly authorized has by default been denied. Saying *non* means you are in charge, and being in charge means you say *non*. *Non*, for that matter, is one of the key ingredients of France's deeply entrenched tradition of bureaucratic obstinacy—even the French know this. In 2013, we watched in awe as the French government tried to force bureaucrats to start saying yes. France passed a law stipulating that all queries to the government would have to be answered within sixty days—revolutionary enough in itself—and if this didn't happen, the official answer, by default, would be yes—*yes*. We didn't have time to see whether this initiative had any effect.

It's hard to imagine it will. The French even say *non* to *non*. Between the French *oui* and *non*, there is *si*, an interesting nuance, completely absent from the English lexicon. *Si* is often translated as "yes," but its grammatical purpose is actually to contradict a negative statement. For the question, *"Luc n'est pas venu?"* (Didn't Luc come?), the proper response—if it turns out that he did—is *si*. In other words, instead of saying yes, the French have a word that says *non* twice.[1]

Luckily, *non* is often a *oui* in disguise. The trick is figuring out how to turn no into yes. Although its uses are broad, there is really only one thing outsiders need to grasp. The French don't take *non* for an answer, and neither should you. It's difficult for foreigners to desensitize themselves to the sting of the *non,* which sounds like a refusal to engage. In fact, *non* is the opposite. When the French vehemently disagree with something, *non* doesn't mean the conversation is over. It's more like a conversation starter, a bargaining position, or an invitation to make a counteroffer. The mistake is to consider *non* a stone wall when it actually operates like a trampoline.

Like negotiations with Mediterranean merchants—and the French do share that heritage—interactions in France tend to begin when two parties have laid their positions on the table. *Non* is what gets things rolling. If everyone agrees, there's nothing to talk about. (Paradoxically, talking is even the key to understanding when a French person *doesn't* want to talk to you. The French don't send the signal with body language or facial expressions. When French really don't want to talk to you, they don't open their mouths. To them, the message is loud and clear.)

The best thing to do when facing a firm French no is to keep talking. The lessons came flying back to Julie when she went to buy her first Paris subway pass. Transport is not exactly a free market in Paris. Monthly bus and metro passes are only available to Parisians who can prove with a utility bill that they live there. Unfortunately, Julie only recalled this *after* she had made the thirty-minute trip to the Opéra metro station to buy her pass. But she thought it was worth trying to talk her way into a pass. She started explaining to the young woman behind the ticket counter: "I live in Paris. But I just moved here. So I don't have my *justificatif de domicile* [proof of address] with me."

"*Je suis désolée madame,*" the agent replied. It was that gently wrapped no. But Julie could tell from the clerk's body language that the door was still open. Julie had used some key French terminology—*justificatif de domicile*—and it was a good start. She scoured her mind for other bureaucratic buzzwords that might break the agent's resistance. "I don't have my lease with me because my husband has it. He went to get our Carte Vitale [France's health card] at the Caisse primaire d'assurance maladie [Health Insurance Primary Fund]," she said. The bureaucratic brand names worked their magic. The agent was still shaking her head, but more gently, so Julie soldiered on. She pulled our daughters up to her side and talked about how fortunate we were to have a school that was right across the street from our apartment.

"What school do your daughters attend?" the agent asked brightly. Julie named the school. The receptionist turned to her computer and crosschecked it with our address, then smiled and took Julie's photo. "Welcome to Paris," she said. "What do you think of the French school system?"

Sometimes the French say no out of pure gamesmanship. It's a curious cultural difference: in some cultures (like ours) agreement can actually lead to sharing and comparing stories. But to the French, "yes" often sounds like a dead end. A frank *non* is a better show of spirit than automatic acquiescence, and it often sparks a discussion. But there is more to the French *non* than just verbal jousting, and foreigners should never take no for an answer in France until they have figured out what it actually means.

The French say no to get around a series of French taboos.

The first of these is the fear of ridicule, and of being blamed for things. North Americans have a quasi-universal fear of being disliked or not being accepted. The desire to be liked produces a culture that values huge smiles, even in the most desperate and unfriendly situations. When disputes arise, North Americans usually try conciliation and consensus building first. We don't like appearing too authoritative.

We even say we don't know when we do. It's a way of reaching out. We also say we're sorry when we're not, and accept blame that's not ours, because it's often just the best way to keep things moving.

This would never work for the French, and for one reason: the French almost universally fear being found *en faute* (at fault) for something. This fear of *faute* is behind many, if not most, of the spontaneous noes you hear in France. It's not that the French are opposed to pleasing people. But pleasing is not nearly as important to them as making sure they never get blamed for a problem or oversight.

The word *faute* doesn't fully translate into English. It's a combination of "wrongdoing," "responsibility," and "blameworthiness." Curiously, the word is used to designate language mistakes: it shows how seriously the French take language. Spelling and grammar mistakes in French are called *fautes,* not errors (*erreurs*) or mistakes (*méprises*). The full meaning of *faute* is much more serious than a mistake or an error. The word actually has strong religious connotations. *Faute* evokes sin. "Worse than a crime, it was a *faute,*" said Napoleon's oft-quoted minister of police, Joseph Fouché. Fouché was referring to a political opponent executed on the emperor's orders. But the word lacks gravity in translation. The notion of *faute* can apply to situations as minor as small professional oversights or as major as criminal offenses. "Not knowing an answer" at work is considered a *faute* in France. So is gross misconduct or criminal negligence.

The big difference between a *faute* and an error is the element of personal responsibility it implies. A *faute* always has repercussions. French law—in particular, labor law—has even created a number of categories for faults—*faute simple* (which poorly translates as negligence), *faute grave* (serious misconduct), *faute lourde* (gross misconduct), *faute inexcusable* (inexcusable conduct), *faute matérielle* (a factual error). These notions, which hardly translate, delineate degrees of *faute*. A *faute simple* refers to a failure to meet one's essential obligations through carelessness, incompetence, or stupidity. A *faute lourde* adds the notion of intention and negligence. That means that the difference between both is not in the actual damage caused by the fault, but in the behavior of the person who committed it. In French law, which is inquisitorial by nature, confession is paramount. Admitting you are at fault is tantamount to pleading guilty. Whatever you argue, don't ever say it was your fault.

It's not hard to see why, no matter how trivial the matter, the French will do anything they can to avoid being accused of a *faute*. It's one reason conversations so often start with no. "No" is a safe default position the French take to reduce the risk of being blamed for something. It even has the added benefit of deflecting responsibility onto someone else.

This universal French fear of *faute* does breed some bizarre behaviors and lead to surreal conversations. In the spring before we moved to Paris, Jean-Benoît was passing through the city as part of a lecture tour and had made an appointment to touch base with one of our publishers at their office near the Luxembourg Gardens. On his way over, he phoned our publicist there, Élodie Royer, on her direct line, just to let her know he was running a few minutes late. "No problem. We're expecting you," she told him with cheery enthusiasm.

When Jean-Benoît arrived on the premises, the welcome was anything but cheery. The receptionist buzzed Élodie to announce there was a Monsieur Nadeau there to see her, after which Jean-Benoît became party to what sounded like a lunatic exchange between them. The receptionist turned back to him. "You had an appointment?"

"Yes, I just spoke to her."

"Your first name is?"

"Jean-Benoît."

"And you are?"

"I'm one of your authors."

The receptionist picked the phone up again, relayed the facts, then turned back to Jean-Benoît and announced, "Madame Royer will see you after her meeting."

Jean-Benoît wondered if he was losing his marbles. Didn't he just speak to Élodie Royer? How could she possibly have forgotten him? Was there some kind of office behavior code he hadn't picked up? After a half hour of waiting, Jean-Benoît started getting nervous. So he returned to the front desk to get to the bottom of it.

"Are there by any chance two Élodie Royers on your staff?" he asked the receptionist.

"No."

"Are you sure? Because I spoke to Élodie five minutes before I got here and this just doesn't make sense. She said she would be expecting me."

"Oh, let me see . . . ah, yes, we have Royer and Royez. Did you want to see *-ez* or *—er*?"

"Royer, *-er*."

The receptionist's final words: "Well you should have said so, *monsieur*."

Jean was stunned. This sort of misunderstanding can happen anywhere in the world, especially when receptionists are new on the job. But this particular exchange had one unmistakably French quality about it: the receptionist blamed Jean-Benoît for her own mistake, then just stared at him, unperturbed. The error was minor, but she could be "faulted" for it, and being French, she would have instantly associated this risk with job security. So she did the one thing she could do: put the blame straight back on Jean-Benoît.

The magnitude of the French *faute* taboo only becomes obvious when you compare the frivolity of a given offense with the amount of effort spent—or the ridiculous things said—trying to avoid being blamed for it.

In the total of four years we spent in France between 1999 and 2014, we hardly ever heard anyone pronounce the words *je ne sais pas* (I don't know). The fear of not knowing is so great in France that people will do anything to cover up their ignorance. In this *faute*-fearing universe, not knowing is even worse than exposing oneself to ridicule, which is bad enough for the French.

Jean-Benoît witnessed this less than twenty-four hours after arriving in Paris when he went to the store to buy margarine. It wasn't located with the butter. At least he didn't see it. So Jean-Benoît went to ask a clerk. His inquiry was answered with one of the usual variations on *non:* this time, the almost farcical "It doesn't exist." Jean-Benoît thought this was pretty amazing since margarine was invented in France (in 1869, for a contest organized by Napoleon III to find an alternative to butter; margarine was patented by the French pharmacist Hippolyte Mège-Mouriès the same year, and then the inventor sold his patent to a Dutch industrialist who went on to found the multinational consumer goods company Unilever). But Jean-Benoît decided against giving the clerk a history lesson.

Instead, he said, "*Si* (no-no). It's like butter, but it is made with vegetable oil."

"Okay, then it's in the oil section," the clerk replied.

"No," Jean-Benoît said. "Because it is refrigerated and it's solid."

"Then it's butter."

"Maybe, but it's not a dairy product."

While the clerk was looking in the cheese department, Jean-Benoît decided to take a second look in the butter section. He found products labeled "butter" and others that weren't called butter but weren't identified as "margarine" either. Then he spotted a telltale "Omega-3" badge on one of the plastic containers and read the list of ingredients, confirming it was oil based, not a dairy product. When Jean-Benoît showed it to the clerk, who, by then, was busy rooting through the cream section of the fridge, she replied with the closest thing the French have to "duh," like Jean-Benoît should have known himself. *"Mais la voilà, la margarine* [well there it is]!" When faced with the irrefutable proof of the existence of margarine, and of confirmation of her ignorance, the clerk actually scolded Jean-Benoît for not having looked more thoroughly. By the time Jean-Benoît realized he'd inadvertently switched on the clerk's fault shield, she had moved on to some other problem.

The anecdote would not seem significant to us, but we lived it over and over. In France, everyone is trained to know. In French labor law, the definition of a *faute simple* (which is sometimes enough to get you fired) includes "incompetence" and "stupidity"—which are also just euphemisms for "not knowing." We estimate that three quarters of the spontaneous noes we heard in France were default noes designed to hide the fact that someone didn't know something. It is a remarkably easy and, on the whole, widely accepted technique for getting out of a fix. (It is also, we noticed, one of the great sociological differences between Parisians and non-Parisians. For some reason, people outside of the capital are more willing to admit they don't know things when they actually don't.)

The astounding creativity the French use to avoid uttering the words

"I don't know" might be a product of France's salon culture, which was at its height in the seventeenth and eighteenth centuries, but is still present in France in modern forms. People were, and still are, invited to participate in salons on the basis of their ability to defend an idea or position, to speak like they "know." The French need to know might also come from their ancient fear of ridicule, which was also part of salon culture. Although there's a French proverb that says *le ridicule ne tue pas* (ridicule doesn't kill anyone), no one in France really believes that. In 2014, the Paris daily *Le Parisien* published an interview with the director Patrice Leconte who had made a popular film called *Ridicule* in 1996. Leconte explained how incredibly liberating he had found it to say "*Excusez-moi, je me suis trompé*" (Sorry, I made a mistake). [2] Apparently, only a famous film director can get away with something as outrageous as admitting he was wrong in France.

Another method the French have adopted to hide their ignorance is making categorical declarations and putting an end to discussions before questions can arise. It's basically another way of saying no. We got a taste of it at the Préfecture de police (police headquarters), where we showed up shortly after our arrival to get our *titre de séjour* (residence permit). The receptionist at the police headquarters told us we had to obtain our working permits before we could get our residency papers, and she sent us across the city to the Centre de Réception des Étrangers (literally, Foreigners Reception Center) in the seventeenth arrondissement. We thought it was strange, since we had arrived in France with what we believed to be a rare visa, the Carte compétences et talents (Skills and Talents card), which we had obtained by virtue of being authors. But the receptionist seemed very sure of herself (and very indifferent to the specialness of our visa).

We should have heeded our instinct. Instead, we spent two hours waiting on the pavement, under a threatening sky, outside an immigration office, only to discover we would have to wait another hour because the police officers had left for lunch. When we finally got inside the Centre, and when our number was finally called, the policewoman behind the desk took a quick look at our paperwork and informed us that the Centre didn't process the type of visa we had. When we told her we were following specific instructions from the Préfecture de Paris, she answered with that kind of absurd bureaucratic logic the French have turned into an art form: she blamed the mistake on us. Then she blamed us for having listened to the staff there. "You had to ask more questions," she said. We pointed out that it's hard to ask a question if you don't know there's a question to ask. But of course, she was right. We really should have known enough to ask, all the more so since no one in France ever admits they don't know.

One final way the French fend off *faute* is by inactive listening, a behavior category they seem to have invented. Actually, they listen. They just don't register information that comes from outside of the box. Julie phoned a photography agency in Paris to inquire about getting new author photos. We knew the studio did author photos because a photographer there had taken one of Jean-Benoît years ago. Still, the first answer was "No, we only deal with publishers, not authors." Julie knew enough to keep talking. She hoped the receptionist would eventually come to the realization that a customer is a customer.

The problem this time was a simple cultural difference. French publishers always pay for their authors' photos (the opposite of the United States, where publishers never pay for author photos). As a result, French photography agencies seem to have developed a firm belief that authors can't have pictures taken without their publisher's permission—or they won't be paid. Once Julie had connected the dots and understood why the agency was shooing her away, she simply explained the cultural difference, citing examples from her own publishing experience. The receptionist grasped the difference between American and French publishers, and once she became confident Julie would pay, told Julie the agency would be happy to take her photo.

Contrary to popular opinion, the French do listen, and well, but this usually happens *after* they say no a couple of times. It takes a certain amount of faith, and sometimes a lot of talking, but you can almost always find the yes hiding behind a French no, if it's there.

～ 4 ～

Schools: The Speech Factory

It was September 4, the day after *la rentrée scolaire,* back-to-school in France. Our daughters weren't in school yet. The four of us were rubbing our eyes after the night flight from Montreal to Paris. When we arrived at the customs gate at Charles de Gaulle Airport, we handed our passports to a placid-looking customs agent. Because of residency requirements, we watched carefully to make sure he actually stamped all passports with the date of our entry, something customs agents used to be rather casual about. He glanced at the first two, then handed them back to us, properly stamped, without a word.

Then something in the machine jammed. The customs agent sat up straight, suddenly looking punctilious. He carefully matched our daughters' (almost identical) faces to their passport photos. Instead of handing the photos back to us like he did before, he held them up in front of us and shook them in our faces. "Your children aren't in school!"

And so they weren't. We hesitated. One should never give customs agents more information than they ask for, and we didn't have the best excuse for missing school anyway. We had arrived in France a day late because it was 25 percent cheaper: airfare to Paris dropped by a quarter after *la rentrée*. Jean-Benoît tried to reassure the agent. "*Ne vous inquiétez pas* [don't worry], *monsieur*, our daughters will go to school as soon as we get them registered at city hall."

Jean-Benoît probably should have stuck to the Golden Rule of customs communications and kept his mouth shut. "*Ça ne se fait pas!*" (That's unthinkable!) the officer shot back. "School started yesterday!" He swung around to his neighboring agent and spread his arms wide so we could see that everyone in the country agreed with him.

We had been expecting a bit of heat from school authorities when we showed up late for school. But we really thought border authorities had bigger issues to tackle. Still, we shouldn't have been surprised. The French don't value education. They exalt it.

France is a country that has turned films about school life into a cinematic subgenre of its own. In 2004, one French citizen out of ten went to theaters to see a film about a school choir, *Les choristes* (The chorus). Two years earlier, one million viewers saw the documentary *Être et avoir* (To be and to have), about a one-room rural school in Auvergne. During the year we spent in France, there were two more documentary film hits about school life: *La cour de Babel* (School of Babel), about a class for immigrants in a Paris school, and *Sur le chemin de l'école* (On the way to school), which follows children in Kenya, Tunisia, Sri Lanka, and Argentina who have to climb mountains and walk through deserts every day to get to school.

After registering our daughters at city hall, we returned to our apartment, across the street from their new school, and walked fifty feet with them on their own *chemin de l'école*. It was day four of classes, and the sidewalk in front of the school was packed with parents, grandparents, and nannies trying to figure out what was going on. France had changed its school schedule the year we arrived, adding a half day of school on Wednesday mornings and shortening the school day on Tuesdays and Fridays. Parents were confused and frustrated, and our principal (the first one; he would go on sick leave the next week) looked as if he were trying to manage some kind of humanitarian crisis. Canada's and France's school years don't quite coincide so we had to talk to him to figure out which grade to put the girls in. We said *bonjour* and began to explain our situation.

The principal cut us off when he heard our daughters speaking English to Julie.

Mais ces enfants parlent français? (These children speak French?) It was more of a cry of distress than a question. Bigotry was not the issue here: his concern was administrative. We had registered our daughters in the regular class. Immigrant students who do not speak French are normally put in special integration classes in another school. Jean-Benoît assured the principal that our daughters spoke French to him.

But when we went to pick the girls up at the end of their first day of school, the hammer fell on their language skills, once again. We were again waiting in the throng of parents on the sidewalk when a tall man in his late fifties waved to us from the back of the crowd. He was dressed in a blue overshirt, and at first we thought he was a janitor. It took us a moment to remember that the smock was the traditional schoolteacher's *blouse*. He was Nathalie's new teacher, Monsieur Laouni. "I'm delighted to have Nathalie in my class," he said with a sparkle in his eye. "There's just one problem. Nathalie needs to speak more." We were dumbfounded. Surely a teacher would understand that a ten-year-old newcomer might not steal the floor on her first day in a new school, in a new country. Monsieur Laouni did understand. But it didn't matter. "Nathalie needs to make herself heard. She needs to take her place in the classroom," he explained.

That's when we understood what we had done. By bringing our daughters to France, we were actually sending them to a boot camp where children learn not just to speak, but to speak a lot, and well.

Although the military image might sound far-fetched, it's not. Public education in France is one enormous centralized machine, with 64,000 schools, a veritable army of 840,000 teachers, and 12 million kids. For the French, the national education system, the Éducation nationale, is a campaign. It has a one-size-fits-all approach: the curriculum is identical from the British Channel to the Mediterranean (including overseas territories).

Making sure citizens master French is the number one objective of French education, and strong oral skills are a big part of the project. "Speaking well is *primordial*," paramount, Monsieur Laouni announced to parents at the first parent-teacher meeting two weeks later, as if everyone didn't know that already. Our daughters' teachers were a master study in contrasts. Erika's teacher Madame Letendre was soft-spoken and methodical, her hair in a neat bob and her classroom suitably tidy and organized. Next door, Monsieur Laouni's classroom had no particular order we could discern. Desks and odd tables were scattered about the room and cluttered with gadgets we couldn't identify.

Yet despite their differences, both teachers agreed wholeheartedly about what was essential: *les exposés,* oral presentations. No other subject—except maybe English instruction—was as thoroughly explained, or aroused more interest among parents. Even before either teacher had a chance to elaborate, parents started blitzing them with questions about the *exposés.* How long would the *exposés* be? How often would students give them? Would they choose their own topics or have them assigned?

That's when we really understood Monsieur Laouni's day-one assessment of Nathalie, and why he felt the need to alert us about what he perceived as her oral deficiencies. The French don't think of oral presentations as something some kids naturally do better than others. To the French, speaking in public is a fundamental part of education, a life skill. All kids have to do it, and do it well.

As far as we could tell, most French kids do end up speaking amazingly well, with confidence and precision. We heard this for ourselves at the end of the school year, when classes put on plays for the parents in the school gym. One grade 6 group performed the Greek tragedy *Antigone,* written by Sophocles around 441 BC. None of the children sounded the slightest bit self-conscious as they bellowed out their lines. And they all knew their lines.

Our daughters were never what you'd call big talkers, except between themselves. Yet after only two months of school in France, friends who had known them in Quebec already heard the difference. "They are more precise," commented Mireille, a French friend who partially raised her children in Quebec. "They're asking questions all the time," another Quebec friend remarked when she visited us later in the year.

Like little French children, our girls developed an impressive stock of rhetorical tools. They beefed up their elocution by marking their intentions with qualifying phrases like *"en fait . . ."* (as a matter of fact) or *"pour l'instant . . ."* (for the moment). Phrases like this flow off the tongues of French children effortlessly, making them sound like little adults. (The influence only went so far in our case. We never heard our own children start a sentence with *"globalement . . ."* [as a general matter of speaking], as one of their friends did on a regular basis.)

Had they been exposed to it longer by staying in France an extra year, the normalizing effect of French school would probably have erased our daughters' Quebec accents altogether and would have vastly expanded their vocabulary. Even by the middle of the year, we noticed that when the girls arrived home at the end of the school week, after five days of instruction, their pronunciation had shifted and their vowels flattened out to a hybrid Parisian-Quebecois accent. After spending the weekend with us, the girls' accents shifted back to the original Quebecois.

So how do teachers do it? For starters, language is the highest priority on the school curriculum. As our daughter Erika put it one night several months after school started, "They don't teach French here. They teach *grammar*." We saw what Erika meant when she brought her first report card home in December. Elementary school report cards in France are not a sheet of paper. They are a ten-page booklet, with a clear plastic cover, which students keep throughout their elementary studies. There's nothing fancy about the marking system: kids get A (for "acquired"), B (for "needs reinforcement"), C (for "in the process of being acquired"), or D (for "not acquired"). But that's where the minimalism ends. The number of "acquisitions" the French evaluate in a single report card is mind-boggling. Kids get 191 different marks (though not all topics are evaluated every year). Nowhere is this level of analysis higher than in French (and they do call it French, contrary to Erika's impression), which is divided into eight subsections—oral skills, reading, calligraphy, literature, composition, vocabulary, grammar, and spelling—and sixty-eight subsections for those categories.

Grammar—the king topic—has no fewer than twenty-two subsections in which teachers evaluate ultraspecialized skills like "using adjectives correctly in possessive phrases" (*manipuler l'adjectif et le complement du nom*) or "recognizing an adverbial phrase" (*reconnaître les complements circonstanciels*). Only math is evaluated with something close to the same rigor as French.

Six weeks after school started we met our daughters' teachers to discuss their progress. Classes in public schools in France are large, with thirty or more students, so we weren't expecting much feedback. We just wanted to make sure the girls were fitting in and keeping up. To our surprise, Madame Letendre and Monsieur Laouni each sized up our girls' strengths and weaknesses pretty thoroughly. Both had the same concern. Madame Letendre tried to be diplomatic. "Children Erika's age," she explained gingerly, "are expected to be in the process of mastering the science of their language." In less diplomatic language: Erika needed to get with the *programme*.

We have never heard anyone in France say learning should be fun, or that kids should do "what interests them." French parents have none of the soul-searching North American parents (and educators) have about what kids should learn (facts or analytical skills?) or how they should learn (by rote, or self-directed learning?). French parents don't mix purposes. School is work. And kids are there to follow Le Programme.

In Le Programme, French children are taught to assimilate material. That means there is a lot of memorizing. Every week, Erika arrived home with at least one assignment that required strict memorization. This applied across the board, to every subject. Madame Letendre had her pupils memorize short descriptions of the political organization of medieval cities and the Five Pillars of Islam. Erika memorized a summary of how the Frankish warrior Charles Martel defeated an invading Islamic army in France in 732. She learned by heart lists of early French kings and their contributions, and memorized the number of towns, departments, and regions in France.[1]

Erika learned "the science of the language"—grammar—exactly the same way. She mastered the definitions of different types of adjectives, learned categories of adverbs by heart, and memorized examples of their use. On written tests, she had to regurgitate these formal definitions verbatim, including the examples.

Both our daughters also memorized poems, which they had to recite by heart in front of the class. Like all French kids, they learned the classics. They brought home verse written by the seventeenth-century poet Jean de la Fontaine and by the twentieth-century writer Marcel Pagnol. By the end of the year, they could memorize up to forty lines of poetry, which they afterward recited to their classmates. (Le Programme evidently hasn't changed much over the years. When we mentioned poems our kids were learning, some French friends recited them spontaneously, on the spot. They had learned the same ones when they were in primary school, decades ago.)

Nathalie was assigned one memorably difficult poem, "Heureux qui comme Ulysse" (Happy the man), a famous sonnet in a collection written by the sixteenth-century poet Joachim du Bellay, a member of the Pleiades group of poets. The theme struck us as slightly esoteric for ten-year-olds: the sonnet is about Du Bellay's longing for his home village in the Loire after a four-and-a-half-year sojourn in Italy. But the most amazing thing was, Nathalie had to learn it in its original form, in sixteenth-century French—the poem was written before the French Academy standardized French spellings. Fortunately, Jean-Benoît found a version of the poem sung by Algerian-born French pop singer Ridan on YouTube. And Nathalie did find it easier to master with a beat.

Our girls had some catching up to do as far as French history and references went, but they never complained about the full-time memorization regimen, even though it was antipodal to the methods used at their school in Montreal, where teachers ask them to "react" to stories. Memorizing is boring but it gives kids instant gratification and a piece of knowledge they can use to show off when the need or opportunity arises. Though it might not be every child's cup of tea, one North American friend whose daughter spent a year in Paris reported exactly the same thing: her daughter didn't mind just meeting clearly set expectations for a change.

We did occasionally meet French parents who bemoaned this regime of constant memorization. "It's futile. You forget it afterward," one mother told us. But few French parents ever said what North Americans might: that rote learning was stifling their children's creativity or stunting their analytical skills. It didn't seem to be doing any damage to French kids. Julie accompanied Erika's class one afternoon on an outing to a small exhibit about Grimms' fairy tales at a German cultural center near the Luxembourg Gardens. The exercise was a three-stage affair in which kids listened to the *contes,* tales, and answered questions. Erika's teacher then read a *conte* to her students and asked them to compare the stories to the versions of the same tales written by the seventeenth-century French writer Charles Perrault, the author of the Mother Goose Tales. The first child to answer said he wondered how some of the stories could be so similar, when they were written in two different countries, and so long ago. Madame Letendre had asked her students to engage in an international, historical exercise in comparative literature and the nine-year-olds in Erika's class didn't flinch.

The upshot of all the memorization is that French kids learn to speak the way they write, or at least as other people write. The French are known, in linguistic circles, for aspiring to speak with the same formality and precision as they use in their written language—as opposed to English speakers, who embrace different standards for written and oral expression. It's one reason the French use more words to express the same ideas. The French language does not lack the capacity for concision. The French just love words.

We often saw how the spoken and the written converge in French education, as when Nathalie mysteriously mastered the *passé simple* (the simple past). The simple past is a verb tense usually described as "literary." Since the nineteenth century, it has fallen out of usage in spoken French because it's hard to learn: there's no formula for the simple past that applies to verbs across the board, as there is for the more popular *passé composé* (past perfect), which has universally replaced the simple past in speech. This is why, today, the simple past is almost never used in day-to-day language, and rarely in speech at all except in formal address and in literature.

Erika learned the *passé simple* by memorizing verb endings and reproducing them, verbatim, on tests. But Nathalie's teacher, Monsieur Laouni, was less systematic about getting kids to memorize (an attitude that enraged one group of parents so much they dedicated the year to getting him kicked out of the school). Monsieur Laouni taught the simple past the way he did everything else, with no particular method we could discern. We never actually saw Nathalie study it.

So we were astonished when she arrived home one evening in March, after six months of school in French, with a short story she had composed *in* the simple past. Nathalie appeared to have mastered this rather obscure and seldom-used verb tense just by "picking it up." It took us a few days to understand what had transpired. Although she hadn't been memorizing it, like her sister had, Nathalie had been using the simple past, and listening to it, for months. Many of the written stories Nathalie read and the poems she memorized were written in the simple past so she learned an unspoken verb tense, at least partly, by ear.

Spoken and written French also converge in the famous French *dictée.* Dictation exercises are a unique French education ritual. They are not like English spelling dictations. In French *dictées,* teachers read a short text with sentences and paragraphs, so students have to produce the correct verb conjugations and grammar as well as word spellings.

The *dictée* was invented in the 1840s when teachers were looking for a new method to teach French. Until that point, teachers in France used the so-called cacophonic method: students were exposed to a list of possible spellings and had to identify the right one, like multiple choice. The method created more confusion than anything and was abandoned in favor of the *dictée,* which tests students not merely on spelling but also on grammar. Like English, French spelling is complicated, but the real difference is that French grammar is often inaudible—most plurals, for instance, cannot be heard, and many nuances of verb tenses are not apparent in oral speech, only in writing. So *la dictée* is a useful tool for teaching and testing and went on to become something of a national obsession.

A few weeks after school started, Erika came home with a question. She had already picked up the French rhetorical tick of announcing that she had a question before asking it. *"J'ai une question.* Why doesn't our school have a name?" For a North American, raised with the ethic of school spirit, Erika was disappointed with the clinical label above the front door of our school: "City of Paris. Mixed Elementary School."

The answer to her question goes to the heart of why the French put so much emphasis on speaking and writing correctly, and why they remain so formal, almost old-fashioned, in the way they teach. French public schools are not viewed as integral parts of communities, as they are in North America, and rarely exhibit their unique identity—though some elementary schools do have names. That's because there is only "one" French education system, called L'Éducation nationale (National Education). It's not even accurate to speak of a French school "system." School is an institution in France. Schools in France are factory outlets of one big company called the French state.[2]

When national education was created in France in the nineteenth century, the objective of schools was not just to educate the population, but to assimilate diverse groups by teaching them a common language, French. The French are generally well versed in their own history, but even some of them forget how recently the French language became a common tongue in their country. At the time of the French Revolution, not even half of the population understood French. Only a quarter could speak it fluently. The rest spoke one of myriad local languages, dialects, and patois, two dozen of which are still spoken in continental France—the largest ones are Breton, Alsatian, Occitan (and its most famous dialect, Provençal), Picard, and Basque. By World War I, most French could speak French, but half still spoke one of what are today qualified as "regional languages."

French had been declared the official language of the kingdom centuries earlier, in 1539, by a king's ordinance. Oddly, the French language made little progress for the next 250 years. During the French Revolution, the government realized that it had to find a way to get its citizens to speak French. But in the upheaval of the Revolution and imperial wars that followed, organizing a gigantic school system proved too daunting a task. It was impossible to train the tens of thousands of teachers that were necessary to teach millions of children. It took France forty more years to get over this hurdle.

The "project" of getting the French to speak French would influence how the language was taught, and how the French came to think about teaching French to this day. In the 1830s France got its first ed-ucation minister, François Guizot, who started building a national education system. From the start, French teaching was, literally, second-language teaching. Many language students today would recognize the methods: students learned grammar and vocabulary by heart. This tendency toward rules-based learning was reinforced by the intellectual climate of nineteenth-century France, when French intellectuals became infatuated with the ideals of classicism and lan-guage purism—two ideas from the seventeenth century that had made a comeback. Purism entered schools and stayed there. As the French writer André Gide (1869–1951) wrote, "En chaque Français, il y a un Vaugelas qui sommeille" (Every Frenchman has a Vaugelas inside him), which referred to a famous seventeenth-century grammarian who was one of the original members of the French Academy.

That spirit lives on, to put it mildly. Today, less than 9 percent of the French, or 5 million, speak one of the regional languages, and less than 1 percent speak a regional language exclusively before attending school. Yet French education never completely shed its original raison d'être. Today's language teaching techniques have retained much of the philos-ophy of the original methods. Rules-based, prescriptive teaching is still the norm.

Even if you don't have children, education is a great topic of con-versation in France. In fact, it's hard to avoid. While with some things, like *dictées,* the emphasis on oral expression and rote learning never seem to change, teaching methods and the education program itself have evolved over the last century and are perpetual subjects of debate today. But of course, in a society whose school system is designed to teach children how to be convincing, it should come as no surprise that when the French grow up, they like to argue about school.

5

The Family Factor

One of the most novel things about living in France for the second time was experiencing French culture with children. Our daughters Erika and Nathalie are gregarious, and thanks to them, we met children from a variety of backgrounds, and families of different types and sizes. We also hung out, for the first time, in places where families congregate in Paris, namely parks, pools, museums, and libraries. Since our daughters have a taste for friends with *caractères forts* (headstrong behavior), their French friends were perhaps a bit more talkative than average. And since we lived in the relatively well-heeled fifth arrondissement, they came mostly from middle- or upper-middle-class Parisian families. But we believe most of what we saw about family life in France was fairly representative of French society as a whole, or at least of the model most French embrace.

The thing that surprised us the most about the group of nine-year-old French girls we got to know over the course of the year was the way they spoke to adults. French children are remarkably articulate, more than many grown-up North Americans. They can hold surprisingly long conversations and ask a lot of thoughtful, sometimes pointed questions. Even the least talkative among them have the good manners to deliver the obligatory *bonjour* and *au revoir* to grown-ups. Whether or not there is a parent hovering nearby, French children say *s'il vous plait* and *merci* clearly, not under their breath, or grumbling. As far as we could tell, French children of all classes are raised with the same basic framework, and from a young age.

We had no trouble meeting other parents, partly because of our daughters' skill for filling their weeks with playdates, and partly because in a city as dense as Paris, where almost all children go to local public schools, you are bound to run into other parents every day. Over the course of the year, talking to a lot of fellow parents about child rearing, we realized that many of the peculiar ways the French communicate—the automatic *non,* the inescapable *bonjour,* and great emphasis on "presentations"—start not at school, but with how parents raise their kids: with a tight leash, and relatively few doubts about the best techniques.

One striking feature of French families is their size: the French have a lot of children. According to official statistics the French have an average of two children per woman. This is the highest rate in Europe, equal to that of Ireland, as well as the United States'. It is also an interesting reversal: between 1750 and 1945, the French were notorious for producing many fewer children than the Germans, the British, and the Italians. Then, starting at the end of World War II, they turned into the European leaders of birthrate.[1]

In our girls' immediate social circle, families of three children were common, and one had four. The girls only had one child without siblings in their group, the daughter of a divorced mother, our friend

Brigitte. As we would discover, a lot of powerful and influential women in France have large families: in the French government, a third of female ministers had three children or more, which is double the national average (itself the highest in Europe). The same holds true for male ministers—the president himself has, officially, four children. And all French presidents since Charles de Gaulle have had four children.

To get to the bottom of the birthrate enigma, Jean-Benoît visited France's national bureau of statistics, the Institut national de la statistique et des études économiques (INSEE), located in a nondescript building with a spectacular view of one of Paris's least attractive sites: the *périphérique* (ring) highway around the city. He went to talk to Pascale Breuil, the head of demographic and social studies, who examines the ins and outs of France's population growth. Jean-Benoît was expecting to talk mostly about numbers. Instead, Madame Breuil explained why she thought the issue of France's birthrate is mostly a cultural one.

Madame Breuil concluded that France's high birthrate was not actually the product of the country's generous social programs, like day care, health care, and family allowances. According to her, what really sets the French apart from the rest of Europe is their attitude about family itself. She compared France to Germany. Sixty percent of adults in France say they want to have three children or more. The same proportion of French men and women say that having a family is essential to their *épanouissement personnel* (personal fulfillment). That's double the rate of Germans who think so. The French say the first condition for having a child is "finding the right person." Germans say it's having enough money and finding proper housing.

French families are not, in themselves, radically different from their North American counterparts. The typical family model is the same: two-generation units of parents and children, though French grandparents are still expected to pitch in and supply child care. (And from what we saw, most step up to the task to some degree.) The real difference is what the French think "family" means or represents. The French think of family as a timeless *institution*. Like all French institutions, it has a well-defined identity and plays a specific role in how society functions. In terms of taxes, for instance, the moment you are married, you declare your income tax as a couple. In France, when you form a family (by getting married or by having children if you are in a common law relationship), you are automatically given a *livret de famille,* an official family booklet that contains the records of marriages, divorces, births, and deaths, as well as the names of everybody's parents and grandparents.[2]

Simply put, there's very little way you can escape from being part of a family, administratively speaking. As a family, you are constantly asked for your *livret de famille* to prove you are entitled to one of the many incentives, allowances, and discounts for families. Even in French tax law, there is no such thing as personal income tax: the tax unit is a couple (even before they have children).[3] When it comes to writing wills, the French have very little freedom over their estates. Most of what they leave behind goes automatically (and obligatorily) to children and the spouse; only a small proportion can be disposed of at will.

The French have never seriously questioned the value of the family unit, not even during France's agitated revolutionary period when revolutionaries tried to rebuild France's institutions from top to bottom— to the point of inventing a new calendar with new names for the days of the week and months. Modern French society is remarkably sensitive about redefining "family." The year we were in Paris, one hundred thousand people took to the streets to protest same-sex marriage, dubbed *mariage pour tous* (marriage for all), an expression that brings the French as close as they'll ever get to being politically correct. That march, impressive on its own, was just a curtain call of protest a year earlier by the same group—a collective of thirty Catholic and right-wing associations called the Manif pour tous (Demonstration for all)—when half a million people marched on the Champs-Élysées to defend "the family" (the Web site of the movement states they want to end "genealogy for all," meaning no family trees for same-sex couples).

The French themselves were surprised by how belligerent, but also how popular, the Manif pour tous became. And France's Left, in particular the Socialist government, in some ways folded to the pressure. It was utterly averse to fiddling with the French definition of "the family." The only idea the government came up with to make same-sex marriage politically palatable was to separate marriage from family: same-sex marriage was authorized on May 18, 2013, but same-sex couples were denied access to assisted reproductive technology.

Julie was relaxing on a bench inside the enclosed children's park in Paris's Luxembourg Gardens one afternoon while our daughters burned off some steam on the park's mini zip line, called a *tyrolienne* in French. There was a mother beside her, tending to a baby in a stroller while the mother's other, four-year-old daughter stick-fought with an umbrella to kill time. Julie was in the little girl's line of fire and, predictably, got jabbed in the upper thigh. The mother shot up from her baby to scold the big sister. In typical North American style, Julie assured her she wasn't really hurt and told her *ce n'était pas grave,* it wasn't a big deal. But it was. The mother shot back to Julie, "*Si. C'est grave!*" (Yes, it is) and turned back to scold her daughter with new vigor. There was simply no way she was going to let a victim undermine her efforts to properly educate her daughter.

French ideas about parenting struck us as conservative, a little authoritarian, sometimes bordering on retrograde. Yet the more we saw how the French parenting philosophy worked out in practice, the less disturbing the techniques seemed.

In France, giving children a *bonne éducation* (a good education) is paramount. The term comes up frequently in discussions about children. It has little or anything to do with school. Rather, it's the formal education the family provides. What exactly is a good education? Our friend Brigitte, the mother of one of our daughters' friends, liked to regale us with stories of her extremely bourgeois upbringing in Paris's "old money" sixteenth arrondissement. Among other things, her grandmother insisted on teaching Brigitte how to perform a proper curtsy. No French citizen of parenting age, in any Paris neighborhood, would call that part of a good education today. But some things haven't changed. Brigitte was determined to instill in her own daughter the basic elements of a good education: teaching her to be *sage* (which literally translates as "wise" but means well behaved, good, calm), to present herself (say *bonjour*), to respect adults, to have good table manners and express herself properly. (The opposite of this is *mal élevé* [poorly raised], meaning bad-mannered, something the French universally condemn.)

Part of what makes French parenting work is that everyone more or less agrees on the goal, and the techniques for achieving it. The American journalist and author Pamela Druckerman, who reports on Paris for *The New York Times,* identified one of the key elements to French parenting as the *cadre,* the frame. In her book *Bringing Up Bébé,* Druckerman describes how French parents just take for granted that kids need structure and rules. And parents don't question what those rules should be.

As she dug into the topic during her research, Druckerman realized that one of the most striking features of French parenting philosophy was the absence of "philosophy." Ideas about the degree and type of authority that should be exercised have evolved. No one would endorse the kind of naked authority their parents or grandparents exercised, at least not openly. But the French have not exactly thrown the old rules out with the bath water. For the French, exercising authority is part of a parent's job. Children are corrected early, and firmly, in the interests of making them *sage*. And most French children, as we saw, pick up a sense of what's right and wrong very early from their parents, who are pretty unequivocal about it. French parents are certainly less strict and authoritarian than they used to be, but the idea of the parent-as-friend is still almost universally ridiculed.

As Druckerman points out, the French don't even have a word for "parenting." The closest equivalent is the expression *éducation familiale*, family education. But there's an important difference between the two. "Parenting" is a verb: it's something you do. The ultimate goal is understated, even up for debate—do we raise kids to be autonomous? Secure? Adventuresome? As North Americans, we consider that parents all have different styles that correspond to their values (which is not to say we agree with the style or the values, just the basic principle that parenting is something of an individual art). The French notion of *éducation familiale* emphasizes both the action of educating *and* the result, which is *une bonne éducation*. We talked to a lot of French people from a lot of different situations and classes, and they all seem to think pretty much the same thing about what family education consists of.

Teaching kids to express themselves is a big part of it. One of the most remarkable features of the French is not just the ease with which they can speak but also the fact that they speak well. Through school and family, the French get the message very early, then consistently throughout their lives, that they are expected to exhibit a certain eloquence in their interactions with others. Children are taught eloquence as a life skill, and not just with the objective of facilitating future careers in the arts and or in show business. It applies to every element of French society. Not all French speak brilliantly, but everyone is expected to demonstrate some polish in verbal presentation—starting with saying the proper *bonjour, merci,* or *au revoir.* It makes a lot of sense for families to cultivate this skill, for the simple fact that people who speak well will always seem more educated than they actually are.

This attitude is not surprising considering what the French consider the objective of raising children. In a fascinating book called *Devenir adulte: Sociologie comparée de la jeunesse en Europe* (Growing up: Comparative sociology of European youth), the French sociologist Cécile Van de Velde identifies four European models for adulthood.[4] For the English (and by extension Americans), the goal of growing up is to *s'assumer* (take responsibility for your life). In the Danish and Scandinavian model, becoming an adult is about *se trouver* (finding one's self). For Spanish and Italians, it is more about *s'installer* (making a home).

For the French, Van de Velde claims, the objective of growing up is to *se placer* (find a "situation"), to find a good job and a good place in the system. The French *éducation familiale* is all about giving kids the skills they need to find the right "situation." That's why a lot of the values and habits French parents teach their kids work to help them be accepted and "fit in." Kids are taught a number of codes very early in life.

The first one is to avoid ridicule, or being laughed at. It's probably fair to say the fear of ridicule is pretty universal in all cultures. But North Americans, for example, believe so strongly in the merits of individuality that they're willing to cut some slack when it comes to not "conforming." Not the French. They pretty much agree that you should avoid anything that keeps you from fitting in.[5]

One of the most outstanding examples is in name choices. Names in France are remarkably conformist. It's nothing like the extreme of Denmark, where 40 percent of the population shares the same twenty first names. But the French are not inclined to go anywhere near the endless innovating that Anglo-American societies do with first names, where anything seems to go, spelling mistakes included. This first-name conservatism in France is partly explained by history. In 1803, when Napoleon was not yet emperor, French law stated that children must be named after calendar saints, biblical figures, and people from documented history. In 1966, the law was loosened up to authorize names from mythology and French regions—the Bretons took to this with a vengeance. But as recently as 1993, French parents still had to get state approval for their first-name choices.

Parents today can choose any name they want, and the state can't legally do anything to stop them, except in extreme cases, where it can prove that a name will "cause prejudice to a child," like, say, Adulterine.

But curiously, the French still stick to the classics when it comes to naming children. Even today, Jean and Marie top the charts of popular French names. And one rarely sees names with really unorthodox spellings. The French just assume having a weird name will limit you in life. Our twin daughters, who are adopted, had as their original Haitian names something along the lines of Mandarine and Mandoline. Before the girls arrived, many of our North American friends were worried that changing their names would damage their identities by depriving them of a link to their Haitian origins. Our French friends uniformly congratulated us for changing the names and helping our daughters avoid (what they assumed would be) humiliation all their lives. *Personne ne pourrait vivre avec ce nom,* they said. No one can get through life with names like those. (The girls themselves thought nothing of changing their names and are very happy with our choices.)

The French would certainly have never voted, as Quebeckers did in 2014, for a government led by a certain Philippe Couillard. The name Couillard comes from *couille* (as in balls, for testicles), though the name actually derives from a medieval catapult in the shape of the male organ. It's a common name in Quebec, but for the French, the link between Couillard and *couille* is just too ridiculous. There are people in France named Couillard, but they would have to change their names if they wanted to be elected. Avoiding ridicule is actually the primary reason people give when requesting an official name change in France. The changes are posted in France's *Journal officiel,* the official gazette that publishes all legal notices, decrees, and decisions. The name issue is so sensitive that the list of people who have been granted new names appears only in the paper version of the document, not online.

A French sociologist, Baptiste Coulmont, carried out an interesting study examining France's conservative name choices. His hypothesis was that names were a self-fulfilling prophecy.[6] The parents who valued success the most would make the most conservative choices. Coulmont looked at the first names of students who had just done the *bac* (end of high school) exam (some seven hundred thousand students). Only 9 percent of these seven hundred thousand students managed to get a *très bien* (a mention) on the exam. So Coulmont studied which first names were on the list of the best students and—big surprise—three quarters of them were straight from the Napoleonic list, including Ulysse, Guillemette, Quitterie, Madeleine, Anne-Claire, Ella, Sibylle, Marguerite, Hannah, Irene, Octave, Domitille. Less than 2 percent of the best students had "modern" names (Asma, Sephora, Hakim, Kimberley, Assia, Cynthia, Brenda, Christian, Bilal, Brian, Melvin, Johann, Eddy, and Rudy). When Jean-Benoît mentioned this to a group of French friends, one woman tersely commented, "*c'est normal*" (it's to be expected). Parents who choose unusual names "watch too much American TV."

As part of their *éducation familiale,* kids learn to respect authority. As North Americans, we have always found French parents' authoritarian streak a little startling, especially when it comes out of the mouths of some particular friends who are extremely liberal, leaning toward bohemian. We used to think French children accepted authority at home because they have to live with so much of it at school. Now we know it's the other way around. School mirrors the values families teach anyway. By the time children find themselves in institutionalized education, whether in a crèche (day-care center), in a *maternelle* (kindergarten), or at elementary school, they have been getting strong doses of authority from their parents for years.

We saw this scenario unfold so many times while we were in France that all the faces melded into one prototypical parent with a child. That mother (it's usually a mother, but not always) is marching somewhere leading a child by the hand, or sometimes by the neck. The child is sobbing. The mother repeats, loud enough to hear from the other side of the street: "You aren't obeying! You aren't obeying!" She says it at least ten times, in a half dozen different tones ranging from stern to completely indignant. The scene lasts between thirty seconds and several minutes. We never actually see how any of these stories start, and we never stick around to see how they end, but the gist is the same: irritated French people order their children to "obey." Parents in New York, Chicago, Montreal, or Monterrey would only insist that their children "listen."

In short, authority is never understated in France. It is probably the central notion that unifies all French families. This is why no one shies away from using words like *enfants sages* (well-behaved children), *cadre* (frame), or *éducation* (the rules of which everyone agrees on). They are universal and well-accepted foundational concepts. Nor do you often see French parents trying to be their children's "friend." Whatever their failings as parents—and France's divorce rate is 55 percent, roughly comparable to that of the United States at 53 percent—trying to be a child's friend is a mistake as far as French parents are concerned.[7] French parents consider it their prerogative to call the shots.

French parents can be strangely permissive: at parks, at parties, even in restaurants, French kids do all sorts of annoying things in front of other parents, and sometimes parents carry on the conversation without seeming annoyed at all. But when enough is enough, parents clamp down and don't apologize for it. French children make demands and parents often give in. But both parents and children know who's in charge. We never hear French parents justify their decisions with long explanations appealing to children's sense of responsibility, for instance. When French parents complain about other parents, the first thing they say is that they "are not strict enough."

So why don't little French kids all grow up to be docile, subservient adults? For one thing, when they go to school, the first thing they learn is how to talk like adults themselves.

~ 6 ~

The Art of Conversation

One drizzly November evening in Paris, we left our daughters at home and headed out to a small dinner party near the Luxembourg Gardens. Our hostess was Guillemette Mouren, the editor of a magazine put out by the lobby group Défense de la langue française (Defense of the French language). A sharp and elegant woman in her early seventies, she had interviewed Jean-Benoît earlier in the year about our book on the French language and, afterward, invited us for dinner.

After a short walk through the winding streets of Paris's Latin Quarter, we found the door to Guillemette's building on le boulevard Saint-Michel and typed the *digicode* to get in. Then we walked through not one, not two, but three inner courtyards before arriving at the door of her elegant ground-floor apartment (which had its own private garden, as we would see). The dwelling was a perfect example of the Parisian bourgeois style, sumptuous and spacious with high ceilings and pristine white walls, furnished with brightly polished antiques.

Guillemette greeted us warmly at her door and invited us into the living room for the *apéro,* before-dinner drinks. Her husband was seated there with another polished-looking couple in their seventies, Corrine and Giorgio. As Guillemette served champagne, cherry tomatoes, and finger pastries, we chatted about current events. The previous week, a Quebec writer of Haitian origin, Dany Laferrière, had been elected to the French Academy. As fellow nationals, we thought we'd share a few thoughts on Laferrière's literary merits.

No sooner had we opened our mouths than one of the ladies, Corrine, veered off into left field with a completely off-color remark about the French Academy. It was what the French call *une énormité,* an outrageous comment. "Everyone knows it's easier to be elected if you are a homosexual," she declared. We stared dumbly for a few seconds. It was the first time we'd heard anything of the sort about membership criteria for academicians, let alone speculation about Dany Laferrière's sexual orientation. We told her that Dany Laferrière was *aux femmes* (into women) as far as we knew and waited for someone to change the topic.

Things improved half an hour later, when we figured out why this particular small group had been brought together. It turned out we were the guests of honor at a small gathering of hard-core Quebecophiles. Corrine and her Italian husband, Giorgio, had met during a snowstorm in Quebec City in the 1960s, when she was a ballet teacher and he was a young diplomat. After they got married, they lived in Montreal for a few years. They seemed to have loved every minute of it, including the snow. Corrine then told us, in delicious detail, about how she met the French president Charles de Gaulle during his famous state visit to Quebec in 1967.

Dany Laferrière was long forgotten and the conversation was rolling by the time Guillemette invited us to *passer à table,* move to the table. Guillemette had placed platters of sauerkraut, sausages, mashed potatoes, and bread on the table so she wouldn't have to run back and forth to the kitchen serving all night, which would interrupt the flow of the conversation, or make her miss out on something. In short, she had put together a meal not so much designed to show off her cooking skills as to keep the conversation flowing. The group regaled us with stories from their long lives in France and overseas. After Quebec, Corrine and Giorgio went on to live in the United States and Australia. Just before Guillemette served dessert—a simple apple pie that we cut and served ourselves—the conversation turned to Paris itself. Over the years, these couples had seen it all and were still reveling in the city's cultural life. We listened carefully, taking mental notes.

And then, more than an hour after we had arrived, we finally woke up and remembered our manners. French conversation does not follow rules so much as adhere to values. The most important one is that you have to give as much as you take. We had been doing a lot of listening that evening. Too much, in fact. The French love to hear foreigners' observations and insights about their own country, and we had been doing that, but it wasn't enough. You can't be a good conversationalist by just being polite. If you spend the whole evening just listening, commenting on other people's observations, and politely agreeing or demurring, you aren't playing fair—or well. Conversation in France is like tennis: to be a good player you have to do more than just return the easy balls.

Julie suddenly snapped out of her reserve just as the cheese course arrived. The conversation had turned to a new Art Deco show going on at the museum of the Trocadéro, behind the Eiffel Tower. She leaned forward and cocked her head to the side apologetically to soften the blow of what she was about to say. Then she just spit it out. "You have to admit, Art Deco was European fascists' favorite decoration."

Julie had just uttered her very own *énormité*. There was a pregnant pause around the table. Then Giorgio smiled and leaned forward like we were about to start a game of poker. "How interesting," he said, with a smile. On the other side of the table, his wife Corrine called Julie "charming," with a wink. And the conversation took off. Everyone has something to say about fascism. And about art. So for the next half hour, we had a spirited discussion about whether one could separate art from politics or enjoy the aesthetic quality of Art Deco independently of its political associations. We hadn't been invited simply as a courtesy, and no one here expected us to be polite or respectful. Our hosts were hoping for some action, some friction. They wanted to have some fun.

As we walked back out through all the courtyards after leaving Guillemette's apartment at the end of the evening, we felt as though we had been to a French salon (partly, of course, because of the swank surroundings). A French person might actually laugh at us for thinking such a thing. Most French consider salons a thing of the past, and strictly speaking, they are. Over the course of French history, forums for conversation have shifted, notably from salons, to discussion groups, to clubs, to *dîners en ville* (our experience at Guillemette's). But one feature unites French conversation wherever it happens: a certain culture of eloquence. In other words, the spirit of salons lives on.

Strangely, although everyone in France knows about the salons, French aren't really conscious their conversation has a particular style. To them, it's simply the way it is. The French don't seem to realize how much their conversation style today owes to rituals that developed centuries ago.

French salons started popping up, in an early form, in the seventeenth century. At the time, they were informal gatherings in private homes, mostly in Paris, called *cercles* (circles) or *académies* (academies). The French were actually emulating the Italians, who, during the Renaissance, had revived the ancient Greek "art of conversation." But if the French didn't invent this art, they certainly succeeded in branding it as uniquely French. The French marquise de Rambouillet, who was born Catherine de Vivonne in 1588, is credited with running one of the first truly influential speaking circles. When she was still a young bride, she got bored of life at the French court and decided to create her own private conversation circle. She moved into a new town house, located on the site of today's Louvre, painted her bedroom blue— pretty scandalous at the time—and then turned it into a reception room.

Until the death of the marquise de Rambouillet in 1665, the Hôtel de Rambouillet was frequented by some of the most intriguing and provocative minds of seventeenth-century France, including the poet François de Malherbe (who invented language purism) and the Cardinal Richelieu, King Louis XIII's chief minister (who was behind the rise of political absolutism). Guests read poetry and letters, criticized the latest literary works, analyzed French grammar, and discussed the state of morals and society's values. After that, salons just took off.

Historians attributed the multiplication of literary circles—which would only later be called "salons"—mostly to the intellectual atmosphere of seventeenth- and eighteenth-century France. Salons gave people a place to talk, away from the stiff rules of the French court. According to the French historian Marc Fumaroli, France's preeminent thinker on the art of conversation and member of the French Academy, salons were practically born of necessity. In his book *Trois institutions littéraires* (Three literary institutions), Fumaroli argues that

French salons were a pressure valve for the increasingly rigid French state, what he characterizes as "the unstable, arbitrary and damaging character of France's political and administrative institutions."[1] According to Fumaroli, salons were also a place the French could rebel against their ultraconservative clergy.

Early salons, like Madame de Rambouillet's, ended up playing an important role in the development of the French language. There was relatively little published literature at the beginning of the seventeenth century in France, and the grammar rules of French had not yet been formalized. Elevated conversation was an ideal forum for hammering out French grammar. In fact, one of Madame de Rambouillet's most revered guests, the Cardinal Richelieu, was so impressed by the quality and nature of the debate at her house, he hijacked another literary circle in Paris and turned it into the French Academy.

But salons weren't exclusively aristocratic think tanks. Figures of relatively modest origin were welcome there, as well as personalities with less stellar intellectual credentials, like soldiers. All they needed was *esprit* (wit) and something interesting to add to the conversation. Each participant's value was measured by the quality of his or her commentary, and how much he, or she (women were welcome, too), contributed to the common pool of topics and ideas. And new participants could truly make their mark in society by perfoming well at a salon. Madame de Rambouillet regularly invited the poet Vincent Voiture, son of a wine merchant who went on to become one of the first members of the French Academy when it was founded in 1635.

Even today, conversation operates as a remarkable equalizer in French society. As Marc Fumaroli puts it, "Joining a conversation, whether it is sophisticated or natural, is a game you play with partners you consider your equals. The only thing one expects from them is to play well."[2] As the French literary critic Emmanuel Godo argues, in the salons, different sexes, different talents, different conditions, and different characters were not considered a source of conflict, but of richness, and promised enjoyment. The French love conversations in which diverse perspectives clash and people duke it out intellectually. That's considered far more interesting than reaching consensus. So it's easy to understand why "political correctness" irks the French. It's boring.[3]

Generations of French thinkers have dissected the art of conversation in attempts to define its precise qualities, essence, and true objectives—which is paradoxical, since reaching consensus is usually the last thing the French really want to do when they enter into conversation. As Marc Fumaroli writes, "Salon participants had to be interesting and informed but not weighty and erudite; they had to speak brilliantly but without humiliating anyone; their words had to be moderate but at the same time spontaneous and personalized, a bit racy, spiced with a bit of irony, but no bad will."[4]

To an outsider, the French art of conversation sounds like a bundle of contradictions and it is. Excelling in the art of French conversation was, and remains, a tall order. Participants are expected to be playful, or, as the modern-day French philosopher and anthropologist Pierre Sansot puts it, in an essay called *Le goût de la conversation* (The taste for conversation), conversation requires a certain "lightness." "Dreary or serious conversations worry us and make us self-conscious about enjoying life," he writes. "Conversation requires good-natured familiarity and a propensity for marveling at life."[5] At the same time, Sansot argues, good conversation requires "impertinence, and a little discomfort." As we were reminded at Guillemette's house, playing the conversation game well does require taking risks: everyone is expected to plunge in at some point. Corrine's early comment regarding Dany Laferièrre's sexual orientation was probably just that— a bit of what the French call *provoc* (short for *provocation,* provocation). And that's a good thing.

Yet provoking just to get a rise out of someone is off limits. Why? Good conversationalists have to be honest ones. Or as Godo puts it in his *Histoire de la conversation* (History of conversation), participants should consider conversation a game, and respond to its rules. You need to listen to other participants rather than make a show of yourself, Godo argues. But then, there are limits to being honest. As Sansot points out, "No one should use conversations as an excuse to spill their guts." Taking the game too literally, he says, and dragging everyone into your drama, will ruin it for everyone.

Then there's the rule of reciprocity. To play the game well, you need to known when to talk, and when to listen. Everyone should try his or her best. But no one should steal the show. That would be tantamount to stealing from the kitty. As Sansot puts it, "I would absolutely never invite back a pedant, an opportunist or a whiner, nor someone pretentious or ironic who breaks up the harmony and mutual trust of the company." And of course, there's spontaneity. If you really want to make your mark as a good conversationalist, you need to have all the above qualities, plus an excellent memory to quickly conjure witty *reparties,* comebacks. Because conversation is meant to be spontaneous, not studied. And finally, you need a fine mastery of the language—because using the language well is paramount, if not the whole point.

In short, the art of conversation in France, as it was originally conceived, and still practiced, is something like an English garden: it's highly cultivated to look and feel natural.

Curiously, talking about literary salons with the French spurs mixed reactions. Modern French tend to associate salons with one of the sillier contingents of young women who attended them, whom the French literary giant Molière dubbed *les précieuses ridicules* (pretentious young ladies), the name of a play he wrote about them. Many French associate the art of conversation itself with the frivolous French court life of the seventeenth century. It's a strange bias, because salons (and the word wasn't actually used until 1783) became serious business with the arrival of the French philosophes and with the events of the French Revolution in the eighteenth century. As Godo puts it, the purpose of salons was no longer to celebrate the present but "to change society, to invent the future."

No one embodied this spirit better than Madame de Staël (1766–1817), a trailblazer in French salon culture who is enjoying something of a comeback among French intellectuals today. Born Germaine Necker, she was the daughter of King Louis XIV's finance minister. She began attending her mother's salon in Paris when she was five. When she grew up she was married off to Sweden's ambassador to France. It was not a happy union and Madame de Staël dedicated the rest of her life to finding more stimulating company. She opened her first salon on Paris's rue du Bac in 1786, three years before the French Revolution, and kept it running during the Revolution and the Napoleonic Wars, even after Napoleon sent her into exile for disagreeing with and defying him.

Madame de Staël kept running her salon in the middle of social and political upheaval and wherever she found herself (at different points she lived in Sweden, Switzerland, Russia, Italy, and Germany). Her years living abroad also gave her a new appreciation for what she came to think of as an innate French talent for conversation. Italians had imagination, she said. English had originality. Germans could write, but not talk—and when Germans did converse, she was stunned to learn they didn't allow interruptions (though this is mostly because of a grammatical feature of the German language itself: German verbs often come at the end of the sentence).

Though it was partly for her own pleasure, Madame de Staël did promote conversation as a way of bringing ideas of great thinkers to a wider audience. By her day, salons had started operating like media at a time when there was no radio and hardly any press to speak of, and when most news circulated through gossip, songs, or poems. The salons served to popularize or legitimize new ideas, in the same way high-standard radio broadcasters like NPR, the BBC, CBC, or France Culture do today. Madame de Staël herself opposed slavery and favored constitutional monarchies like England's. She argued for a society founded on justice and humanity and was a great advocate of political power heeding public opinion—one of her biographers, Michel Winock, describes her as simply "modern."

Like that of her predecessor Madame de Rambouillet, Madame de Staël's salon was frequented by some of the most brilliant minds and influential figures of her era: the philosopher Denis Diderot, the author of France's first encyclopedia; Charles-Maurice de Talleyrand-Périgord (1754–1838), the French ambassador to the United Kingdom, considered the best conversationalist of his time; the Enlightenment philosopher Nicolas Condorcet; and the scientist Georges-Louis Leclerc, Compte de Buffon.

In her salon, participants discussed religion and literature; argued about the limits of the power of the state, the place of individual liberties, and the nature of the institutions being established in the new French Republic; and talked about how to defend individual liberties against the power of the king and avoid authoritarianism in all its forms. Even in the middle of a revolution, wars, coup d'états, and regicide, French salons kept honing the art of conversation, with all its idiosyncratic rules and built-in contradictions, no matter how serious the topic. That is, the salons never became simple debating clubs. In *Trois institutions littéraires,* Fumaroli argues that the French love of conversation contributed to the loss of the colonial empire. He describes an eighteenth-century French diplomat who visited the United States and pointed out that there were many more French talking in cafés in New Orleans than there were working the land on their farms in rural Louisiana. Indeed, the French threw in the towel on Louisiana a few years after this visit and sold it back to the United States for $15 million. It just wasn't a place where their true talents could flourish.

Literary salons more or less disappeared from France in the years following the French Revolution.[6] The aristocracy was not gone—nor the monarchy, as the French would see when the king returned in 1814—but in this new middle-class era, aristocratic activities like salons became stigmatized. As Fumaroli puts it: "A violent prejudice against conversation came crashing down on France." Nineteenth-century writers like Guy de Maupassant and Gustave Flaubert even made fun of organized conversation in their works.

But the French love of conversation didn't evaporate. In the nineteenth century, artists took over from aristocrats as the cream of the crop of conversationalists. As Fumaroli says, in the new utilitarian, businesslike society of nineteenth-century France, the artist was the only one who could claim to be "a genius in leisure" (*avoir du génie dans le loisir*). What were originally circles, academies, and salons became *cénacles* (clubs). Flaubert himself had his literary club where Maupassant was a habitué. The period had its own renowned conversationalists in

the form of the romantic novelist Stendhal and the writer and historian Prosper Mérimée. Victor Hugo had a club, as did Alfred de Musset
and Théophile Gautier. The gatherings had all sorts of names, one more
imaginative than the next: *camaraderies, phalanstères, bandes littéraires, sociétés d'admirations mutuelles*—as did the groups themselves: there were
Les Réalistes, Les Parnassiens, Les Vivants, Les Hydropathes, Les
Zutistes, Les Zutiques, Le Doyenné, and Les Buveurs d'eau.[7]

Instead of aristocratic homes, artists, poets, and the other talkative
free spirits of nineteenth-century France headed to cafés. It was an
important change: for the first time, conversation became an integral
part of the French dining experience. In 1803, France's very first food
critic, Alexandre Balthazar Laurent Grimod de la Reynière (1758–
1837), set out the rules for table talk in his *Almanach des gourmands* (Al-
manac for gourmets). Rule one: never talk about politics. "There are
so many more lively and appetizing subjects . . . like literature, artistic performances, gallantry, love and art," he wrote.[8] Jean Anthelme
Brillat-Savarin (1755–1826), an Epicurean who launched the first
French gastronomical journal, *La Physiologie du Goût* (The Physiology
of Taste), in 1825 had the same advice: avoid politics. It would be "trou-
blesome to both ingestion and digestion."

The love of conversation for its own sake lives on in modern France,
and the French still embrace its contradictory values. So it's no wonder
outsiders find French conversation so baffling. There is, however, a
dark side to the art of French conversation. Although meant to be
amicable and inclusive—yes, even when it's confrontational and
contrarian—it produces a culture of people who feel silly if they can't
come up with a good *replique,* or comeback. Put simply, French culture
penalizes people who are not voluble. In 2007, the French author and
literature professor Pierre Bayard published a bestseller called *Com-*

ment parler des livres que l'on n'a pas lus? (How to talk about books you haven't read) that sold eighty thousand copies in France and was translated into thirty languages. It was a perfect product of a culture where the worst thing you can do is be at a loss for words and not know what to say about a book you were supposed to have read.

That said, the French always know when a discussion has run its course. As Godo writes, conversation is *"cet art de l'instant,"* the art of the instant. It is *"par nature fugace et insaisissable,"* fleeting and evasive by nature. During the rest of our evening with Guillemette and her guests, the conversation remained stimulating and polemical, warm but never argumentative, and no one stole the show.

Then, at the strike of midnight, Giorgio gently announced he was tired. Everyone understood that the conversation had run its course and that it was time to go home.

~ 7 ~

Très *Talk*

Swimming is the most popular recreational sport in Paris. Julie learned this and other interesting facts after she asked the lifeguard at our local pool why he wasn't doing his job. In the months she had been swimming, she hadn't seen the young *maître nageur* (master swimmer) intervene a single time in the unruly waters. Now he wanted to talk about anything but his shabby work, and being French, he expertly deflected the *faute* for the whole problem straight back to Julie. "With so many swimmers, who could really expect Paris pools to be safe?" he asked. "Personally, *madame,* I would never swim here."

In his defense, Paris's pools are always full, and with good reason. Swimming is an inexpensive and accessible sport. Paris has thirty-seven municipal pools where swimmers can do laps for three euros. The pools are also quite nice. When we lived in the eighteenth arrondissement, our local pool faced an interior garden that provided natural light.

Julie swam in half a dozen Paris pools before she bought a membership card at the pool in the Latin Quarter, named after the former French world swimming champion Jean Taris. It wasn't the worst place she'd swum, just the most lawless. With up to ten swimmers per lane, there was so much water being pushed around that Julie felt seasick after five laps. But the particularly high volume of swimmers just made a bad situation worse because all Paris pools have one thing in commom: a total absence of etiquette.

There are rules in a pool. Before she moved to Paris, Julie assumed these were international. You choose a lane that corresponds to your real (not imaginary) speed and you don't kick off the wall when another swimmer is arriving; if you have a faster swimmer on your heels, you shift toward the lane marker and let her pass or wait at the wall while she turns. If French pools have similar policies, no one respects them, and lifeguards don't enforce them. (At one of the other pools, when Julie complained about kids jumping into the lanes reserved for swimmers doing lengths, a lifeguard told her, "Children pay to swim just like you do, *madame*.")

Given how fixated the French generally are on the notion of the common good, Julie always found it perverse that they put individual freedoms and laissez-faire ahead of safety the second they dive into water. Yet strangely, as soon as French swimmers left the pool and returned to the change room, Julie noticed that they snapped back into their old French ways and talked civilly. Julie even heard swimmers having a spirited discussion about their own near collision, before heading off to the hair dryers, no offense taken, apparently.

The explanation for this anomaly, we realized, is actually pretty simple. Talking is the key to all French social interactions. Since there's no way to say *bonjour, je vous en prie,* or *pardon* under water, the speechless French revert back to a state of nature, and the swimming pool becomes a free-for-all. In chapters 1 and 2, we explained in detail why phatic terms are so important in how the French define who's *in* and *out*. But pool tourism got us wondering: since talking is so important to the French, maybe *being able to talk* is an essential condition to keep French society functioning.

Jean-Benoît went to a cocktail party where he met a sociologist who studied that very issue: Professor Jean-Pierre Brun, a consultant in labor relations from Laval University in Quebec City who works in both Canada and France. Indeed, according to Brun, French companies systematically run into management problems whenever they make the mistake of not letting their employees discuss things, or not letting them debate enough. "The minute employees are deprived of the opportunity to express an opinion, all work relations become difficult," he told Jean-Benoît. French employees demand and exercise this right even in situations when they know their superiors have already made up their minds, he added.

We observed the same phenomenon over and over during our year in France, including in our own business of journalism. That year there was a dispute between staff and the editor in chief of the French daily *Le Monde*, Natalie Nougayrède, after she announced she would be cutting some sixty jobs or be transferring them to the digital version of the paper. The editor in chief wanted to turn *Le Monde* into "the premier global francophone media," she said. She had even tested out her ideas during consultations with staff. Her mistake, apparently, was that she presented the final plan as "final." The staff of *Le Monde* never had the opportunity to discuss or express their opinion about the plan. So middle management turned around and had Nougayrède fired.[1] French businesses are notoriously hierarchical, even at newspapers like *Le Monde* (or *Libération*) that have strong traditions of egalitarianism. But employees have to have their say anyway.

Spontaneous expression matters a lot to the French. Their entire political system is built around it. For most elections, they favor a two-round system. In the first round, voters choose their favorite party (and candidate) from a list of up to fifteen parties. Then in the second round, the voters choose between the two finalists from the first-round vote.[2] The French love for protests and other public demonstrations is a direct product of their need for spontaneous expression. Demonstrations and protests are political forums in France. After the slaughters at *Charlie Hebdo* and the Hyper Cacher grocery, 5 percent of France's total population took to the streets. North Americans, who don't protest in the street nearly as much as the French do, interpret it as a sign of unrest, if not political chaos. In fact, it's the opposite: if the French couldn't protest, that would lead to political chaos.

It's hard to overestimate how important oral expression is in France. In the previous chapter, we explained how salon culture raised conversation to the level of an art. However, the French also have a distinct conception of this art. It's one of the fundamental differences between the French and North Americans, and it's nothing new. Gustave de Beaumont, the travel companion of Alexis de Tocqueville, the French author of the classic study of American culture *Democracy in America* (published in 1835), was also a keen observer of American political and social mores. He wrote: "They don't chat in the United States the way they do in France. The American always argues. He has no knowledge of the art of lightly skimming the surface of topics in a large group, where each one puts in a remark, brilliant or dull, heavy or light, where one person finishes a phrase begun by someone else, and where everything is touched on but never in depth."[3] Tocqueville, himself, had great admiration for American practicality in speech among other things, even though it contradicted everything he had been taught about talking growing up in France. "The sole object of the people I was raised by was amusement and diversion. They never talked about politics, and I believe they scarcely thought about them. . . . One studied how to please as today one would study how to gain wealth or power."[4]

We were struck by how these different conceptions showed up in pop culture (even when French pop culture is getting more American day by day, as it is). On American talk shows, hosts invite guests for a chat. When new guests arrive, the old guests take a backseat and listen, maybe laugh or add a thing or two, but leave the floor to the new guest. French talk shows are just a free-for-all. There can be up to eight guests, each of whom the host introduces, then releases into the ecosystem with the other guests. The point of the French talk shows is not really to hear what each guest has to say. It's to see how they all play together, or survive each other. Each guest is expected to shine in his or her own way, while the host just makes sure the newcomer gets a chance to get a word in.

In other words, it's a conversation. In France, *conversation* focuses on the relationship between interlocutors. Discussions are different. They are about examining a topic. Two or more participants dig into a topic in depth, considering different elements and perspectives. As much as the French shine in the art of conversation, discussion comes easily to them, too. And like conversation, they are practically raised to discuss. In particular, French students have been doing compulsory philosophy studies since the French Revolution (which was at least partially a product of Enlightenment philosophy itself), partly to train them in analyzing and expressing ideas. Today, all French students get a huge dose of philosophy before the age of seventeen.

The goal of philosophy studies in France is to teach kids to think, and by extension talk formally. The by-product is the French get early formal training in how to discuss issues intelligently. It shows whenever they open their mouths. Most French have been given the challenge, early in their lives, of discussing a topic, that is, carefully studying an idea or issue by analyzing it or at least weighing the pros and cons. The French are trained not to think about things in simple binary terms (good and evil, black and white, good or bad) but rather to cultivate nuances. Not everyone is good at discussing ideas and issues, but everyone understands the exercise.

French education at the *lycée* level (the equivalent of high school) strongly emphasizes philosophy. In the last of the three years of *lycée,* known as la Terminale, literature students do as much as eight hours of philosophy per week, studying as many as fifty authors in their thirty-week program. Even students who specialize in economics and social sciences do four hours of philosophy per week; science students do three hours and technology students do two. Students in vocational programs are the only ones who get to avoid philosophy altogether. This adds up to more philosophy than most university students in any American institution ever do, and it is mandatory.

Nothing illustrates the importance of philosophy quite like *le bac* (short for *baccalauréat*), and the exam that *lycée* students take at the end of their final year to get it. The *bac* exam was introduced by Napoleon in 1808. Today, every second week of June, the French media speculate about and comment specifically on the philosophy exam, which they call *l'épreuve reine* (the mother of all exams) for the *bac*. Some seven hundred thousand students across France are given four hours to produce about ten pages of copy answering one of a selection of questions. The stakes are high. The *bac* is a high school diploma but also very narrowly, an entry ticket to university. Students who get a *très bien* (a mention) on their *bac* exam get access to the best programs and institutions in the country. Everyone else has to settle for second (or third) best. It is so big that even a daily like *Le Monde,* for instance, publishes the full list of questions for the philosophy exam as well as the *corrigé* (an untranslatable term that means both answer booklet and past papers).[5]

Predictably, the students in Bac L (for literature) have to tackle the most difficult philosophy questions or topics. In 2014 they had three choices: Do works of art educate our perception? (*Les œuvres éduquent-elles notre perceptions?*), should we do everything to be happy? (*doit-on tout faire pour être heureux?*), or, finally, discuss an excerpt from Karl Popper's *Objective Knowledge: An Evolutionary Approach.* Students in Bac ES (Economics and Social) and students in science, who do half as much philosophy, have it slightly easier.[6] Students in technology had it easier still, but most North Americans sophomores would probably have trouble making a convincing philsosophical case even for the questions these French students faced: Are exchanges always self-interested? (*Les échanges sont-ils toujours intéressés?*), can a truth be definitive? (*une vérité peut-elle être définitive?*), or discuss an excerpt from Plato's *Gorgias.* Statistically, at least the French are getting better at the art of discussing as every year passes: Only 20 percent of kids passed *le bac* fifty years ago. Today, some 80 percent do. (That hasn't stopped philosophy professors from complaining about how "mediocre" students are getting. On the other hand, professors are still teaching philosophy the same way they did in 1945, when not more than 5 percent of French students got to the *lycée.*)

Not surprisingly, because of the high value the French place on the art of discussion, philosophy has a high premium in French society. Even the École Polytechnique, France's celebrated engineering school, has an in-house philosopher. Respect for philosophy also explains the high status of the intellectual in French society. Whether or not France is still producing thinkers of the stature of Jean-Paul Sartre or Michel Foucault is debatable, but it's also slightly beside the point. The French admire their intellectuals. However, French intellectuals aren't "experts" in the way we North Americans think of them. They are expert "discussers," people who can express themselves forcefully or brilliantly about a topic, either because they have studied it thoroughly or because they just feel strongly about it. In other words, intellectuals become prominent in France not because they know the most about something, but because they talk the best about it.

Arguing is part of discussion, and the French do it well, but formal debating is another matter altogether. Curiously, as comfortable as the French are with contradiction and with juggling different perspectives, their education doesn't serve them when talking becomes a formal showdown. Early in our stay, Julie was invited by Hélène Guinaudeau, a young press attachée at Québec's diplomatic offices in Paris, to attend a verbal "joust" at a Paris courthouse, on Île de la Cité. In her spare time, Hélène acts as secretary general of the Conférence Olivaint, France's oldest student society, founded in 1875. Public speaking is the raison d'être of this exclusive society, whose membership is limited to just 150 and whose alumni read like a *Who's Who?* of France: from Laurent Fabius and Hubert Védrine (respectively the present and former ministers of foreign affairs) to Jacques Attali (a former adviser to President François Mitterand), actress Isabelle Huppert, and TV news anchor Christine Ockrent, among others.

Hélène invited Julie to watch a debating contest between two clubs, La Conférence Olivaint, whose members are law students, and La Conférence du Stage, whose members are business students. According to

Hélène, formal debating contests fell out of fashion in France but are now enjoying renewed popularity. "The French are suddenly realizing it's a skill you have to learn," she said. At the end of the debate, she agreed that when it came to debating, this particular cohort of students still had some learning to do. At least one person saw it coming before the debate even started: the president of the jury opened the event by warning the jousters that they weren't just there to exchange ideas (*converser*) or throw insults. "Debating is the opposite of conversation," he said. "It's about combining eloquence and conviction. And it's about winning."

The joust took place in a dark wood-paneled courtroom. Each team had four members. About a hundred of their classmates huddled in camps on each end of the room while nonaligned observers like Julie sat in the middle. The candidates (all men) had all drawn a topic from a hat earlier that afternoon and had had five hours to prepare their arguments, either for or against their topics, which were a mix of current events and philosophical questions like, "Should women be allowed in the Pantheon?" or "Must one listen to one's enemies?"

When it came to presenting their cases, the debaters showed themselves to be incredibly inventive. There was no rigid rhetoric, no stiff monologues. It was all smooth talking, theatrics, and strategically placed hyperbole. The participants bounced from one position to another like acrobats. One delivered an entire argument in rhyming couplets. Another fell on his knees to plead his case before the audience.

The winner of the event, a law student of East Indian origin, simply did the best job of using creative oration to make a compelling argument. He had drawn the "No" side of the question, "Does integrating mean renouncing your identity?" and built his case on the idea that it was ridiculous to expect immigrants to parrot their culture of adoption. For his concluding remarks, he assumed a mock Italian accent and did a breathtaking parody of the Italian comedian Roberto Benigni first in French, then in English. Everyone was smiling. The contest was only half over, but the audience could see the law student had it in the bag.

Then again, the spectators probably knew the second half of the debate would not be as entertaining as the first. After their orations, candidates began the actual debate segment, during which they paired up with a participant from the other team to argue out the topic. Even the brilliant East Indian student couldn't quite pull this off. Without preparation, these brilliant young French elocutionists just lost their panache. For starters, they couldn't seem to snap out of conversation mode. Instead of attacking his adversary, one jouster posed rhetorical questions to himself, then answered them himself, seemingly because he wanted to demonstrate, once again, that prized rhetorical tool of *la réplique,* the smart comeback. It sounded like he had rehearsed it. None of the participants could think on their feet; some just fell back on name calling. In his closing comments, the president of the jury characterized the jousting as "disappointing." It was the understatement of the evening.

What the French call "debating" is usually just an in-depth discussion. True debates—where confrontation serves to establish a winner—seem to go against everything they learn about oral expression. We spoke about the issue with Stéphane André, an actor and opera director who has a master's degree in psychology from one of the most prestigious business schools in France. For the last twenty years, he has been running a school, L'École de l'Art Oratoire, to teach the art of public speaking and debating to French managers and executives. The problem, says André, is that French education places too much emphasis on writing. "The French are very talkative, and often brilliant at *la discussion du Café du Commerce* [everyday discussions]. But when they have to use talking to win—whether it's to change an opinion, win a negociation, or get a new client—they tend to overprepare in writing. They prepare, prepare, prepare." It was exactly what Julie had witnessed at the Paris courthouse. "Then they have trouble getting outside of what they have prepared," André continued. "Debating is about improvisation and coming up with arguments that change people's minds. It's about being ready to listen, and [being] prepared for surprises. It means dealing with *l'imprévu* (the unforeseen). And naturally, when they find themselves facing *l'imprévu,* they think they are in danger. So they tend to wrap up with repartee that is stupidly aggressive."

There is another French cultural trait that works against the art of debating. The French almost universally value expression over communication. We observed this ourselves, again, in the journalism world. French journalism tends to put editorializing ahead of content, or even the facts. In French news articles, the point of view of the writer is often clearer than what happened. Even when the French speak, expression is paramount, and is often carried out at the expense of connecting with the very audience to whom that expression is directed. (For that matter, public personalities in France can say the weirdest, most senseless things, and no one seems to care.) This tendency to editorialize (and esoterize) pops up in all communications. The French seem more interested in the act of passing a message than in how it will be received, or whether it will be understood (which is the essence of communication). The "meaning" is often left to the reader or listener to divine. The same reflex also operates in the arts. French universities have always resisted teaching writing workshops or courses in literary creation owing to the belief that learning would be too technical and too formulaic, contradicting the essence of artistic expression.[7]

You see this posture everywhere in France, not just in highbrow culture, or among France's elite. French beggars don't simply ask for change. They are more likely to construct a three-point argument to explain exactly how they ended up in their present plight and conclude by asking for help. Of course, the emphasis on creative expression can backfire anywhere. We witnessed this watching two panhandlers one morning near Paris's Métro Capucines. The pair had developed a truly eye-catching technique. They sat on the edge of the street holding long fishing rods with cans at the ends of the lines. That got people's attention. Unfortunately, the mixed message turned most people off—were the beggars reeling us in like fish? We didn't see anyone reaching into their pockets. But the fishing pole beggars made another, more fundamental mistake. They sat silently waiting for donations. They should have been talking to people. The beggars had missed the essential point: nobody gets anything in France by keeping his mouth shut.

Part Two

❦

Content

8

Food for Talk

No matter how much the French love food—and they do—they will never let eating get in the way of a good conversation.

We vividly recalled how much French dining rituals are made to get people talking the first time we were invited to a friend's house for lunch in Paris. Our hostess Janine, a friend from the hiking club Jean-Benoît joined fifteen years ago, had invited us to her apartment in the nineteenth arrondissement for a casual, midweek meal with a few other hiking friends. An elegant widow in her early seventies who walks twenty-five kilometers in the woods every weekend, Janine is also what the French call a *redoubtable* (a mix of excellent and formidable) cook. She has been known to show up for hikes with fifty *crêpes au rhum* in her backpack, "just in case we need a snack." Fortunately, the other lunch guests, all fit, active retirees like Janine, were *bonnes fourchettes,* healthy eaters: we were about to spend five solid hours eating lunch.

We started with an *apéro* of champagne, which took about an hour. Then Janine set bowls of cold escargots, small cheese pastries, and shrimp *hors d'œuvres* on the table. That took another hour. For the main course Janine served steaming bowls of *bœuf carottes,* beef and carrot stew, with linguine in butter. After another hour passed, she brought out a cheese plate with Camembert, a goat cheese, and an Emmental. Then Janine appeared with the grand finale, an *île flottante,* floating island, essentially a soft mound of meringue bobbing in crème anglaise (caramel cream sauce). But that wasn't the final curtain. Another hour passed and we moved back to the living room for the coffee and *limoncello,* an Italian lemon liqueur, which we drank while Janine told us about her holiday in Italy.

By the time we finished eating lunch, it was practically supper time.

You have to hand it to the French: they know how to pace a meal. French meals have a fixed order for courses. Hosts rarely deviate from these, though some simplify or combine courses to speed things up or cut down on cooking time. First comes the *apéro* and *hors d'œuvres.* Then the *entrée,* which can be more *hors d'œuvres,* or soup, and doesn't necessarily have to be eaten at the table. The main course is normally served in large dishes guests help themselves to. Then comes the cheese course (cheese is *never* an appetizer or an *hors d'œuvre* in France), then dessert, then a *digestif* and coffee. It sounds like a lot of food to consume, but it's not really when you consider meals can last five hours.

Do the French eat slowly and methodically in order to allow plenty of time to talk? Or do they talk in order to kill the time it takes to eat? They probably don't know themselves. Though French meals are undeniably longer than they need to be, eating rarely feels tedious, partly because the food is so good, partly because the French know how to combine food and conversation and make the whole production feel effortless. After fifteen years of dining with the French (in France, and elsewhere), we've come to the conclusion that as much as the French love food, they love talking more. Even food takes a backseat to conversation at the dinner table. The point of the slow pacing is not to fill stomachs gently—it's to build a frame for conversation.

In other words, talking is the real point of it all.

French meals are built on a series of rather complex table codes meant to give people time to talk. Our friend Janine followed French eating rituals to the letter, creating perfect conditions for her guests to say all the things we had to say. As she served consecutive courses, the conversation topics glided from serious health problems to lighthearted nostalgia, reports on recent trips, intercultural comparisons, and plain old gossip. Over the course of the meal, we compared notes about international adoption: the other couple there, Liliane and Alain, had adopted their son Stéphane, and one other guest, Jacqueline, had a four-year-old grandson adopted from Russia. Then we moved to a heartbreaking subject: one of the guests, Denise, had just been diagnosed with Parkinson's disease, and in a streak of disastrous luck, was knocked down the stairs of the Paris metro while her five-year-old granddaughter was watching, traumatizing them both and worsening Denise's Parkinson's symptoms overnight.

French dinners come in many shapes and forms, but French meals almost universally share a certain rhythm. That's because the French believe conversations need time to breathe, like wine. Having many courses is a built-in mechanism to ensure a lot of different topics get on the table. Courses insert into the conversation breaks that give everyone the opportunity to change topic or tone. Otherwise, the French would probably feel like they were eating the same dish all night long.

After the first course, Denise herself changed the topic from Parkinson's disease. Like all French, she knew that conversation is a shared resource, just like the bowls of escargots, and if you hog it—even with the best of intentions—you might ruin the experience for everyone. The end of the *hors d'œuvres* offered an elegant opportunity for us to switch to reminiscing about memorable hikes and gossiping about a few unforgettable hikers. One former member we had all known had to leave the club when he became a *préfet* (prefect), the state's representative in one of the ninety-nine French *départements,* and began moving from post to post. We chuckled as the hikers reported all the privileges they had garnered from visiting him at his succession of residences. As the meal progressed, we worked up to some cross-cultural analysis, which gave the hikers the (always) welcome opportunity to vent about France going down the tubes, an eternal complaint. Liliane swore the French "don't like to talk to each other anymore."

We told her that was impossible.

French anthropologists who study food and the table recently revived an old, archaic term, *commensal* (table companion), and turned it into a new concept: *commensalité,* or table companionship, the ritual of sharing one's meal. They simply found a name for the quality that is at the heart of France's relationship with food. To the French, dining is about expressing relationships with others. The idea of *commensalité* applies to all French, regardless of their background, education, or social class. In contrast to the custom in the United States, in France meals are taken at a fixed hour, at the table, and they avoid eating alone if possible.[1] They are akin to Catholic rites, like communion. To be capricious is to exclude oneself, or to excommunicate. If we sent French people to live on Mars and served them dried food out of packets, they would still eat together and observe the same rituals.

Dining rules have been passed down from generation to generation in France—probably not since the days of the Roman Empire, as many

French believe, but long enough to convince everyone in the country that there's no other way to eat properly. Since the nineteenth century, dining rituals have been a subject of serious, even academic, study in France. In one treatise, called *Le goût de la conversation* (The taste for conversation), the historian Pierre Sansot (mentioned in chapter 6) argues that a table with no ceremony, one that does not respect the order of servings, will "drain conversation." Nor should the service itself be so elaborate that it "steals the show," he says. In reality, though French eating habits are deeply ritualized, there's no philosophy of "appropriate" topics of dinner conversation. You can talk about anything the French will talk about. The idea is to let conversation enjoy its natural lifespan, whatever that turns out to be.

Of course, the French spend a lot of time talking about food itself. You can talk about food anywhere in France, anytime, with just about anyone. Talking about cuisine is not particularly class dependent in France. It's also a great way to talk to one of the most famous stereotyped characters in France: the waiter (or restaurant owner, as the case may be). North Americans tend to look at people waiting tables as part-time or temporary workers: waiting tables is not a highly respected vocation. But in France, waiting tables is a career. Good waiters have a solid knowledge of the menu and type of cuisine they are serving. Outside of lunch and dinner rushes, when waiters are not pressed for time, most are happy to discuss food at great length. (French waiters also tend to welcome criticism of the food they serve, not just compliments, as long as it is informed.)[2]

But don't try to talk to the French about food unless you have at least a basic understanding of *terroir*. The word itself is difficult to translate. The French originally used it to describe the particular taste wines get from specific soils, growing conditions, and techniques used to create them. It was gradually applied to food, starting in the 1930s, when the French historian Lucien Febvre introduced the concept of France's "map of food," which consisted of four territories delineated by the type of fat each used in cooking: butter, olive oil, goose fat, or lard. Some French still refer to France's four distinct regions and their *fonds de cuisine.* The actual word *terroir* only started being used for local specialties around the middle of the twentieth century.

We discovered the concept of *terroir* during our first stay in France when we heard locals boast about their culinary specialties in almost the same terms, everywhere we went. But when the French talk about *terroir,* they are not just bragging. Though some of France's territories are naturally better endowed for culinary achievement than others, discussions about food rarely pit one region against another or place local foods in a hierarchy. *Terroir* is a synonym for authenticity. Eating *cuisine de terroir* is a way of connecting to regional identity, and to a certain extent, a gesture of solidarity with the few small-scale farmers left out there who stubbornly resist the trend to industrialize production.

The idea of *terroir* is not really about taste or quality. Food in France is not for "foodies" (hobby gourmets). In fact, you meet relatively few foodies in France, probably because most French have at least a rudimentary knowledge of French cuisine and no one thinks anything of it. So North American foodies traveling in France are bound to end up feeling foolish unless they know the basics of where things come from in France—which boils down to having a basic knowledge of French geography.

Although France is not the only country in the world with excellent regional cooking, there's a reason it was the French who branded the notion of *terroir:* the country does produce an incredible variety of food. France has a natural advantage over most nations (with the possible exceptions of Italy and China) because its territory is remarkably varied, with landscape ranging from high chalk cliffs on the Normandy coast to mountains and volcanic plateaus in the Massif Central, stretching from an almost subarctic climate in the North to a semiarid climate in the Mediterranean and boreal rainforest where the Pyrenees descend into the Atlantic. France even has a natural advantage in climatology: since the average altitude rises almost evenly from the western shores to the eastern interior, rain falls evenly over the country. In short, France has excellent growing conditions from one end of the country to the other.

Famous for his writing on food and eating habits, the French anthropologist Claude Fischler developed a theory in his book *L'Homnivore* (The Omnivorous Man) that different eating styles of different cultures boil down to the way each determines what is good and bad to eat. North Americans, he argues, use nutritional quality as a benchmark. (Indeed, we spend a lot of time talking about fats and carbohydrates.) The French talk about fat content, too, but they definitely think it's more interesting to talk about where food comes from than what it's composed of, or how much fat it contains (though they do worry about this these days).

There's another reason the French are so focused on food. In a country as politically and administratively centralized as France, food is a politically acceptable way to talk about one's local origins. Talking about local cuisine allows the French to brag about their native regions without breaching republican doctrine. When the French talk about food, they are talking about themselves. The French are almost always ready to tell a story about the food or the eating habits of their hometown or region. When we served a humble leek and potato soup (the French call it vichyssoise) one night to our friend François, he reached over to the bottle of bordeaux on the table, picked it up, and started pouring wine into his bowl, as one might garnish soup with cream. We thought he was crazy. But all he was doing was showing us that even though he lived in Paris, he was a local boy from Tence, a town near Saint-Étienne in southwest France. "This is how the *paysans* eat vichyssoise," he told us proudly (and to our surprise, it was delicious).

When we were eating at François's house another night, he served us a *jambonnette*—essentially a sausage made of ground beef rolled in pig's skin and stewed—that he brought from Saint-Étienne after visiting his father there. We raved about it so he handed us another local product, a *saucisson* (dried sausage) to take home. Jean-Benoît shared it with his hiking friends the next morning, and they were utterly enraptured. They demanded he supply details about it. Fortunately everything was explained on the package: it was a mountain *saucisson,* from a charcuterie in Lisieux, address: 43200 Saint-Jeures, Haute Vienne, a town of 950 people located at an altitude of 1,045 meters. That's the kind of detail the French love getting when they talk about food.

The danger of emphasizing *terroir,* however, is to over-romanticize it. Insofar as regional specialties are considered to spring from age-old "traditions," the idea of *terroir* is often a stretch. As the British writer and historian Graham Robb points out in his remarkable book *The Discovery of France,* until the beginning of the twentieth century, most French lived on a diet of boiled cabbage, dry bread, and an occasional piece of meat. Many local food specialties were actually luxury products regions exported to Paris and few locals consumed themselves. In other cases, they were the products of the intense efforts the French made, starting in the eighteenth century, to develop the countryside. We visited friends in the department of the Landes, for instance, and stayed in their village, Castets, about an hour north of the Spanish border on the Atlantic coast. Bayonne, just north of the area, is famous for its ham, and the whole area is heavily Spanish influenced with tapas and abundant Basque specialties, including one we loved, *piperade* (a garlic, onion, and pepper dish). But the fact is, until the nineteenth century, the Landes was pretty much a sandy swamp. Nothing grew there until huge parts of it were drained and planted with pine trees.

And as well endowed as France is geographically, scholars agree that the French attachment to *terroir* is not about geography so much as the peculiar history of France's economic development. France industrialized later than the United Kingdom, Belgium, and Germany. Contrary to the British and the Germans, the majority of French didn't live in cities until the 1950s, when factory jobs attracted them away from their villages. So by the time French peasants started migrating to the cities, education had been in place for decades (the school system was built in the nineteenth century), so they were relatively well educated. Suddenly plunged into modern urban living conditions, the French began to idealize country life. By the 1970s, urban French were taking vacations in the countryside. Urban workers brought the food of their *terroirs,* and the nostalgia that went with it, back to the city. In other words, French cities to some extent "created" the French countryside. (And, as Graham Robb points out, much of the French countryside itself actually was created by enormous public works projects during the eighteenth and nineteenth centuries, like the one in the Landes.)

Some culinary "traditions" in France, for that matter, are entirely fictitious, like the Savoyard specialty *tartiflette,* a gratin of potatoes, bacon, and Reblochon cheese. The word *tartiflette* comes from the Savoyard for potatoes, *tartifla.* But far from "traditional," the dish was invented in the 1980s by the cheese association of the Savoie department, ostensibly to find a way to sell more local cheese. The recipe quickly became a classic of French ski resorts and voilà!—a French tradition was born. (A similar dish predated *tartiflette,* so a case could be made for it being "traditional"; it uses the same ingredients—potatoes, onion, bacon, and cheese—but the potatoes are fried with the skin, and the cheese is dropped in the skillet. *Tartiflette* has boiled potatoes and is cooked in the oven.)

Today, the French are resolutely urban. According to France's National Institute of Statistics and Economic Studies (INSEE), about 20 percent of the French population lives in a rural setting, but only 2 percent work on a farm. In other words, the French attachment to the land is more about postcard rurality than actual country living. For that matter, though the French strongly embrace the idea of small-scale agricultural production, over 80 percent of what they actually eat is the product of industrial processing. The French have one of the most mechanized and productive agricultural industries in the world. French frozen foods are of such high quality that restaurants regularly use them and pass them off as their own. In April 2013, French chef Alain Ducasse sparked a scandal when he claimed that 75 percent of French restaurants served meals made from ready-cooked ingredients, either frozen or vacuum-sealed.[3] There was no official study to back Ducasse's claims, but the words of a celebrated chef carry weight in France. The city of Paris reacted by creating a new label for restaurants that could prove they actually cook their food from scratch.

Though the French may be hazy about the time line of some of their traditional culinary specialties, that doesn't change the fact that they know a lot about food and always have a lot to say about it. Even in urban France, people pride themselves on understanding and appreciating what the French land produces. Historically, the French state has been dedicated to centralizing the country and erasing differences, to the point of eradicating local, pre-French languages. But the French learn geography and are remarkably well versed in the various cuisines produced across French territory.

Nothing demonstrates the intensity of French interest in *terroir* better than France's Salon international de l'agriculture (International Agriculture Fair) held at Paris's Parc des expositions. In 2014 the Salon set a new record with seven hundred thousand visitors—that's one French citizen in a hundred—and made the agricultural fair the second most popular exhibition in the country. In 2014 there were over 130 acres of culinary specialties, as well as machinery and live-stock, from twenty-two French regions and four overseas territories. With enough appetite, a visitor could sample every imaginable delicacy in France (though we headed straight for the foie gras sandwiches when we got there and didn't have room for much more). The French president spends a day at the Salon every year. His visit, highly cov-ered by the media, is considered a litmus test. If a president can handle livestock competently (as Jacques Chirac famously did) then he's deemed a leader. President François Hollande stuck to tasting food on his visit, without so much as picking up a piglet. His weak performance did nothing for his popularity, which was already on a downward spiral.

Most Parisians, of course, have roots in some other region of France (or another country). This physical distance can serve to heighten passions for *terroirs,* and the French who holiday in their hometown invariably bring back wine and other products to share with friends in Paris. The rest of the time, Parisians love to talk about where they *buy* their food, and in the process, unveil their secret knowledge both of food and of the city. We spent hours listening to Parisians tell us about the "best" places to find everything from *macarons* to choucroute.

One Sunday, when Julie was getting ready to leave Paris's Luxembourg Gardens, after the girls had been playing in the children's park, Erika announced she had a question: "Why is everyone speaking English today?" The park did have a remarkably high proportion of English speakers. Julie thought it over, then realized what was going on. It was Sunday morning. The French people were all out grocery shopping. She and the girls walked back to la rue Mouffetard, near our apartment, to see for themselves. La Mouff', as it is known, is one of Paris's oldest streets. An ancient winding path (a plaque on the street claims it has existed since Neolithic times), the street somehow survived the renovation of Paris during the nineteenth century, when Baron Georges-Eugène Haussmann, the prefect of the Seine department, cut straight through the maze of streets and neighborhoods to create the long boulevards and avenues you see in Paris today. After having hit bottom in the 1960s, when it was ghetto, La Mouff' morphed into a lively street of bars, boutiques, small groceries, specialty food shops, and eateries that cater mostly to tourists and students (the Latin Quarter is full of schools, as the name suggests). But on Sunday mornings, the local French residents literally take it back, arriving in waves and lining up at gourmet bakeries, butcher shops, cheese stores, wine cellars, and fruit and vegetable stores. They are shopping for Sunday dinner.

Meals and meal times in France are amazingly ritualistic. Children are taught the rituals from infancy and those habits are reinforced when they go to school. Specifically, French parents are spared the morning ritual of packing children's lunches because French schoolchildren either eat at their school's *cantine* (cafeteria) or they go home for a proper meal. A quick glance at the *cantine* menu will teach an outsider a lot about French dining habits. The objective of the *cantine* is not just to fill children's stomachs. It's to edify. Each meal has an appetizer and a main course, followed by cheese or yogurt, then a dessert (often fruit). Children (except our own) do not bring snacks to school, nor are they supplied, even during the after-school programs. In other words, kids are expected to eat what's on their plates at the proper time, just like everyone else, and then wait until it's time to eat again.

To many North Americans, the school menu at our daughters' school would sound pretty grown-up. At lunch, our girls dined on roast pork *à l'orange,* Comté or raw milk cheese, vegetable potages, turkey escalope *à la meunière,* veal blanquette, ratatouille, paella, braised pork in Basquaise sauce with Piedmont salad, and rémoulade. Admittedly, it's not stuff all kids like—even French kids. And the quality of the food varies enormously from school to school. But children in France learn to eat what the rest of society eats. And they learn the rules that French people follow when they eat.

French children are also expected to eat like adults and sit at the table for as long as it takes. It's not that the French are cruel. On the contrary: they assume children will find the dining experience as pleasant as adults do. At the most, French parents make adjustments to the menu, but they never deface a meal by offering kids fish sticks or chicken nuggets in the middle of it. We'll never forget a four-hour, nine-course meal we had with our daughters at an avant-garde restaurant, François Gagnaire, in the small city of Puy-en-Velay. The chef and owner marched up to our table, greeted our daughters—who were only six at the time— and told us not to worry. (It seems even French kids are averse to oysters and mushrooms.) A father himself, he told us to order off the menu for the girls, and he would just substitute offending ingredients with carrots and sweet potato purée (he even threw in a lollipop made out of red beet reduction as a garnish). But the most spectacular aspect of it was the dessert: a sugar shack and logs made of crêpes covered with a caramel made of maple syrup. He was remarkably accommodating. On the other hand, he didn't serve us any faster.

French food habits are changing, though not as thoroughly as many French will lead foreigners to believe (see chapter 10, on French negativism). The French anthropologist Claude Fischler published a book in 2013 called *Les alimentations particulières* (it translates roughly as "individual eating") about the arrival in France of special diets, like gluten-free or vegan. During our stay, the populist Parisian daily *Le Parisien* published an article on an "alarming" development: the French had started to snack. In fact, the article was about a study that found two out of three French now eat between meals. The journalist's conclusion: the French model of three meals per days was eroding. *That* seemed alarmist to us, but we had to admit, some attitudes did seem to be changing. When we lived in France fifteen years earlier, McDonald's was regularly decried as the model of *mal bouffe* (bad eating). In 2013, *Le Figaro* classed the fast-food chain among the fastest growing employers in France. With some twelve hundred McDonald's restaurants, France has more McDonald's than any country except the United States. So people can't hate it that much.

More people eat as they work, and lunch breaks are getting shorter, with less wine. The French are also starting to carry lunch in a bag. According to a study of the Mutuelle Malakoff Médéric, in 1990 only 3 percent of employees brought a lunch to work.[4] That had grown to 20 percent by 2009 and is now 27 percent. A survey of health and eating habits conducted in 2010 by the National Institute for Prevention and Health Education found that the number of people who only eat one or two courses for their evening meal had risen steadily, from 38 percent in 1998 to 49 percent in 2008. But one thing does remain stable: even if the French agribusiness is one of the most aggressive and productive in the world, portion sizes in France are still relatively small.[5]

We witnessed a few new rituals that had developed since we lived in France the first time. One that threw us off was *l'apéro* (before-dinner drinks). There's nothing new about getting together for drinks. The novelty was that it had become code for a casual light dinner. Our first was at our upstairs neighbors', a friendly couple whose young school-age children attended the same school as our girls, across the street. Our children met riding scooters and playing soccer in the tiny interior court of our building (kids in Paris work with what they have). A month after making our acquaintance they invited us upstairs on a Saturday night, at 7:30 P.M., for an *apéro*. We still thought this meant we would have drinks. It turned out to be more of an informal meal of finger food. And at any rate, no one gets together in this country to talk and eat for an hour. We headed home at 10:00 P.M.

We decided to host our own *apéro* and invited another neighbor we had met at the building Christmas *apéro*. Gauging the ceremony on our past experiences, we made the invitation for 7:30 P.M. And we made sure we had enough warm pastries, smoked salmon blinis, and canapés to last eight people for a couple of hours. Evidently we overdid things. Our guests good-naturedly complained that they wouldn't have any room for supper! But then they stayed until midnight. We remain puzzled about this particular ritual.

So what's the *apéro*, we wondered? It's an excuse to get together and talk but without the onerous task of actually cooking a full meal. The unspoken agreement seems to be that you supply just enough food to keep hunger at bay for as long as the conversation lasts. A year, and many *apéros*, later, the precise characteristics of this mysterious ritual still escaped us: it seemed to assume a new shape every time we attended one.

The late afternoon *goûter* is another ritual we encountered for the first time, mostly because we now had kids. The verb *goûter* means "to taste" but as a noun, *le goûter* stands for a "substantial snack." Like every food ritual in France, *le goûter* is governed by unspoken rules: in this case, we discovered (by trial and error), it must be something sweet, like cookies or cake—we had cold slices of French toast one afternoon. Beyond that, there are only guiding principles. *Le goûter* can happen as early as 4:00 P.M., but can be partaken as late as 6:00 P.M. The idea appears to be to hold children over until supper, and as far as we could tell, adults eat it, too, but only if they are with children. Again, children don't snack casually, stuffing things in their mouths whenever they are hungry. They partake in a ritual called the snack.

But things in France aren't changing that quickly, or profoundly, no matter what the French might say themselves. One afternoon, we visited the Musée Rodin, in the seventh arrondissement, with friends visiting from Montreal, Joëlle and Paul and their two sons. By the time we remembered what a food desert this neighborhood is, we had four hungry children on our hands. We finally found a bakery near the Solférino metro, but there was nowhere to sit. So the eight of us piled into the metro, then just pulled out our sandwiches and ate them en route to our next destination. Big faux pas: our fellow metro passengers observed us with a piqued look. You still don't eat on the run in Paris, especially not when you are in a group.

We got the message loud and clear through the stern glares: no responsible parents should be teaching their children such atrocious eating habits.

~ 9 ~

Know-It-Alls

"So, what region are you from?" As casual icebreakers go, the question would sound a little too specific for North Americans, who normally ask new acquaintances, "So where are you from?" But in France, an open-ended inquiry about someone's origins is an outright insinuation.

Assimilation is one of the core values of the French Republic, meaning all national identities (theoretically) are supposed to blend into the national melting pot. Taken to its logical conclusion, questioning anyone's origins, even subtly, is taboo. If you ask an immigrant, even second generation, "Where are you from?" the question will be interpreted as a subtle challenge to the person's right to be in France, or worse, to *be* French. In the case of the "old stock" French—and you would never know unless they told you—even raising the possibility of not being French sounds derogatory, if not accusatory. For everyone between these two poles, the question is unsettling: no one in France likes having his or her membership credentials challenged.

On the other hand, if you ask precisely what region the French are from—*De quelle region êtes-vous?*—there's no harm done and no offense taken. If your interlocutor is from a different area of France, he'll likely tell you what department, region, or even town he's from, then branch into some trivia about local geography, history, or culinary achievements. If the person turns out to live in the very *commune* you are standing in, she could take the question as an invitation to expand on her family origins. You never know where the question will lead, but it's rarely a dead end.

What gives the word "region" its magic power? The French like talking about themselves as much as anybody, but the word "region" helps them avoid a touchy topic: identity, either personal or national (we address this more in chapter 18). On the other hand, asking the French about regions, or towns, allows them to talk about two topics they love: geography and history. The French know a lot about geography and history, particularly their own, and they delight in displaying their knowledge.

Learning history and geography are practically republican duties in France. Both are fundamental components of what the French call *culture générale* (the term translates literally as "general culture" but has the sense of "good education"). The French have iron faith in the idea that there are a certain number of things everyone should know. It is something like the universal ideal of the humanities (the study of culture), but it applies to everyone, of every age and stage in life.

The concept of *culture générale* is so deeply engrained in France, it has its own niche publishing industry. A few months before we arrived in France a 160-page quarterly magazine called *L'Éléphant* was released with a subtitle that said it all: *La revue de culture générale* (the review of general culture). The first issues had a profile of the writer Alexandre Dumas, a list of key dates in contemporary art, an article about black holes, another explaining the international currency system, an essay on the philosophy of comic books, a piece on existentialism, and finally—just in case anyone needs to know—an article on the taste of an obscure citrus fruit called a *cédrat* (citron).

Displaying one's *culture générale* in France is not considered elitist behavior. On the contrary: *L'Éléphant*'s manifesto is "to know is to be equal and free." Its founders, Guénaëlle Le Solleu, a former journalist, and Jean-Paul Arif, an engineer who worked in geomatics, set out to make a publication with information people could both read and memorize easily. To this end, the pair conscripted the Laboratory for the Study of Cognitive Mechanisms (Laboratoire d'étude des mécanismes cognitifs) at the University of Lyon II to design the magazine's quizzes, crossword puzzles, and other mental games.

Nor is *culture générale* written in stone. The actual facts that constitute it change over time, which is why yet another French writer, the journalist François Reynaert, published a book called *Le kit du 21e siècle* (The kit for the 21st century), subtitled A new guide to *culture générale*. Reynaert argues that no one can really function in today's world without knowing about antioxidants, carbon footprints, the human genome, or George R. R. Martin's *A Game of Thrones*. To say that the French openly embrace the power of knowledge is an understatement.

Before there was *Wikipedia*, the French had their own homegrown paper version of it in the form of a reference book called *Le Quid*. *Le Quid* had more than twenty-two hundred pages with 2.5 million entries on topics about France and the world—or everything that is supposed to matter to the French. In its heyday, *Le Quid* sold 250,000 copies a year. Unfortunately it didn't adapt well to the arrival of Web-based, free reference tools (like *Wikipedia*); it stopped publishing its paper version in 2007, then closed definitely in 2010 when the Web version didn't break even. But until its demise, *Le Quid* had sales comparable to those of popular dictionaries like *Petit Larousse* (which adapted very well to the Internet). For that matter, *culture générale* is a recipe for success in France. Even the American "Dummies" got in on the action, publishing *La culture générale pour les Nuls* (General culture for dummies) in 2008. And every week, an established author or philosopher releases a new dictionary or volume designed to quench the huge French thirst for general knowledge, like author Charles Dantzig, who sold seventy thousand copies in France of his 970-page *Dictionnaire égoïste de la littérature française* (Egotistical dictionary of French literature).

As far as the French are concerned, you are never too young to start acquiring *culture générale*. By the time they get to school, French kids are supposed to be primed to acquire the knowledge and information they will "need." School is not considered the exclusive repository of *culture générale* in France, but it's expected to play a big role in fostering it. It's an enormous difference in philosophy from North American ideas about education. Only real outliers in France question the value of acquiring factual knowledge. The gap between French and North American teaching philosophies sunk in when we returned home and our daughters started grade 6 in Canadian school. One of the first things their teachers told us at the September parent-teacher meeting was that students would be reading a lot and would be expected to "react" to books. We had to pinch ourselves.

In France, we learned, children are expected to assimilate what they read. It goes without saying. For her first school research project in French school, Nathalie was instructed to choose a French classical painter and write a short report on him. (Nathalie was perfectly able to do this: she just googled "French Classical Painters" and came up with Nicolas Poussin (1594–1665), the most famous artist of the seventeenth century. She did need some help interpreting the information; on the other hand, she ended up learning some basic concepts of art history that she would apply over the course of the year.) Back in Montreal the next year, our daughters' first school assignment was to write about "my favorite body part." Again, our jaws dropped. The idea (we assume) was for them to learn how to organize information. The content didn't matter. In France, form also matters, but never at the expense of content, especially when children are supposed to be building their *culture générale*.

To be fair, the universal French faith in knowledge acquisition means they end up cramming a lot of stuff into children's heads that probably doesn't belong there: some of it doesn't stick no matter how hard teachers try. Julie accompanied Erika's class one morning to Paris's "Festival du Pain" (Bread Festival), held in an enormous tent erected in the open square in front of Paris's Notre Dame Cathedral. Before entering the bread tent, it dawned on Erika's teacher that there was a great learning moment standing one hundred yards behind her. "That's an example of Gothic architecture," she told the class, pointing to Notre Dame Cathedral and slowly enunciating. Her tone suggested the children should have known that already (and since most of the kids lived a twenty-minute walk from Notre Dame, they probably should have). But the kids just shrugged. Even French kids can't know everything.

That doesn't stop the French from trying. Nobody questions the necessity of children learning La Fontaine's fables, or the ancient Greek tragedian Aeschylus's plays, even if the content is not exactly appropriate for children (by our standards). At the end of the year, our daughters memorized a forty-line fable by La Fontaine called "The Wolf and the Dog," the moral of which was "better to starve free than be a fat slave." Children start learning the names of France's rivers and the major dates of history as early as first grade. When a French teacher asks ten-year-olds, "Marignan?" children are supposed to be able to automatically answer, "1515" (1515 was the year King François I waged the famous battle of that name near Milan). There's no pedagogical "approach" backing up all that memorization, just the rock-solid certainty of the French that everyone should learn as much factual information, especially about France, as possible.

Geography is the most concrete and the most unifying among the topics that constitute French *culture générale,* so it's always a good bet for starting conversations. History is fascinating, but it can be polemical. Geography is neutral. It's also a topic that shows France in a flattering light. France is a geographical wonder with a wide range of geological, agricultural, and climatic conditions packed into a relatively small territory. What the French don't learn in books, they get to experience themselves during the country's abundant holidays.

However, with geography, as with almost all topics of French *culture générale,* a certain French tunnel vision can make foreigners feel foolish. In a typical conversation, one friend of ours told us she had a summer home in Plougasnou. When we asked her exactly where that was, she just answered, "It's in Brittany." We continued to probe, "Okay, but where in Brittany, exactly?" To which she answered: "Between Le Trégor and the Coast of Armor." It would have been a lot more helpful for us to hear that Plougasnou was one hundred kilometers west of Rennes, Brittany's capital city. But that's typical North American reasoning. The French give directions strictly with reference to other French landmarks (to be fair, Germans do the same). They never use cardinal points (though strangely, they do learn these in school) and hardly ever talk about numerical distances. Everyone is supposed to know where places are so they can figure out where other places are in relation to them.

French schoolchildren memorize things like the exact height of France's highest summit, Mont Blanc (4,807 meters), all stuff that can make grown-up North Americans feel ignorant, all the more so because French kids are taught to demonstrate their knowledge, so they tend to flaunt it. A popular gauge of good education in France is being able to recite the names and numbers of all of France's ninety-five *départements* by heart. Children are supposed to know this by the end of middle school. (French license plates all indicate the car owner's department; when driving, parents quiz their kids on these numbers.)

It probably struck us because as North Americans, we have to grapple with the vast distances of our continent so much: although France is by far the largest country of Western Europe, the French look at their country with a completely different mindset. They squint at it as if they are examining its features through a microscope, dividing it into the smallest units possible and contemplating the sometimes minute differences between, say, two neighboring towns. Administratively, France has thirteen *régions* that split up France's ninety-five *départements,* which in turn are split into thirty-seven thousand *communes* (towns). France has more towns than England, Germany, Spain, and Belgium combined. Unofficially, the country is also divided into 420 *pays,* distinct zones with their own geography and cultural particularities. (And those, in turn, are divided into 1,800 *micro-pays.*)

The reason French wine labels don't have grape types listed on them is that the French are expected to know, by seeing a department number (indicated on all wine labels), where the wine comes from, then deduce from their general geography knowledge what kind of grapes grow there (or simply what type of wine is produced there, skipping the grape types altogether; or by the shape of the bottle, which differs according to wine type). Learning France's minute territorial divisions at school means this should be part of one's *culture générale* by drinking age. Although French winemakers have added grape types to export labels to appease foreign markets, the French still like labels that are exclusively geographic because they don't insult their intelligence. *L'héritage de Carillan* is from le Pays d'oc, and that's that. The back of the bottle may tell you it is from Nîmes, but more often, it will simply give the number of the department, 30, by which you know that the wine comes from Le Gard, northwest of Marseille. A Saint-Pourçain is from Saint-Pourçain, in the Loire valley. The smaller and more specific the geographic area on the label, the more exclusive (and generally higher priced) the wine will be: the little known Bonnezeaux wine, for instance, comes from a small estate of one hundred and twenty hectares in Anjou, a minuscule patch within the seventy thousand hectares of the Loire Valley (to put this in perspective, Saumur wine is produced in an area of fourteen hundred hectares).

This splintered vision of their geography means the French have to look elsewhere to get a unified view of their country and that seems to be the job of weather reporting. The French view weather with a very wide lens. French newspapers' weather sections start with seventy-five-word paragraphs, rather poetic in tone, which convey the overall mood of the country, not meteorological conditions anywhere in particular. For example, one chilly May morning, *Le Parisien* newspaper wrote: "The Ice Saints Days Are Here. It's St. Servais' Day, after St. Mamert's and St. Pancrace's. The three Ice Saints are bringing back the North Wind and adding a chill to the beautiful spring sky. 'Beware of Frost,' say gardeners, who won't plant anything before the Saints have passed." The paragraph wrapped up with jaunty advice, ostensibly for anyone on French territory who might be thinking of leaving their house: "It might be a good idea to take a little scarf with you this morning." The story gives the French the illusion that the weather has some overarching grasp on the nation and that there's something "French" about the weather no matter if it's in Paris or Rennes.

The French also love to talk about history, which of course they know well, having started learning major dates in first grade (or earlier). Every day, every week of the year, either one of France's public television channels runs a special about a historical event or period, or a magazine publishes an entire issue about a historical period, or a new book on history is released—and that's not counting the many museum exhibitions about history. Whether it's ancient Egypt, the Freemasons, or Roman Gaul, the French just lap it up. Any major event is a good excuse for delving into related history: just before the World Cup started in Brazil, *Historia* published a special edition on the Portuguese colonial empire. World War II and the Algerian War are perennial topics.

The risk in talking about history with the French is that the book is never shut on it. The French have many parallel histories: there is the official timeline, but also local and personal histories that fit into that timeline. The two only converge in rare cases, as in World War I, during which 15 percent of France's population was either killed or injured and which everybody experienced more or less the same way. That's one reason the World War I soldier, called a *poilu* ("hairy," because they never got to shave), became an iconic figure in French history.[1] But in other cases, like the violent upheaval in Paris that happened a few decades earlier, La Commune, in 1870–1871, there is no consensus about what happened to this day.[2] World War II is even touchier. The country was divided. Some French collaborated with the German occupiers, some resisted, and in many ways, the war has not yet ended. When our young landlady visited us in our apartment, she made a point of telling us that her father had been a Grand Résistant, a fighter in the French Resistance. "But I can't say as much for other owners in this building," she alluded. It still mattered. Then again, people who experienced it are still alive. One friend from Jean-Benoît's hiking club, Huguette, still remembered Germans arriving in her village of Sarthe in 1940, when she was ten—a story she told for the first time as we were hiking on the seventieth anniversary of D-day.

Even beyond the great conflicts, the French have a complex, conflicted relationship with the past. The French Revolution aside, the French on the whole love the symbols of France's defunct monarchy, the ancien régime. Since 1984, Paris has celebrated something called Les Journées du Patrimoine (Heritage Days), by opening some seventeen thousand national buildings, normally closed to the public, to visitors. One Paris daily speculated about the curious popularity of the event, where people flock to admire the vestiges of a regime they love to hate—not just in Versailles Palace, but at the Luxembourg Palace (which houses the French Senate), the Élysée Palace (where the president lives), the Panthéon, and the Palais Bourbon (which houses the National Assembly). People still want to feel close to the monarchy, and they do it through historical monuments associated with power.

Then there's the issue of official history versus local history. Official history in France is essentially "Parisian" history. It is the official narrative of France that Parisians supply to the rest of the country. This is partly because Paris is where France's national institutions are located but also because throughout France's history, the government, located in Paris, has bulldozed local cultures and identities. Unofficial history is the history of the rest of France, the local history, which local people know very well. The relationship between the two is as fraught as that between a Native American or an Afro-American version of history and mainstream American history (or Canadian, for that matter). Naturally, a lot of local history is left out of France's official history, including local heroes one only hears about outside of Paris (and even Paris has its own local history). The French love supplementing "official" history with tidbits about their local history. Knowing just the smallest details about a place—not to mention having a decent grasp of official history—can go a long way in breaking the ice with people. When Jean-Benoît visited the town of Bourges, he only had to mention the name of the local hero Jacques Cœur (c. 1395–1456) to get people talking. Cœur was a local hero, a very rich merchant in the fifteenth century, and a famous treasurer of the king whose career ended as a result of an unfair trial. In remote French departments like Guadeloupe, locals told us about the slaves' heroic struggle for liberation, an episode that is ignored in official history—and here again, knowing about local fighters like Louis Delgrès (1772–1802) or La Mulâtresse Solitude (circa 1772–1802) makes it easy to talk to people.

As with geography, the French love their own history, even if it's not all glorious. This fascination can leave outsiders with the distinct impression that the French are backward looking, not to mention inward looking, victims of a giant case of nostalgia. There is no doubt that a sizable portion of the French population is falling back on tradition as an answer to challenges of the present. But France is not alone in that respect. And the French have not always been fond of the past. Classical art was about the rejection and destruction of Gothic art, which owes its name to the fact that the French regarded it as barbaric (the word comes from *gotico,* in sixteenth-century Italian, and originally meant "savage despoiler," in reference to German tribes who invaded the Roman Empire).

The present fascination of the French for their history is actually quite modern—it dates back to the romantics, particularly Victor Hugo's fascination for the Gothic and the grotesque. And for a country that boasts one of the biggest tourist industries on the planet, the past is very good business. Jean-Benoît visited Bourges, the capital of the Berry and very close to the geographical center of the country. His hostess, Michelle, belonged to a historical society that organized Veillées aux Flambeaux (candlelight vigils) and other events to celebrate local historical anniversaries. She knew a lot about the city's superb cathedral, which competes with Salisbury's in beauty and luminosity, and about Jacques Cœur, the local grandee whose remarkable Gothic house is still open to visitors. Bourges is a superb city with hundreds of timber-framed houses, built after the city burned down in the mid-1400s. A century ago, most of these timber frames were hidden under mortar to prevent fire. They were uncovered when architects and developers understood their potential as a tourist attraction.

In short, the French are a furiously modern people that live with a combination of beautiful things and ugly memories from the past. When you are talking about history in France, you need to tread carefully to avoid inadvertently stepping on toes. It's always a loaded topic. But there is one advantage to being an outsider: you are usually perceived as neutral. If you inadvertently ruffle their feathers, the French are likely to cut you some slack.

After geography and history, art is the third pillar of the French conception of *culture générale*. Because it is linked to taste, art is a more controversial topic than geography, and equally as debatable as history. But like Julie's famous Art-Deco-is-fascist declaration at Guillemette's table, the French *love* to hear opinions about art and culture—the more provocative, the better.

Though they tend to forget it themselves, the French have not always been geniuses of taste. The interest for art in France goes back to the French king François I, who reigned from 1515 to 1547 and brought the Italian Renaissance to France at the beginning of the sixteenth century. Prior to François I's rule, the French were considered rather crude. France was known for religious fanaticism (they led the Crusades), and for excelling in trade and the military arts, but not culture. François I did more than import Italian art (and cuisine): he was the first French ruler to make cultural promotion into a royal policy. The French have placed a high premium on art and culture ever since. According to a report from Ernst and Young, France's cultural industry employs 1 million people—that's one job out of forty—with half of those in Paris alone. A full 21 percent of the jobs in culture are in the film industry, and an amazing 19 percent are in live performance.[3] Not surprisingly, Paris has more public libraries and art galleries than any other capital city in the world.[4]

Art is the small talk of high talk in France. Almost all conversations veer toward some field of art at some point. Whether you are at a business lunch or having a picnic with friends on the lawn of the Louvre, you're bound to talk about the latest art shows, films, plays, or productions going on, and not just in Paris but anywhere in France. People like to know what's going on, but mostly, they want to hear what you think about it. While discussions about art, or the arts, often have a predictable element of evaluating the other's taste, the real goal—as in conversations about anything in France—is to spar. For that matter, when the French can't come up with something interesting to say about an event, they tend to fall back on the acceptable French default position of "hating it." And as we know, in French conversation, this is often just part of the opening remarks.

Knowing about art—any kind of art—is, of course, a mark of good *culture générale,* but writing is the most universal, and most highly respected, art form in France. The message comes straight from the top. Highly placed figures of all types in France almost universally aspire to publishing at least one book. They write books not to share wisdom or lessons learned from their experiences but to demonstrate that they can exercise France's cherished art of self-expression.

Yet there is one distinct feature of art and culture discussions in France: they are not especially class dependent. The subjects interest pretty much everyone, and to some degree they connect social classes. That might be because like good food, art is not considered a luxury in France but a basic necessity. It's also because the French state does its part to make sure the French "consume" art in whatever form, encouraging the film industry, offering free admission to museums, and even setting a TV schedule that gives cinema (and French cinema in particular) an edge. Everyone in France is expected to have some kind of cultural varnish.

Art has another distinctive quality in France: it excuses just about any kind of behavior. The French have an uncanny sympathy for artists turned criminals, or vice versa. Illegal actions or questionable gestures are not enough to get a brilliant artist expelled from good society, particularly if that action has nothing to do with the person's art. To the French, the fact that the film director Roman Polanski was charged with unlawful sex with a minor, or that Woody Allen essentially married his stepdaughter, is beside the point. In French minds, bad morals just do not trump artistic achievement. Particularly if there is no link between the action for which an artist has been criticized and his or her artistic production.

There is also a side of French culture that just loves equivocal artists. Famous criminals can change public opinion about themselves just by producing something of artistic value. The petty criminal Henri Charrière, aka Papillon (1906–1973), wrote a brilliant biography, mostly fictional, about his time in, and escape from, the famous island prison Île du Diable (Devil's Island) in French Guiana—the book inspired a Hollywood film starring Steve McQueen as Papillon. Another thief and murderer, Jacques Mesrine (1936–1979), became a popular hero when he published two books about being a convict, then a fugitive. Not to mention Pierre Goldman, half brother of the famous composer Jean-Jacques Goldman (who penned hits for Celine Dion among others). While serving a life sentence for armed robbery, Goldman wrote and published his autobiography in 1975. The book impressed certain left-wing intellectuals, like Jean-Paul Sartre, so much that Goldman ended up winning an appeal and being acquitted for his crime. He went on to work as a high-profile journalist, interviewing the likes of Gabriel García Márquez, before being assassinated in 1979.

If artists or writers are good enough, they're also allowed to say just about anything without jeopardizing their careers. The most blatant case is the author Louis-Ferdinand Céline (1894–1961), still revered for having modernized French literature in the 1930s by introducing argot among other things. Céline was a rabid anti-Semite who collaborated with the fascist regime of Marshal Pétain during the German occupation of France. In 1950 the French state convicted him for collaborating and declared him a national disgrace, but Céline bounced back and restored his literary reputation when he published a trilogy about his exile (he fled France for Denmark before the liberation) in 1957. In 2011, the French government refused to include him in a list of five hundred literary icons, but that didn't change the fact that Céline is a revered writer in France (this is partly because his novels actually contain little of the violent racism he expressed in pamphlets).

Though the French view of art often comes across as elitist, they don't systematically eschew lowbrow or vulgar entertainers or creators. Rather, they transform low art into a kind of high art of its own. For example, the French take circus arts, comic books, and drag queens quite seriously. This is a country where a man led a successful music hall career by farting in a microphone every night. Joseph Pujol's (1852–1945) stage name, le Pétomane (flatulist or fartist), said it all. In 2014 Paris's Musée d'art et d'histoire du judaïsme (Museum of Jewish Art and History) held a five-month exhibition of the work of Marcel Gotlib, an illustrator and comic book author who is the closest thing the French have to Monty Python.[5] Gotlib's zany weekly series and his humor magazine, *Fluide Glacial,* profoundly influenced French comedy, not to mention the entire comic book industry. The venue was also surprising given that Gotlib is spectacularly irreverent when it comes to religion—he is famous for a six-page cartoon entitled *God's Club* in which Monsieur Jupiter invites his friends Gaston Jéhovah, Louis Buddha, Jesus Christ, and Claude Allah to get drunk and watch a porno film together.

While we were in France, the National Library had a five-month-long exhibition about the comic book series *Astérix,* about the adventures of a diminutive hero in Roman-occupied France. The series has sold over 360 million copies in 107 languages and dialects and its authors, René Goscinny and Albert Uderzo, are national celebrities. The French are voracious consumers of these *bandes dessinées,* and comics, usually referred to by the acronym *BD* ("*bay-day*"), are considered an art form of their own. France is the world's third market for comics after Japan and the United States, but it represents a staggering 12 percent of the publishing business, compared to 8 percent in the United States.

One peculiarity of the French relationship to art is that they never divorced masculinity from artistic taste, which has been the case in North American society since the nineteenth century. That probably explains why one never hears diatribes about how the arts are "useless" in France. On the contrary. What Americans qualify as a "liberal arts curriculum" is just considered plain old education in France. Children are initiated into the arts—whether it's Rodin's sculptures or Gothic architecture—starting in *la maternelle,* kindergarten. The French are willing to invest a lot of personal time and collective resources to make sure the lessons stick. Public museums grant free admission not just to children under eighteen, but to all students under twenty-six, as well as card-carrying journalists (so that's where we spent our free time in Paris).

France also has extensive cultural policies that encourage new creation in all fields. All public works projects have architectural design contests before they are built. Not all the architectural projects selected turn out to be popular—many French think Paris's high-tech

Georges Pompidou Center, with its multicolored exposed skeleton (the plan was chosen from among 681 entries), is a horror. But no one questions the need to make buildings that are more than utilitarian.

Just as no one questions the need to know a thing or two about architecture. Because that, too, is just part of what the French consider a good *culture générale*.

~ 10 ~

Down by Nature

Although there's no specific rule against it, French schoolchildren never eat out of lunch boxes. They either go home for lunch or eat at *la cantine* (school cafeteria). That means that in addition to registering children for school, parents have to trek to their local *mairie* (town hall) to sign them up for lunch service.

And that's how we ended up in conversation with Monsieur Fitoussi, the director of the Caisse des écoles (the body that manages cafeterias and after-school activities) in Paris's fifth arrondissement. We had to show him our tax return so he could decide what fiscal category we belonged to, lunch prices being scaled to family income, and in the process, we mentioned we were freelance journalists. Fitoussi jumped on the opportunity to boast about some of his office's achievements, starting with the fact that 60 percent of the food served in all *cantines* is organic. Monsieur Fitoussi was quite proud of this. He reported that a delegation of Canadian school officials had just visited our arrondissement to talk about lunch menus. His next plan was to make sure all the fish in his *cantines* are "caught by French fishermen."

Taking his cue from Fitoussi's buoyancy, Jean-Benoît decided to relate some observations about other things that we, as foreigners, felt worked quite well in France, like good access to medical care, the excellent road system, reliable fast trains, high-quality teachers, and universal pre-school starting at age three. In our research we had also learned that life expectancy and productivity rates in France were high, and energy consumption low (the French use half the energy North Americans do). Jean-Benoît even backed up his claims by mentioning a fascinating study he had recently come across by the Atlantic Council, called *Companions in Competitiveness,* which concluded that France outranked the United States in infrastructure, education, and health care.[1]

Monsieur Fitoussi didn't buy it. "You can't possibly believe France has anything to teach to the world?" he replied. A mere thirty seconds earlier Monsieur Fitoussi had been bragging about foreigners who were interested in his achievements. Now he refused to believe that his country could do a single thing right. Monsieur Fitoussi's reaction actually highlighted the one field in which the French do demonstrate unparalleled excellence: the art of extreme and extravagant self-criticism. When it comes to systematic pessimism, nobody does it better. The French are the world's undisputed heavyweight champions of negativity.

While French bashing is practically a subgenre of the Anglo-American press, what amazed us when we lived in France was the degree to which the French press parrot it, almost to the letter. We considered it a bit of a riddle: are the French regurgitating criticism from outside the country, or are foreign journalists simply reporting all the bad things the French say about themselves, verbatim?[2]

We tend to believe the latter, based on the extent to which negativity, pessimism, and skepticism are permanent and universal features of

French discourse. The form and intensity of this negativism have varied over time. On our first visit to France in 1992, the country was in
the middle of severe budget cuts. The mood was foul. Then when we
moved to France seven years later, the economy was vibrant and this
negativity had waned. On visits and stays in France between 2004
and 2008, the mood slipped and pessimism seemed to be on the rise.
But in 2013, we arrived in an all-time low (for us). France was grappling
with economic stagnancy and fiscal reckoning. Even the French Left
had lost its pluck. It normally blamed France's problems on the usual
suspects—capitalism and the United States. Not anymore.

Whether we were discussing language, the quality of cafeteria
food at Radio France, or even bread, wine, or cheese, the prognoses
were uniformly bleak. If we had written a travelogue about France
after our year in France, we would have at least subtitled it *Tout va mal*
(nothing works).

But things in France always sound worse than they are because of
the simple fact that the French are chronically negative. The systematic pessimism we are describing goes well beyond the universal "no"
with which most verbal exchanges are initiated (which we discussed
in chapter 3). French negativism is a customary starting point in almost
any French conversation. It is a form of hypochondria that frames almost everything the French say. In France, it's as polite to start speaking to a stranger by complaining as it is to comment on the weather
(as long you are complaining, that is).

French negativity doesn't require any prompters. It is spontaneous
and always presented as self-evident. If you contradict an assumed negative stance off the bat, the reaction will often be a baffled stare. After
Julie finished an interview one evening with the director of one of
France's language-protection groups, she walked with the gentleman

to the metro station where they were both leaving, in opposite directions. He asked Julie what she thought about public transport in Paris, evidently expecting a familiar complaint to ensue. When Julie answered, "It's great," the man just looked at her blankly, then turned on his heels and walked off. Witnessing unexpected satisfaction is one of the few things that leave the French speechless.

The popular expressions used to characterize France's decline change over time, we noticed. Fifteen years ago, we frequently heard: "*La France, ce n'est plus ce que c'était*" (France is not what it used to be). Today, the French are so down they don't seem to think their country was anything to start with. They have a new maxim: "The way the country is going today . . . ," alluding to the supposedly self-evident "decline" in French values. Then there is the good old "*Ça, c'est la France!*" (That's France for you!), which actually translates as, "Of course things in France are getting worse."

When it comes to negativism, defeatism, alarmism, and catastrophism, the French make full use of the resources their language offers. Expressions we heard describing this sentiment included *morosité* (morosity), *sinistrose* (malingering), *vague à l'âme* (melancholy), *abattement* (dejection), *idées noires* (gloomy thoughts), *spleen* (melancholy), *cafard* (the blues), and *la déprime* (depression). Thanks to the unique ability of the French language to transform adjectives into nouns, the French also have a special category of titles for the different groups of people affected by bad times. There are *les insatisfaits* (the dissatisfied), *les agacés* (the irritated), *les énervés* (the irritated), *les impatients* (the impatient), and *les exaspérés* (the exasperated), not to mention *les râleurs* (the moaners), *les rouspéteurs* (the grumps), and *les mécontents* (the malcontents), to name but a few.

Even the motto of Paris, *Fluctuat nec mergitur* (tossed by the waves, it doesn't sink), has a curiously negative ring to it. France's institutions seem to cater to a preordained pessimistic mind-set. When we left France, we had to close accounts for a number of utilities. After wrapping up our business with France's electric company, we received a survey asking us to evaluate waiting times on the phone, quality of answers, the level of courtesy (*amabilité*), and other aspects of customer service. The four choices were *nul* (lousy), *pas à la hauteur* (not up to standards), *correct* (fine), and *bon* (good). In other words, on a French rating scale, the opposite of "lousy" is not "excellent." "Good" is as good as it gets.

There's an old joke that when two British people meet in the street, they shake hands, then get in line, but when two French people meet, they shake hands and start complaining about France. For the French, the glass is either half empty or totally, desperately empty. The French even have a way of presenting their pessimistic starting points so they don't seem to require substantiation. It's more of a state of mind than an opinion, but more of an opinion than an observation.

Because the French tend to be so negative about so many things, it's hard to get an unbiased assessment of their actual feelings. Still, it's a mistake for foreigners to take French negativism at face value—the same way it would be a mistake to think that everyone is happy in North America when they smile. (It's just our peculiar way of being polite.) Over the years, we have learned to take the overly pessimistic viewpoints of the French with a grain of salt.

Though it seemed to go against the grain of everything happening in France, the spring of 2014 in Paris was Le Printemps de l'Optimisme (The Spring of Optimism)—at least thanks to a Frenchman named Thierry Saussez. It was actually a three-day event, the first of its kind, and consisted of high-profile round tables and workshops on positive thinking. Jean-Benoît met Saussez, the event's founder and a right-wing political organizer, public relations specialist, former communications adviser to Nicolas Sarkozy, and author. Prior to the event, Saussez had commissioned a national survey on optimism. What he discovered was that the French were, in fact, optimistic about their own prospects, but pessimistic about their society. "This is bizarre," he told Jean-Benoît. "Think about it. How can 80 percent of people be optimistic about their own lives, while only 20 percent are optimistic about the society they live in and whatever doesn't concern them personally?"

National statistics in France reveal the same dichotomy between high personal optimism on one hand and high "societal" pessimism on the other. Aside from France's sustained high birthrate (which we discussed in chapter 5), generally considered a sign of optimism, the French, historically, have never felt things were so bad they had to leave their country. The French have always emigrated less than other European nations, and by a large margin. According to the latest figures available, the French have created six times more businesses than Germany, the UK, or the United States over a five-year period, a phenomenon generally considered to be a sign of optimism.[3] In a recent survey by OpinionWay, 66 percent of French youth between eighteen and twenty-six stated they were "rather optimistic about the future," a score 20 percent higher than that of older generations, which is surprising given that unemployment rates among French youth are high, above 20 percent. The French appear to be closet optimists wrapped in a thick cloak of pessimism.[4]

In April, just a month before Saussez's Spring of Optimism event, the French TV channel TF1, roughly the equivalent of the BBC, launched a publicity campaign that made fun of France's split personality. The concept was simple: a voiceover expressed a series of common gripes, then contrasted them with images that showed the exact opposite. "The French are sulky" was illustrated with an image of people around a table, laughing; "the French are lazy" showed a tractor tilling a field at dawn; "the French believe in nothing" showed a newborn; "the French are racist" showed a pair of black feet and white feet interwoven on bed sheets; "the French are losers" showed a French soccer team cheering a victory. It ended with TF1's new slogan: *Partageons des ondes positives* (let's share positive vibes). It could have been an ad for Saussez's Spring of Optimism event. Sales of books on personal motivation and positive thinking are at an all-time high in France with sales of two hundred thousand or three hundred thousand copies now common.[5]

So why exactly do the French refuse to sound optimistic even when they are, or at least want to be? The answer is: some posturing mixed with philosophy and a few deeply anchored French taboos. Xavier North, a high-ranking French civil servant, was one of the first people to talk to us about this contradiction. We initially met North when he was in charge of cultural cooperation at France's Ministry of Foreign Affairs, then talked to him again, years later, when he was head of France's main language regulation body, the Délégation générale à la langue française et aux langues de France (DGLFLF). It's a mistake to take the French attitude at face value, he told us. French negativism is simply the French *manière d'être* (way of being) with foreigners, a bit like the Japanese who tend to portray their culture as impenetrable to outsiders. "Negativism is posturing. To a lot of French, being happy seems naïve." A number of famous French people have said the same thing in different terms, including the French actor Jean Gabin, who, in *Mélodie en sous-sol* (*Any Number Can Win*, 1963), declared, "*L'essentiel, c'est de râler. Ça fait bon genre.*" (The important thing is to moan. It makes you look respectable.)

To be fair, as a general manner of speaking, the French do consider criticism to be more honest than praise. To the French, unbridled optimism, enthusiasm, or unwarranted contentment all scream simple-mindedness. As France's most popular stand-up comedian, Jamel Debbouze, put it, you have to sound pessimistic to look intelligent in France.[6] Overt pessimism has an elegant antiestablishment quality about it, like wearing all black. In a society where everyone is expected to produce opinions, negativism is a convenient form of intellectual prêt-à-porter (ready-to-wear), a ready-made opinion that doesn't have to be substantiated. The French even coined a metaphor for this, inspired from rugby: *botter en touche* (drop back ten yards and punt). The idea is, you proffer an *énormité,* then let people fight over it while you buy time to think of something interesting to say.

But French negativism is more than just posturing. French pessimists are on solid intellectual grounds, the product of an intellectual tradition favoring doubt over certainty that dates back centuries. The philosopher René Descartes (1596–1650) philosophized about the necessity of doubt. In his play *The Barber of Seville,* the French playwright Pierre Beaumarchais (1732–1799) writes, "*J'aime mieux craindre sans sujet que de m'exposer sans précaution*" (I would rather fear without reason than expose myself carelessly). Then the philosopher Jean-Jacques Rousseau followed up with the claim that man was "born free and everywhere is in chains," meaning things necessarily go downhill.[7] In 1932, a young Albert Camus crossed happiness off the list of noble goals in life, writing: "You will never be happy if you continue to search for what happiness consists of. You will never live if you are looking for the meaning of life."[8]

But the most forceful attack on optimism came from a contemporary of Rousseau, the French Enlightenment writer Voltaire (François-

Marie Arouet, 1694–1778) in his satiric novella *Candide, or The Optimist*. Voltaire actually wrote the novella in response to the new word "optimism," which only entered the French lexicon in 1737. The story is of a young man, Candide, who grows up living a sheltered life in a castle, which gave him the naïve belief that "all is for the best in all possible worlds." After a series of catastrophic misfortunes Candide is reduced to misery and concludes that "not all is for the best" and, as a result, that "one must cultivate one's garden" (protect yourself). It is an astute description of the French mind-set that sounds familiar even today and fits the paradoxical findings of Thierry Saussez's survey.

But it's probably fair to say that French pessimism is a healthy reaction to another French tradition: excessive and unrealistic official boosterism. The eulogy of France is a subgenre of French poetry dating back ten or even twelve centuries, which French poets produced in an attempt to win their king's favor through flattery. Such writings were commonplace until the Enlightenment, when a new form of hyperbolic and all-encompassing criticism—the pursuit of truth beyond authority—established itself as a type of counter-discourse. Perhaps because authority in France remained absolute (and in many respects, still is today), the French criticism of authority became absolute as well. Artists are automatically expected to embrace this.[9] For that matter, absolute criticism lives on as a literary genre of its own. Some creators have built entire careers on pessimism, the prize going to French-Romanian writer Emil Cioran (1911–1995). Born in Romania, Cioran moved to Paris in the late 1930s where he published *A Short History of Decay, The Temptation to Exist,* and *The Trouble with Being Born.* Cioran was known for claiming that the only thing that made it possible to keep living was the possibility of suicide (he ended up dying at eighty-four, from Alzheimer's disease).[10]

Negativism is also a ploy the French use to address taboo subjects like money, nationalism, and racism. Given the extent to which money is a private topic in France, speaking negatively about economic matters is the most acceptable way of broaching the topic. In a culture where the tax system tends to be punitive and people want to avoid attracting the attention of their neighbors or of tax inspectors, casting a negative light on anything relating to money, status, financial questions, or estates also operates as a smoke screen.[11] The French don't want to look like they are hiding anything, and the best way to deflect attention is to complain. According to historians, this tactic dates back centuries.[12]

Many extreme expressions of negativism in France also stem from repressed nationalism. One effect of the two world wars was that overt nationalism was virtually banned from public discourse in all of Europe. The only political party in France that openly embraces "love of country" is the far-right National Front Party. The love of country exists among the general population, but more often than not, it is expressed in the form of regret: "France is not what it used to be." The same logic applies to the topic of race relations, yet another taboo in France (we address this topic at length in chapter 18). The French (except National Front members, anyway) are generally quite careful when they discuss the topic and tend to express their concerns, whatever they are, again, in the form of "France is not what it used to be."[13]

Thierry Saussez's Spring of Optimism event actually had a political agenda behind it that was surprisingly nonpartisan (given that Saussez ran President Sarkozy's communications department from 2008 to 2010). Saussez denied being a proponent of positive thinking but said he hoped the event would lead to a lucid assessment of the risks of intractable French negativism. In his view, unrealistic negativism was politically dangerous. "It produces a discourse of victimization, impotence and malingering and pushes people to look for scapegoats. That's dangerous."

The French use the term *sinistrose* to describe this discourse. Though a synonym of pessimism, *sinistrose* is actually a term from psychiatry; it describes a condition best translated as malingering. The French term was created in 1908 to describe people who, having suffered a wrong owing to an accident, do everything they can to exaggerate the effect of it in order to gain compensation. That's when negativism stops being mere posturing and starts acquiring a really ugly side. It has happened before in France. In a memoir called *Strange Defeat,* the revered French historian Marc Bloch (1886–1944) documented the experience of the first days of World War II, when the French army caved in the face of the Germany army. The capitulation was completely out of proportion with the actual threat France faced: the French army was a large, well-equipped army at the time. Bloch attributes the defeat to an excessively pessimistic, fatalistic attitude among French elites in the 1930s. What he describes is eerily similar to the mind-set the French have now, seventy-five years later.

The saving grace for the French this time may be that they have no objective enemy.

~ 11 ~

Fixation on French

One of the most endearing idiosyncrasies of the French is their passion for words. The French adore linguistic nuances, revere dictionaries, and collect new words and expressions like precious artifacts. There is probably nothing they love talking about more. One of the best ways to make conversation with the French is to mention an interesting word or novel expression. Over the years, we got into the habit of doing this by translating English metaphors, or using French expressions we picked up on our travels in North Africa, Belgium, or even Louisiana. The French always take the bait. They can't help it. Pondering language is a national reflex.

Introducing exotic expressions is also a great way to change the subject when you need to. Jean-Benoît resorted to this one evening during an Arabic class he was taking at the Arab World Institute in Paris. Just before the end of class his turn came to read a particularly difficult selection. To buy some time, he described his situation with a common expression from Quebec, but unheard of in France: *C'est un cadeau de Grec* (literally: "It's a Greek present," meaning a Trojan Horse). The half-dozen other students and his teacher forgot about what they were doing and zoomed in on the new phrase, even though it was totally off topic. They wanted to know everything about it: where it came from, how long people had been using it, who used it, where. In the excitement, everyone forgot it was Jean-Benoît's turn to read and he was off the hook.

Jean-Benoît had gotten the idea from French politicians, who frequently use this trick to avoid having to deal with topics that are potentially detrimental to their reputations. For instance, in January 2014 we watched in awe as President François Hollande used a particular term to get out of talking about the painful love triangle he found himself in. Paparazzi had discovered his love affair with the actress Julie Gayet, and Hollande's "First Girlfriend" Valérie Trierweiler was refusing to talk to the media. With a verbal *pirouette* (about-face), Hollande completely diverted media attention from the love triangle to— get this—the economy. On January 15 he announced to French media that he was a *social-démocrate* (social democrat), a controversial term in socialist circles because it implies sympathy to the market economy. Hollande was the first socialist leader to ever openly embrace the term, and the surprise effect worked its magic. The media dropped the Julie Gayet story and spent the rest of the month speculating about what exactly Hollande meant by "social democrat."

Languages come with their own narrative. English speakers think of their language as "open," "flexible," and "accommodating." The French story is exactly the opposite. In French minds, their language is a particularly complex and nuanced tongue with no gray zones and little, if any, *à peu près* (approximation). Words are right or words are wrong. Every word has a precise meaning distinguishing it from other words. Grammar is correct or incorrect. The French even think about synonyms differently than do English speakers. *Roget's* English thesaurus

is a cornucopia of synonyms organized in categories with no definitions. French dictionaries of synonyms have few words per category
and more definitions. In the French mind-set, it's virtually impossible
for two words to mean the same thing. So the French want to know
the exact nuance that differentiates one word from another.

Not surprisingly, given this mind-set, linguistic nitpicking is a pretty
popular pastime in France. It's not the exclusive domain of France's
elite or literary circles. French people from all backgrounds talk about
semantic nuances. It's one of the most startling particularities of French
culture. As self-employed writers we are constantly asking for receipts
for deductible expenses. The French, we learned, have four different
words for the word "receipt": *reçu, ticket, fiche,* and *quittance,* each with
a slightly different meaning. A *reçu* is the generic term, but implies a
detailed statement with tax numbers. *Le ticket* is produced by a machine
and is less detailed. *La fiche* is similar, but handwritten. *La quittance* is
the most formal kind of receipt, something like a discharge: it states
the name of the payer and payee, what the payment is for, and is often
signed. Needless to say, we still get them confused.

The French are so bent on being precise that they'll resort to hijacking a word from another language to add some nuance they can't
get in French. That's how "weekend" ended up becoming a French
word. Quebeckers translate weekend literally into *fin de semaine,* end of
the week. But the *fin de semaine,* in France, signifies "end of the working
week," or Friday. So the French decided to call Saturday and Sunday—
which come after the *fin de semaine*—*le week-end.* As far as Quebeckers
are concerned, this is pointless hairsplitting, but Quebeckers are a lot
less picky about language nuances than are the French.[1]

However, it's fair to say that all French speakers share a certain level
of interest in linguistic precision. Every March, the fifty-four member

countries of the *Francophonie* (plus three associate members and twenty observer countries) celebrate the Semaine de la francophonie (Francophonie Week). In almost every country, organizers set up local *dictées* (dictation contests) for the general public or members of associations. Throughout the 1990s and until 2005, there was even an international contest, called *La dictée de Bernard Pivot,* named after a famous literary critic, which was broadcast to millions of viewers who actually did the exercise at home. *Dictée* contests are still organized locally, but since 2005, official francophone celebrations have been more geared toward celebrating regional differences in the French-speaking world. *Francophonie* celebrations in France are called *Le mois des mots* (the month of the words). A typical activity is to have people submit lists of their "favorite ten words," often with a specific theme, like language, love, or travel. Governments in French-speaking countries also publish their own lists of favorite words. In 2014, France's Ministry of Culture and Communications produced a series of twenty words that the organizers had chosen because they expressed the variety and creativity of the francophone world, including the Senegalese verb *ambiancer* (to liven up) or the archaic expression *à tire larigot* (continually, to one's heart's content).

Among French speakers, the release of a new edition of any dictionary is an event amply covered by the press, which then turns the event into a topic of conversation. French dictionaries share one feature with French wine: both industries are built on strong local consumption. Larousse and Robert became international references in the dictionary business (and not just in French, but in English, German, Spanish, Italian, Arabic, and Chinese) because the French themselves buy so many dictionaries, creating a solid base for companies so they can expand. The Paris Book Fair (le Salon du livre) has two

Journées des dictionnaires (Dictionary Days), when dozens of lexicographers present their new work. The dictionary sensation at the 2014 Salon was *Le dico des mots qui n'existent pas, mais qu'on utilise quand même* (The dictionary of words that don't exist but that we use anyway). In this genre, nothing is too specific.

Words constantly make the news in France: literary newspapers, like the Paris daily *Libération,* even cover the appearance of new words entering the French lexicon like current events stories. Shortly after we arrived in France 2013, there was a story in the news about a jeweler in the southern French city of Nice who had shot a thief in the back. It was widely covered and stayed in the news because a Facebook page, created to support the jeweler, got a surprising 1.6 million "Likes" in less than a day. *Libération* ran as many stories scrutinizing the meaning and significance of a Facebook "Like" as it did on the actual event.

French TV and newspaper interviewers often wrap up by asking their guests what their favorite word is. To the French, word choices are revealing both of someone's character and of their ability to use the French language to its fullest potential. When asked what his favorite word was, the actor Fabrice Lucchini, known for being irreverent, answered archly, *"croquis"* (sketch), apparently because he liked the way it sounded. The actress Fanny Ardant answered, *"tant pis!"* (too bad) to show her insouciant side. The filmmaker Louis Malle answered *"bonheur"* (happiness); the actress Brigitte Bardot said *"harmonie"* (harmony); the actress Isabelle Adjani chose *lumière* (light); and Salmon Rushdie, *métamorphose* (metamorphosis).

French newspapers frequently use a single, often enigmatic word as a title to catch readers' interest. In February 2014, following a week of protests against same-sex marriage in France, *Libération* ran an editorial denouncing the lack of reaction by the government. The title was simply "Aboulie," a word that means an absence of willpower. In profiles of French personalities, French journalists expand on their encounter by branching off to examine a new term. In a profile of the actor Guillaume Gallienne, when he was playing the character of Oblomov in a play inspired by the 1859 novel by the Russian writer Ivan Goncharov, a journalist devoted part of the article to exploring the meaning of the word *oblomovisme* (a kind of slothful laziness). It was a strange angle for an article about a hyperactive actor like Gallienne, who has starred in forty plays and twenty-seven films over the last twenty years, but the word was evidently just too interesting to leave alone.[2]

For outsiders to French culture, language is among the easiest topics to talk about with the French, on par with geography, food, and culture. The French are usually willing and eager to immerse foreigners in the minutiae of French grammar rules, etymology, and spelling, and they enjoy comparing languages. The discussions often have a barely concealed tone of proselytization. The French want to educate and enlighten us. They think their language is fascinating and they assume we do, too.

In addition to their fascination with words, the French love picking apart other people's language use. For all their love of nuance, when it comes to language standards, the French are curiously binary. Language use, in their minds, is either good or it's bad; it conforms to the norm or it doesn't. They like to think there is a right and a wrong. It's one reason they constantly correct each other. It's an old cultural reflex tied to the doctrine of language purism, which was first formulated by the French poet François de Malherbe (1555–1628) at the beginning of the seventeenth century. Like many of his contemporaries, Malherbe was motivated by a desire to make a break with the previous century in France, marked by the wars of religion, atrocious massacres, and civil war. Malherbe was an influential poet and took it upon himself to "clean" French of what he considered filth, including archaic terms, regional terms, synonyms, and technical terms. His idea was to make French into a concise, clear, and coherent language. Malherbe's ideas struck a chord in France's circles of power and one of Malherbe's followers, King Louis XIII's chief minister, Cardinal Richelieu, would go on to create the French Academy largely based on Malherbe's ideas. In the meantime, French scholars started producing grammars and dictionaries. French salons saw the arrival of figures known as *remarqueurs* or *remarquistes,* whose remarks and pronouncements on language were considered authoritative.[3]

Modern France still has *remarqueurs* in the form of linguists and language experts whose comments frequently appear in the press. But even if the French media dutifully report on the election of new members to the French Academy, they pay little attention to what the Academy is actually doing. This is particularly hard for foreigners to grasp. Like Perrier, Roquefort, and bordeaux wine, the French Academy is an international brand recognized across the world. But as conversation topics go, no one has much to say about it. The French Academy is more symbolic than significant. It doesn't really do anything but hand out second-tier literary prizes and rubber-stamp the work of actual professional lexicographers (which Academy members are *not*). Foreigners typically attribute to the French Academy more influence than it has, and certainly more than it deserves. Nor does the French Academy "rule" over language. Its pronouncements, which are rare, hold no legal weight and rarely any influence. In short, no one in France has much to say about it because there isn't much to say. (Though if the French understood how heartily the outside world be-

lieves in the importance of their Academy, *that* would make an interesting topic of conversation. The French would be all over it.)[4]

It's another French institution that really carries the torch of language purism: the schools. French teachers have been shouldering most
of the responsibility of preserving French for the last two centuries.
Many French have forgotten this, but two centuries ago, most of France
was not French speaking. As Graham Robb writes in *The Discovery of
France,* "The process of forgetting was one of the great social forces in
the formation of modern France. Middle-class children would forget
the provincial languages they learned from nurses and servants, or remember them only as a picturesque remnant of the past." And he adds,
"In the land of a thousand tongues, monolingualism became the mark
of the educated person." But turning French into the language of the
land was not an easy task. The legacy of this uphill battle explains, at
least partly, why the French remain so firmly convinced that their language is such a difficult one to master. It's also why they are so adamant about children learning it properly and thoroughly.

Language is a matter of national identity in France. In fact, language
is so deeply embedded in the French national identity the French don't
seem to even consider French as a language among others. French
children are theoretically supposed to learn two or three foreign languages by the time they finish *le lycée* (high school). The process starts
in grade 6, where kids become acquainted with a second language
(usually English or German). Then in grade 8, they are introduced
to a third language (the choices are generally English, German, and
Spanish). And when they start *le lycée* (grade 10), students have to
choose yet another language (from a wider selection that may include
Arabic, Italian, or one of France's regional languages). But curiously,

regardless of what language kids choose, the French don't call it a "second" language but a "first" language, *une première langue*. The one after that is the second, *la deuxième langue* (second language), even if it comes third.

In other words, as far as the French are concerned, French is not a mere language. It's part of what it means to be French. Learning the French language properly is considered a duty in France. That's one reason language teaching in French schools is so rigorously structured. By the time French children are nine, as we learned, they are expected to demonstrate proper spelling skills and even penmanship.

Language is a key tool of social promotion in France, in virtually any professional domain. Bad French will get you nowhere in France. Good French opens doors that might not have opened otherwise. French teachers and parents aren't worried that telling children they are wrong might damage their self-esteem. All the mistakes our girls made in their written work were flagged and corrected—and not just in the *dictées* and grammar exercises, but in all their work. No written *faute* goes without censure in France, even if students aren't actually penalized for it. In elementary school the general philosophy is not very punitive, but that changes as kids get older. The really severe marking kicks in during *collège* (roughly grades 6–9) and *lycée* (grades 10–12), where 10 out of 20, or 12 out of 20 is considered a good grade. Students who commit numerous *fautes* can end up with marks of *minus* 10, 15, or even 20.

We already touched on why the fear of *faute* makes the French deflect responsibility for even the most mundane oversights. School performance in France is fueled by the fear of committing *fautes*. The fixation on *fautes* even got so out of hand in France that the government tried to ban the term *faute,* itself, in 2007. Teachers cannot, technically, refer to errors as *fautes* today. But it's not easy to erase age-old teaching (and parenting) mentalities. The philosophy of the *faute* remains firmly anchored in the French psyche. It has been at the heart of French teaching for centuries. In 2014, France's education minister passed a reform that would require teachers to reward students for improvement, as opposed to penalizing them for shortcomings. But to this day, a child who reduces his *dictée* "errors" from 40 to 20 still gets zero over 20, or less.

It will be difficult—likely impossible—to completely revolutionize French *faute*-based teaching techniques, mostly because the French hold their language up to an imaginary mirror of perfection. In this "ideal" French, spelling, diction, and grammar conform to strict rules—some real, some imaginary. No one, of course, writes this "perfect" French in real life. But the idea still has a hold on the French: almost everyone strives to reach it in some way or another.

The same ideals, unrealistic as they are, even apply to spoken French, which is supposed to mirror the written standard. Ideal spoken French is supposed to be perfectly precise. So there should be no approximations (and definitely no mumbling). According to the ideal, every word uttered counts, and each one should convey an exact meaning. Basically, ideal spoken French is school French—and since all public schools in France follow the same curriculum, the language they produce is remarkably uniform from one end of the country to the other (and even across oceans, to France's overseas territories). Local inflections and vocabulary are supposed to disappear in this French, which should sound more or less like you are reading a book. Of course, few people actually speak this "ideal" French, even in formal situations, but in typical French fashion, that doesn't erase the expectation that everyone *should* speak it.

The other places we have lived, besides Paris—Montreal, Toronto, and Phoenix, Arizona—all shared a high tolerance for poor language use (though of course, we only know that because we lived in a place that doesn't tolerate poor language skills). It is common in North American restaurants, stores, or taxis to be served by people who don't speak the greatest English, and it's tolerated. While it happens in France— there are people who slip through the cracks—a visitor is unlikely to meet people who speak French poorly to them. It's not because there aren't any. French society just hides them in back store jobs; they never serve customers, largely because the French themselves have little or no tolerance for bad French.

Nor do the French have the slightest qualms about passing judgment on how others speak. As a matter of fact, they often end up talking about language when they want to criticize something totally unrelated. Language is an easy shield for other less acceptable prejudices. The French use language to editorialize on all sorts of things that politeness or political correctness would normally forbid. It's a common way they criticize *les jeunes,* youth (who supposedly can't speak properly anymore), or immigrants (they refuse to learn French), or technology (it's eroding the French language), or class differences.

In fact, picking on someone's language is an acceptable way of bad-mouthing or mocking them, even if the real complaint has nothing to do with language. Jean-Benoît witnessed this dynamic one afternoon at a café on avenue Montaigne, in Paris's swish eighth arrondissement. He was interviewing the director of a drone flight-test center near Bordeaux for a story on France's civilian drone industry. (The French are world leaders in developing civilian uses for unmanned aerial vehicles, mostly because the French government opened its own skies to civilian drones earlier than most other countries did, including

Canada and the United States.) Throughout the interview, the director, a chain smoker, tapped his cigarette ashes on the ground below the table, unaware that the wind was picking the ashes up and depositing them in the pant cuffs of a neatly dressed older gentleman at the next table. At one point the gentleman in question turned to the director and told him to stop flicking ashes on him. He either forgot or ignored him and continued tapping his ashes until the gentleman turned around a second time and snapped: "*Mais quel malotrus!*" (What a lout you are!) The gentleman was asserting his class status, but knowing that using class was an outmoded way to belittle people and hearing that the director, who is from Bordeaux, had a slight southern accent, he turned to language instead: "*Vous parlez français?*" (Do you even speak French?) It was the ultimate insult.

When it comes to the French and their language, the Anglo-American media seem convinced that the French are obsessed with protecting their language from outside threats. But what worries most French are the threats from the inside. We had lunch with a friend, Sophie Maura, a lawyer in Essonne, a department just southwest of Paris. As her name suggests, she is of Spanish descent. Her father was a Spanish petroleum engineer from Burgos who immigrated to France and spent most of his life working north of the city of Pau, in the French Pyrenees. We were amazed by her assessment of her father's experience as a hard-working immigrant: "I don't understand how he got through his life speaking such horrible French!" She was being perfectly candid. She really was puzzled, but mostly embarrassed for him.

But it would be a caricature to present the whole population of France as dyed-in-the-wool language purists. Despite the norms and standards that form the bedrock of French purism and that justify the custom of correcting incessantly, day-to-day French are constantly shifting and everyone knows it. Conservative circles constantly bemoan changing standards in phonetics, grammar, and vocabulary, citing them as evidence of the "decadence" of French. Progressive circles celebrate the French language's power of invention. Most of the French are on the fence about the issue. But everyone knows that real-life French is not the same thing as school French. People never speak like books or walking dictionaries.[5]

All French go through the purist drill at school. But when they grow up, most become the linguistic equivalent of regular churchgoers, not religious zealots. Many words one hears in France are not in any French dictionary. In any language, even French, speech is much freer than writing. And in a purist culture like the one surrounding French, the spoken language operates as a pressure valve, allowing speakers to occasionally turn their noses up at the purist ideology they have to respect in their day jobs. In other words, as in any case of extremism, French language purism just begs for a backlash. For all their purist posturing, the French love to lapse, and relish the rebellious side of their language.

Needless to say, true French, the language that comes out of the mouths of millions of French people every day, is much more truncated, and less tidy, than school French. Fifteen years ago, people started speaking of *résa,* for ticket reservations. Today it's so common that you see *résa* followed by a phone number or an e-mail address in ads for any performance. Journalists, the chroniclers of day-to-day language, are great popularizers of new expressions. The French daily *Le Parisien* had no compunction about using the term *niaque* (from the Gascon word *gnaca,* meaning to bite) in its headlines to describe a particularly combative political candidate.

One of the best places to see how French is changing is in the world of texting. Most of what is written there is a transcription of real speech, not school speech. Jean-Benoît ran across a fascinating sample of this French when he went searching online for a good hamburger restaurant in Paris, hamburgers being among the few dishes the French are far from mastering. The sentence he found was: "*Je bosse rue de Bercy, j'ai grave la dalle, et je me mangerai bien un hamburger*" (I work on De Bercy street. I'm starving. I would really like a hamburger right now), but almost all in French slang). Although a teacher would mark seven mistakes in the seventeen words (for the sake of cross-cultural clarity, we removed the spelling and conjugation errors), nobody in France would pretend they didn't understand it. *Bosser* is popular slang for "to work," but means something more like "to slog." You could never find *J'ai grave la dalle* (I'm starving) in a dictionary. Normally, *grave* is slang for "serious," but it is also used colloquially as an adverb in the sense of "very." *Avoir la dalle* can mean being either thirsty or hungry, depending on the context. While *je me mangerais un hamburger* (I would really like a hamburger right now) is a faulty pronominal use of the verb *manger* (to eat), it is a common speech pattern in the Southwest of France, probably from the influence of nearby Spain. (Reflexive verbs are very common in Spanish.)

One side effect of universal school purism is that subverting language rules has become something of a national pastime in France. And schools being the churches of purism, not surprisingly, that's where the backlash begins. It didn't take our girls more than a month to start parroting the schoolyard slang they heard during recess (and with two-hour lunch breaks, there was a lot of time for schoolyard French practice). They started by picking up the French accent and cadence, then quickly began truncating words and adding "*o's*" to the end of them, just like their friends. They arrived home from school talking about the *collo* instead of the *collation* (snack). Everyone in France (except their parents) knew that a school principal, a *directeur,* is called a *dirlo. Adolescents* (teenagers) are *ados.* At Christmas, Nathalie declared she would henceforth be her sister's "*coiffeuse perso*" (short for *coiffeuse personnelle,* meaning her sister's personal hairdresser).

The truncation with the *o* is one of the most common techniques the French use today for generating new slang. But there are others, like altering the meaning of words by adding the endings *-ant, -oche, -ouille,* or *—ard,* or even combining these. These endings go back centuries in the history of popular French and argot. In 1980, the word *branché* (plugged) came to mean "informed, aware" and then "trendy." A few years later, the term *branchouille* popped up, meaning trendyish, or hip, followed by *branchouillard,* which means the same thing but implies identity in a group (as in "hipsters"). Meanwhile, people who felt they had moved beyond *branché* developed a new term to describe themselves: *câblé* (being plugged into cable).

One of the modern-day argots in France is called Verlan, a process in which the syllables of a word are reversed. The word *Verlan* itself comes from *envers* (reverse) with the syllables reversed. So *branché* becomes *chébran* in Verlan, and and *câblé* became *bléca.* It's similar to Cockney rhyming slang, or Thomas Jefferson's pig Latin, with the distinction that everyone in France is acquainted with Verlan, which turned *femme* (woman) into *meuf, fête* (party) into *teuf,* and *discret* (discrete) into *scred.* Although Verlan was *branché* twenty years ago, it became somewhat institutionalized over the decades, and today the French hardly mention it because Verlan expressions have even become a sort of mainstream code used by all classes. Some words, like *arabe* (Arab), were verlanized twice: it produced *beur* in the late 1970s and was reverlanized into *rebeu* in the late 1990s.

The most popular French film of 2014 was a comedy called *Qu'est-ce qu'on a fait au Bon Dieu?* (What in God's name did we do to deserve this?), about a provincial, traditional bourgeois Catholic couple whose xenophobic tendencies come to the surface when their four daughters take, in turn, a North African, Chinese, Jewish, and African husband. Verlan is used liberally throughout the film, which was targeted to a general audience: the Chinois (Chinese) is a *noiche,* the *arabe* is a *rebeu,* and the *juif* is a *feuj.* Audiences had absolutely no trouble understanding the jargon. In fact, part of the comic effect of the film came from the way the characters' vocabulary clashed with the conservative milieu in which the story unfolded.

In a way the film was an allegory of the French relationship to their language: they are as firmly attached to tradition as they are open to change.

~ 12 ~

English Envy

We were in France for the seventieth anniversary of D-day, in June 2014. It was the third time we'd watched the French commemorate the Normandy landings, but it was the first time we heard them refer to it as *le D-day,* using the English term. The previous time, the French called it *le Jour J,* which is an exact translation. Jean-Benoît scoured French media databases to see when the switch to the English term had actually occurred. He found 2,900 articles published after 1999 with *le D-day* in the title, but only 900 before 2013. The English translation had taken over in 2014.

From our first days in France, we felt like we were in the middle of another kind of "landing." English was everywhere: on billboards, in TV commercials, in storefront windows, in political slogans, protest posters—French cafés even advertised happy hour in English. The French capital is home to almost every international franchise on the planet, from Tie Rack and The Body Shop to Starbucks, so English has been part of the Parisian landscape for decades.

But what we witnessed went beyond major brand names. Our apartment was in the Latin Quarter, virtually the world headquarters of French, and yet someone had opened near the Luxembourg Gardens an outlet of a British chain called Eat Well: Bagels, Cookies and More. The French were even giving their homegrown businesses English names. A clothes store in Paris's Marais neighborhood called Kulte advertised itself as "The French Brand." The streets were full of stores with English-French hybrid names, like the lingerie shop Woman Secret, which advertised "Sexy Daily" sales in its window. English was even creeping into places where it had no business we could imagine. Paris's Palais des Beaux-Arts held an exhibition on international cuisine and called it *Cookbook, l'art et le processus culinaire* (Cookbook, culinary art and process). We couldn't believe our eyes.

The phenomenon wasn't limited to Paris. We spent a weekend in the southern department of the Landes, which shares a border with Spain and whose economy runs on tourism and lumber. Two lumber shops in one village we visited were called, respectively, Gascogne Wood Products and All Wood. Later, Jean-Benoît went to a literary event in the town of Bourges, in central France, at a bookstore called Cultura, and discovered the store's catalogue was called *Creativ by Cultura,* in English, even though it only listed French books being sold to French people.

Talking to the French we had the impression that the whole country had come down with a serious case of English envy. The French were either open to English or fatalistic about it—it was hard to tell the difference given the French knack for putting a negative spin on good news. Whatever the case, there had been a conspicuous shift in attitudes. Our friend François Digonnet informed us that he thought English was "liberating." This was startling, since ten years ago, this French anarchist (who actually doesn't speak English) routinely recited

anti-American rants like the rest of the French Left, and he still claimed
he wouldn't travel in the United States on principle. Judging by
François's rhetoric, English was no longer part of the package of what
the French used to roundly consider American cultural imperialism.
In fact, it had freed itself from the stigma of being American altogether.
François said he liked the *côté rebelle* (rebellious side) of English.

And that's when we first understood that in France, English is a new
argot. It has become a jargon that people use to flout the wordy precision of French purism. "Things in English are shorter, more concise,"
François concluded. "*Fuck* just says everything, don't you think?" We
weren't sure what to say.

At our daughters' school in Paris, parents couldn't get enough of
English, though for different reasons than François's. At the first parent-
teacher meetings for both our daughters' classes, English instruction
turned out to be parents' next big concern after the oral *exposés*. Parents' attitudes, again, were a strange mix of enthusiasm and defeatism.
"You can't get a job without English," one parent whispered during the
meeting. In Erika's class, no fewer than four parents asked how much
English would be taught that year. Madame Letendre reassured
parents—four times—that there would be an English class, taught by
a special instructor, to be announced. "My accent is too strong," she
said apologetically. In the classroom next door, Nathalie's teacher
turned out to be the only qualified English instructor in the school.
He promised parents he would go beyond basics and actually use
English regularly in his class (and he actually did). He had already
identified the three English-speaking pupils in the class and conscripted
them for tutor duty.

The sense of urgency about learning English is new in France, but
English isn't. Word borrowings are part of the normal life of any lan-

guage. Foreign words come (and go) in any language as countries or cultures gain (then lose) international stature in a specific area. French is no exception. It started absorbing English words in the seventeenth century, and that was after it dipped enthusiastically into Italian (French acquired two thousand Italian borrowings over the course of the Renaissance), Spanish, and German. English borrowings picked up over the eighteenth century with the popularity of British Enlightenment thinkers, then again at the beginning of the twentieth century when the United States became a dominating force in science, business, and diplomacy. (Borrowings, of course, go both ways: between 30 percent and 50 percent of basic English comes from French, though that is a much older story).[1]

Some English borrowings have become thoroughly French with time. At the beginning of the twentieth century, the French developed a soft spot for the English ending -ing, which they pronounce something like "eenyna." It's common to hear the French refer to un happening, le planning, or le meeting, which have roughly the same meaning as in English. But the French also apply the –ing to words, either English or French, to create expressions that only make sense to the French, like pressing (dry cleaner), footing (walking as an exercise activity), and even now séjourning (renting a furnished home). (It sounds a bit silly to English speakers, but English speakers do the same with the French suffix –ette, creating words that sound equally ludicrous to French ears, like "launderette," "luncheonette," "kitchenette," or "suffragette.")

There are of course plenty of voices in France protesting l'assaut de l'anglais (the English onslaught). But professional estimates of the situation don't actually support alarmist outcries. As it turns out, it is quite difficult to quantify the presence of English words in France, or compare it to past situations to establish a trend, let alone evaluate the impact of English on the French language itself.[2] At a symposium on English in the media held at the Collège de France, the French linguist Bernard Cerquiglini said, "We notice borrowings like moles on a face, but we don't notice when they disappear, which is the case for the vast majority of them." His point of view is important. Cerquiglini is one of the few French who have tried to scientifically study the impact of English on their language by looking at the number of borrowed English words in the French press. He has long argued that the actual impact of English on French is minor, and according to his study, 1 in 170 words in a newspaper (he chose *Le Monde*) is a borrowing.

Other borrowings stick, but then take on a different meaning in French, or become so thoroughly assimilated into the French lexicon that they are no longer recognizable as English. The verb "to clash" is used in French in sentences like *Ma mère m'a clashé* (My mother clashed me), meaning, "my mother scolded me and we clashed," a pretty big semantic leap. Even more amusing is the case of *les pipoles* (celebrities). The term comes from the name of *People* magazine, although there never was a French franchise of the weekly. In French media jargon, *un pipole* is a star that plays the public celebrity game. The word is now enjoying a great career of its own, spawning weird neologisms like the verb *pipoliser* (to Peoplize) and the noun *pipolisation* (the process by which things are being Peoplized), and the adjective *pipolisable* (the degree to which a candidate is People-able). Ironically, the English word "people" comes from old French (*pople,* now *peuple*)——the study of anglicisms is full of such historical ironies.[3]

While researching a story on English in France, Julie visited France's Délégation générale à la langue française et aux langues de France (DGLFLF), the closest thing the French actually have to a "language police," to see what they thought about the English onslaught. The DGLFLF is an agency of the French government but relies mostly on volunteer efforts. At the time of writing, it coordinated and compiled the work of seventeen separate committees, composed of twenty or thirty volunteer members each, who monitor their own professional field and then report back on English or other foreign words creeping into French vocabulary. The organization then comes up with equivalents for these words, or finds already existing French ones, which they often get from Quebec. After the new terminology is accepted specific professional and governmental sectors are required to use it, but not, obviously, the French public at large.

Bénédicte Madinier, senior director at the DGLFLF, claimed she wasn't losing much sleep over the English problem. "The French adore using English," she said. Although the government doesn't actually keep statistics on it, in the last ten years, she explained, English was being used much more, particularly in business and the financial sectors, in technology industries and on the Internet. Madinier thought that there was much more English in French publicity, and that this was creeping into daily use. "We used to say *rouge à lèvres*; now we say *lipstick*." On the other hand, she said, English words have been used in French for many years and have become more or less implanted in French. She cited examples like *un sandwich, un steak, un club, le football, un clown, le dumping, le cockpit, un show*. "They're French now," she said.[4]

A conversation about anglicisms between a French person and a Quebecker can quickly degenerate into a blizzard of accusations. That's mostly because the two people don't incorporate English into their speech the same way. When they talk about parking, for instance, French people will say: *je me gare au parking,* while the Quebeckers will say *je me parque au stationnement.* But it's also due to the fact that the two societies have almost completely different relationships to the English language itself. Because of the enormous presence of English in Quebec (there are almost a million native Anglophones in a population of 8 million, not to mention over 300 million English speakers surrounding Quebec on every side), Quebeckers have created language laws that limit the use of English and affirm the place of French in public. Unlike in Quebec, French companies and institutions tend to flash English in public to show they are modern. English is less visible in Quebec, but far more present in day-to-day conversation than it is in France.

It's fair to say the French are obsessed with their language. But contrary to what most of the outside world believes, the French are not especially concerned about English as a threat to the survival of the French language. At worst, they think French is becoming "less relevant," though in French minds, this is bad enough. In the spring of 2013, France's minister of higher education and research, Geneviève Fioraso, introduced measures in the hope of improving France's universities. One of the proposals was to officially allow universities to teach a limited number of courses in a foreign language—which of course meant English. *The New York Times* reported on a "swift and fierce" reaction to the law. In fact, opponents were mostly a case of "the usual suspects." They were familiar voices with predictable objections. (Contrary to Quebeckers who study the matter carefully, French authorities do not seek to understand the opinion of the majority of French regarding English.) The French Academy accused the French government of "marginalizing" French; the renowned French linguist Claude Hagège, a longtime critic of English, declared that the French government was "setting a bad example." The controversy was intense, but the French government went ahead and passed the law;

French universities had been teaching some courses in English for years anyway.[5]

Discussions in foreign media about English in France invariably veer to the topic of the so-called language police, the French Academy. It's worth underlining: the French don't have a language police, or anything close to it. At best, they have something like unarmed vigilantes. Unlike Quebec, France doesn't have a specific law that limits, let alone prohibits, English. Aside from the Ordinance of Villers-Cotterêts—the law passed in 1539 declaring French the exclusive language of the French administration—the only legislation the French have ever passed to protect their language is the 1994 Loi Toubon. It states that official government business in France must be carried out in French and that French companies must communicate to the French public in a way that is understandable to them. The same year, France's Supreme Court declared it unconstitutional to actually forbid English, on grounds that it violates freedom of expression. (By comparison, Quebec's legislature ruled that certain limits on freedom of expression are acceptable in the name of protecting a common good, the French language. Canada's Supreme Court agreed.)[6]

It's important to understand what the French Academy does, and doesn't, do. All societies have a body of some type, whether an "office," an "academy," or an "institute," that establishes standards for the official language and develops policies to promote it. This is true of small languages like Catalan and Hebrew, and big languages like Spanish, which has twenty-two separate academies, one for each Spanish-speaking country (and two in the United States, in Puerto Rico and New York City). Many, if not most, were modeled on the

French Academy, and some do a much better job of promoting and protecting their language.

Contrary to an almost universal belief, the French Academy doesn't do anything to eradicate English creeping into French, at least not where mainstream vocabulary is concerned.[7] None of its pronouncements have ever had the force of law. The Academy mostly rubber-stamps the proposals the DGLFLF makes for French equivalents to English terms (the recommendations of the DGLFLF concern mostly language used in the French administration and other professional domains). Approved words are not *forced* either on the media or schools or society—there's no legal way for the French state to do that anyway. Furthermore, regular French folk often have a good laugh when they hear about new words the French Academy has "approved" in the news.

The real particularity of the French language isn't the Academy, but the strong culture of purism in France. This purism both helps stave off English, and, perversely, encourages its use. Purism, or its effects, is one reason the French welcome English words into the country. The French reflexively call English "simple." Few of them actually know enough about the language to make an educated assessment of its complexity, and many would be surprised at how difficult English spelling can actually be. But the French aren't talking about the English language as much as they are talking about the culture that goes with it, which does tend to value simplicity.

Given this perception, many French see English as an escape hatch from their own purist language culture. The French consider the use of an anglicism as less of a *faute* than bad French. Even respected French editors tow this line. Jean-Benoît was writing back-cover copy for a book we published in France and wanted to use the term *mondialisa-*

teur (globalizer, as a noun). The editor refused outright. "You can't say *mondialisateur*, it's not French," she declared. She proposed using an English borrowing, *globalisateur,* instead. Jean-Benoît replied that the French term *mondialisation* (globalization) had been accepted in French dictionaries, as had *mondialiser* (the verb to globalize). But the editor countered that the form *mondialisateur* had not yet been accepted in dictionaries, so readers would consider it a *faute*. And that was the end of the discussion. (*Mondialisateur* has since come into use—though not without a fight—and no one would regard it as un-French today.)

For that matter, class is a driving factor in the rising popularity of English in France. It is the exact opposite of the situation in Quebec. In Quebec, traditionally, less educated people speckle their French with English words, mainly out of ignorance. Historically, Quebec's industry was so strongly dominated by English speakers that the largely francophone working class was often forced to speak English to their bosses, not to mention that they were deprived of proper schooling. (The stigma is still there today, even though educated Quebeckers certainly recognize the utility of speaking proper English.)

It's the opposite dynamic in France. English pops up in French speech because the French think it makes them sound worldly, sophisticated, or cool, as in the case of our friend François. The French speak much less English, on average, than Quebeckers do. But to them, English sends a signal of modernity. That's the best explanation we can come up with as to why the French version of the televised singing competition *The Voice* is called *The Voice* (pronounced "zee voyiss" with a heavy French accent). Quebec just translated the show as *La Voix,* as Hispanic TV did with *La Voz.*[8]

To their credit, the French do put English to good use and manage to come up with some creative linguistic innovations in the form of puns and witty combinations of English and French vocabulary and syntax. The newspaper *Libération* published a profile of a thirty-six-year-old female butcher who had gone into the business against her parents' will at the age of fourteen. They called the piece "Very Good *Tripes*" (the French word *tripes*, for pork chitterlings, is pronounced exactly like "trip" in English). France's Limousin region had an advertising campaign in the Paris subway with the slogan "Are You Lim?" (Are you in?), which was rather cute. *Elle* published an article about the Australian actress Naomi Watts with the title "Watt's Happening?" *Libération* even used English to make fun of a French acronym: "Don't Worry, Be HADOPI" was the title of an article about France's Internet copyright protection agency, the Haute autorité pour la diffusion des œuvres et la protection des droits sur Internet (HADOPI). In other words, the French are helping themselves to English like everyone else on the planet, and having a lot of fun with it.

The controversy erupts, and purists' feathers consequently get ruffled, when the French maladroitly conscript English to substitute for perfectly good French words. We saw a French ad for a running-shoe brand describing the footwear as "*sneakers casual et trendy,*" using the English words "casual" and "trendy" even though the French equivalents, *décontractés* and *tendances,* mean exactly the same thing. In an article about "*le baby shower,*" one clumsy reporter translated the phenomenon as a "*douche de bébés*" (a special type of shower for babies? Or a shower *of* babies?), not a shower of gifts for *bébé*. In 2012 France's industry minister, Arnaud Montebourg, developed a program to boost industrial promotion in France that he bizarrely dubbed "Made in France," in English. Then there was the French press that dubbed the rampant criticism of President François Hollande *le Hollande-bashing,* and the business press that used the neo-English *manageurs* instead of *gestionnaires* or *cadre* (distinct French terms for two different types of manager) and *trader* instead of *courtier*. Of course, the French are still coming to terms with discussing business and money, so using pseudo-English might also be a way of subtly distancing themselves from a subject they don't really like talking about anyway.

French businesses themselves have a long love affair with make-believe English. Outstanding examples are the grocery chain Leader Price and the pizza chain Speed Rabbit Pizza. In recent years France's famous retail chain, Monoprix, launched a catering service called "Monop Daily"—they tried "Mono Deli," but "deli" wasn't quite English enough, not to mention very close to the French word *délit* (offense), so French marketers went all the way and made it "daily." For that matter, the French have adopted a number of English borrowings that English speakers would never even understand, like *Recordman* (French for record holder), *babyfoot* (table football), or the slang *besta* (children's lingo for *best ami,* friend). Other English words have entirely separate careers in French, like *zapping* (channel surfing) or *brushing* (a blow dry for hair), destined exclusively for French consumption.

But the main drive behind the rise in English borrowings and pseudo-English in French business is simple: English sells, or at least that's what French marketers believe. Although coffee is marketed as "Italian" in France, its mother tongue is English. While we were in France, Nescafé ran a campaign with the English slogan "Coffee is not just black." Nespresso ran commercials with the English slogan "What else?" in which George Clooney and Matt Damon delivered their lines without subtitles. In 2014 Nespresso even hired the French actor Jean Dujardin for the campaign, then had him speak English.

The European Union is another factor behind the rise of English in French advertising. We discussed the issue with Catherine Grelier-Lenain, the director of ethics at the Autorité de régulation profession-nelle de la publicité (ARPP), France's regulatory agency for the publicity industry, and she confirmed our impression. As Grelier-Lenain ex-plained, large European companies now produce pan-European ad-vertising campaigns in English, then adapt them for each European market, so English is a convenient common tongue. "English also sells," she told us.

Another part of the problem is ARPP itself. The ARPP is one of a group of agencies and associations officially mandated to enforce France's Toubon law, which has the rather open-ended goal of making sure "French companies communicate to the French public in a way that is understandable to them." But it is a self-regulating body com-posed of advertising professionals, so members cut each other a lot of slack. For that matter, the ARPP has very loose criteria for what con-stitutes a violation of the Toubon law. As Grelier-Lenain explained, words that have already become part of current French vocabulary are exempt. She cited the French slogan for the hotel chain Sofitel, *"Life is magnifique,"* as an example. "That respects the law," she said. "The word 'life' is part of mainstream French vocabulary, so the Frenchness of the advertiser is made clear."

The only legal actions actually taken in France to counter "abusive" uses of English have come from the Direction générale de la concur-rence, de la consommation et de la répression des fraudes (Directorate-General for Competition, Consumer Affairs, and Prevention of Fraud). However, with fraud investigations part of the organization's mandate, English has never been a high priority. Another organization that has been mandated to monitor English, France's Conseil supérieur de

l'audiovisuel (French Broadcasting Authority), took almost two decades
to act. Jean-Benoît attended its first ever symposium about monitoring
French, in December 2013, eighteen years after the CSA got its mandate. In short, stomping out English is not a high priority in France's
power circles.[9]

Though a struggle against English seems increasingly futile, France
has its qualified "resistors." Most of them belong to one of fifty volunteer "language protection" associations scattered across the country.
And curiously, almost all of them are volunteers. When it comes
to language protection, the French government itself is amazingly
low-profile—or recalcitrant, the language protection groups would
say. That's because the government has only given five of these organizations any real power to do anything about protecting French.
According to the Toubon law, these five, and only these five, can file
formal complaints about language violations to the government on
behalf of citizens. (That means citizens can only file complaints *through*
these organizations.) The problem is, the associations rely almost entirely on volunteers and receive only tiny subsidies from the government. When Julie visited one of them, Avenir de la langue française
(Future of the French Language), she found herself in a cramped,
run-down office with a broken printer and barely enough space for
her to sit down and take notes. At another meeting, she spoke to Marc
Favre d'Echallens, the spokesman for the biggest of France's private
language defense groups, Défense de la langue française (Defense of
the French Language). "A lot of people, especially in publicity, don't
even know there's a law to protect French!" he told her, exasperated
by the lack of interest in what he considered an urgent problem. But
the French don't see the emergency.[10]

French multinationals, meanwhile, are pushing English down

employees' throats—in some cases they actually force French employees to use English terminology while serving French clients. At the
French distribution giant Carrefour, employees in the TV department
get training on *le cross merchandising, le remodeling, la supply chain, le
e-learning*. Sometimes the training is actually *in* English. Language protection has long been designated as a right-wing issue in France, but
that is changing as blue-collar and service-industry workers are starting to revolt in the face of what they see as unjustified requirements for
English proficiency. "English is a job requirement for workers who only
interact with French people," complained Georges Gastaud, a Carrefour employee who launched a new language-defense association supported by none other than France's Communist Party. Gastaud filed an
official request to France's National Assembly for the creation of a
committee to examine "linguistic abuse." "We are stuck fighting for
the elementary right to work in French in France. Isn't that crazy?"

But French language purism will help fend off English even if it's
only subconsciously. The French are the first to say they are "bad" at
learning foreign languages. One of our daughters' principals (they
had three over the course of a year) announced fatalistically, "It's not
worth teaching English to the French. They can't learn second languages." The French, of course, don't suffer from some collective
congenital language-learning handicap. What they have is a mental
block due to their own purist culture. The French try to teach English
the same way they teach French, with rule-oriented methods and a purist approach.[11] They are, of course, missing the point. English is not
purist in spirit, and English grammar and spelling rules have so many
exceptions the language cannot really be mastered using a rote-learning
approach. To obtain her *aggregation* (professorship) credentials, our
friend Anne Dupont, a qualified English teacher, had to learn by heart

some twelve hundred ways the English language represents forty-four different sounds. English-speaking teachers who teach English don't even learn this. Aside from the fact that rule-based language teaching methods are not effective, they create a blind spot among the French when they are learning English. When François Hollande wrote to Barack Obama to congratulate him for his reelection in 2012, he added a handwritten "friendly" to his signature, thinking he was using an adverb (like "sincerely"), unaware that in English, the -*ly* ending can actually make an adjective.

Purism will always have the last word in France. At our daughters' school, the parents' enthusiasm for English teaching had worn off like a back-to-school crush by November. There was only one qualified English teacher at the school, and parents literally chased him out of the school because of his unorthodox teaching methods, and the fact that he didn't give enough French *dictées* to his class.

The French government doesn't need to pass more laws to fend off English. French parents are doing the job very well on their own.

~ 13 ~

Looking Out for France

Fifteen years ago, anti-Americanism reared its head pretty much every day in France. The French press routinely blamed the United States for encouraging "rampant capitalism," lambasting American leaders for their supposed "blind faith in the market economy." Journalists made fun of America's "puritanical culture" and penchant for political correctness, and of course, accused Americans of carrying out linguistic imperialism.

We hardly heard these things in 2013.

Another thing had changed. French newspapers used to constantly use the expression "Anglo-Saxon." With its strange, nineteenth-century undertones, this quasi-ethnological term was a derogatory catchall for anything Anglo-American, Protestant, British, or just English-speaking (East Indians were Anglo-Saxons, too). The French even lumped Quebeckers into the so-called Anglo-Saxon world, and that despite the fact that the majority of Quebeckers are French-speaking and Catholic. Anglo-Saxon just served as a convenient tool to dismiss values foreign to the French. The term is still kicking around, but it has almost disappeared from newspapers.

Another word has practically disappeared from public discourse: *universalité* (universality). Fifteen years ago, French journalists and politicians referred to the "universality" of the French political and social model, *le modèle français,* as though it was self-evident, the implication being that French values—*liberté, égalité, fraternité,* social security, and political centralization—do, could, or should apply anywhere. That discourse has also waned.

We noticed yet another change when we arrived in France in 2013: there was a new tolerance for accents, especially our own. When we lived in Paris fifteen years earlier, people routinely greeted us with a uniform salutation at once warm and patronizing: "*Cousins!*" (in the sense of "our long lost cousins"). We weren't fooled. Back then the North American branch of the French-speaking family was still considered something like country cousins. For that matter, strangers openly mocked our Quebec accents on more than one occasion, laughing or feigning incomprehension to amused onlookers.

The condescending attitude toward Quebeckers has almost disappeared. Most people who greeted us in 2013 with the "*cousins!*" salutation knew they were spouting a cliché, or were being ironic. Far from mocking us, the French tried to impress us with a show of their familiarity about our homeland. They would ask, for instance, "Which part of Quebec are you from?" Jean-Benoît used to answer Montreal, because it was simply too complicated to say the name of his real hometown, Sherbrooke. The French thought he was saying Cherbourg or Tobruk. But now he said Sherbrooke and some French asked, "Which neighborhood?" The question would be followed by an anecdote about some Quebec friend, or a French friend's Quebec friend, or someone who took holidays in Quebec, or who lived there, or wanted to live there—anything to demonstrate they had some general knowledge about Quebec. A North African baker outside the Porte Maillot metro station heard our accents and told us, "*Continuez d'être vous-mêmes*" (Keep being yourselves). Then he threw in an extra chocolate croissant for our girls.

Quebec's newly won celebrity status seemed sudden to us in 2013, but even we knew it had been increasing gradually over the last sixty years. The French started thinking positively about Quebec during World War II when part of the Parisian cultural elite—including many publishers—fled there. In 1950, the Quebec folk singer Félix Leclerc became a sensation in Paris, a first for a Quebec artist. In 1961, the Quebec government opened an official office in Paris, with quasi-diplomatic status. Its sustained efforts in cultural promotion played an important role in what followed. A new generation of Quebec musicians entered the French musical scene in 1969, starting with Robert Charlebois, and culminating with the famous Quebec rock opera *Starmania,* which debuted in Paris in 1979. In the 1990s, there was a bona fide Quebec cultural invasion with Celine Dion and musicians like Garou, Lynda Lemay, and Isabelle Boulay. A decade later, another cohort of Quebec artists, including Cœur de Pirate and Ariane Moffat, made breakthroughs in France. In 2014, the status of Quebec culture rose a notch again when the Haïtian-born Quebec writer Dany Laferrière was elected to the French Academy.

Yet despite all this, a slightly condescending attitude toward Quebec culture prevailed until recently. What changed things? One factor, no doubt, is the upswing in French tourism in Canada and Quebec. It's pretty rare to meet a French person today who has absolutely no connection to Quebec, either through travel, or through friends or relatives who have lived there. Studies among France's 2 million expatriates also show that Canada is the sixth most popular destination, and the second outside of Europe.[1] You can even hear the Quebec influence in French speech. The French used to snicker—some still do—at Quebec's policy of feminizing titles and functions (Quebeckers say *"Madame LA Première ministre"* (prime minister), while the French say *"Madame LE Premier ministre."* This Quebec custom, while still hotly debated, is actually becoming the norm in France. French translators, terminologists, and lexicographers also closely follow the work of the Quebec Office of the French Language.[2]

The idea that Quebec represents something modern can be traced back to 1967, during President Charles de Gaulle's famous trip to Quebec. In Quebec, de Gaulle's visit is remembered for the French president's famous *"Vive le Quebec libre"* (long live free Quebec) declaration, which catalyzed Quebec's growing independence movement. But footage of the visit reveals a change in French thinking about Quebec too: the president is constantly commenting on how modern Quebec is, and how Quebec is leading the way.[3] Five decades later we heard echoes of this in remarks from French people who commented on how Quebec was *dans le coup* (in the know), *en phase avec le monde* (in tune with the world), and even *en avance sur son temps* (ahead of its time). As Quebeckers, we know our society has its own strengths and weaknesses. But for the French right now, Quebec represents everything France is not. The French talk about their country as "out of sync with the world" and *dépassée* (falling behind the times). Then they turn around and hold up Quebec and Canada as models for everything from university financing to public finances, language policy, and even gender relations. Quebec, it seems, can do no wrong.

The new admiration for Quebec would only be a footnote in this book if it didn't signify something more fundamental going on in French society. Quebec embodies two things the French, especially the Parisian elite, have long rejected: America, and the *francophonie,* the French-speaking world beyond France's borders. The new attitude toward Quebec owes at least partly to the fact that French attitudes about these two entities have also changed radically over the past decades.

To understand the change, it's important to grasp that French anti-Americanism started out as a rejection of the whole idea of the New World, not just the United States. The French historian Philippe Roger traces the origins of this anti-Americanism to the middle of the eighteenth century. In *The American Enemy* he argues that sentiment owes to the writings of the French naturalist de Buffon (1707–1788), the founder of natural history in France and a precursor of the theory of evolution. De Buffon never actually set foot in the Americas, but nevertheless, on the basis of very questionable evidence that its mammals were smaller than those in Europe, Africa, and Asia, he claimed it had to be "inferior." A Dutch philosopher, Cornelius de Pauw (1739–1799), chimed in a few years later with the same conclusions, though he never actually went to the New World either. The negative views of America then migrated from biology to political philosophy and sociology, where they spawned even more dubious claims. Even though later thinkers like the French marquis de Lafayette and Alexis de Tocqueville made sophisticated, insightful conclusions about America based on their actual experience there, their writing didn't make a dent in the popular anti-American prejudice that had become solidly implanted in French minds by that time.

Enlightenment thinkers like Voltaire who denounced the French colonization of America as costly and pointless just reinforced the already negative view of the New World. The case against colonialism was not hard to make. Not enough French had ever immigrated to the New World to give France a shot in empire building against competitors like Portugal, Spain, or England. When colonization began, France had a population of about 20 million, or four times the population of England, Spain, or Portugal. By the time France abandoned New France, in 1763, it had only sent 15,000 settlers, or ten times fewer than the British (and a paltry number next to the 750,000 Spanish or the 600,000 Portuguese colonists in the New World). Although French explorers scouted the continent aggressively, their discoveries didn't impress the French back home. On the contrary, the pre-existing negative perception of the colonies left the field wide open for nonsensical propagandists like de Buffon and de Pauw. And the tradition of European anti-Americanism lived on.

What struck us about the anti-Americanism in France fifteen years ago was that the United States was used as a scapegoat to make the French feel better about themselves (Americans do the same thing with France, by the way). The French would criticize American race relations as if there were no such problem in France, with the subtext that France would somehow be safe if it avoided "importing" this American problem. That, of course, was ridiculous. French commentators would dismiss any positive measures in the United States as "Anglo-Saxon," therefore incompatible with French values. Anti-Americanism was a form of chauvinism that united both France's Left and Right for different reasons—the Right because it flattered their nationalism, and the Left because it buttressed their ideology.

Of course not everyone in France bought the anti-American crusade, even fifteen years ago, at what was probably the peak of anti-American sentiment in France. There have always been plenty of Americanophiles in French society. But they were strangely silent. Those who were not, like Jean-Jacques Servan-Schreiber, who founded the magazine *L'Express* as a French version of *Time,* paid the price for expressing admiration of the United States. The magazine still exists but Servan-Schreiber's attempts to start a political career (he was a centrist) fell flat. In 1974, he became a minister in Jacques Chirac's government but only lasted thirteen days before being fired. Back then, the pro-American discourse was just too much for the French to take.

The reasons anti-Americanism is waning in France are complicated but mostly boil down to the fact that morale has gotten so low in France, and criticism of French society so harsh, that the French are only blaming themselves for their problems. Now they are looking beyond France for solutions, not scapegoats. The startling Anglophilia in French society (discussed in the previous chapter) is one by-product of this.

But the French also have a new scapegoat for their problems: the European Union. The EU is increasingly perceived as a dangerous, even nefarious, external influence, especially in populist circles. Though the reasons, again, are complex, popular support for Europe is much lower than it used to be, and the French are quick to blame the European Union for many of their challenges, notably immigration controls, the liberalization of labor laws, and forced austerity measures.

It is very possible that the terrorist attacks of 2015, first at Charlie Hebdo and Hyper Cacher grocery in January, and again on November 13, will shift the French worldview by creating a new declared evil called Islamism. Yet because the attacks involved a large proportion of French nationals, the effect could be greater on how the French view themselves.

When we were in France in the years 2013–2014 we also saw a France that was opening up to the rest of the French-speaking world, a very recent change in thinking. Despite being a founding member of the *francophonie* organization (akin to the British Commonwealth), France has always kept the French-speaking world at arm's length. The issue was just too close to home for the French, too wrapped up in their colonial history, something the French wish they could forget. For France, the decolonization process that lasted roughly from 1945 to 1962 was painful and drew them into two wars (in Indochina, from 1946 to 1954, and in Algeria, from 1954 to 1962). While France watched its colonial empire explode into two dozen independent French-speaking countries, English was supplanting French definitively as the preeminent global language. It wasn't until the 1990s that the French began to wake up to the fact that there are considerably more French speakers outside France than inside. The numbers today are significant: 275 million people speak French in the world, in four dozen countries.[4] France accounts for only a quarter of the total, but has never considered the French-speaking world as a potential source of strength, even in an increasingly globalized world.

Much of the "declinist" thinking in France today owes to the fact that the French are still grappling with what it means to be outnumbered. Some don't even realize it; others are still struggling to understand what their role in the French-speaking world should be, or if they even have one.

The history of the term *francophone* provides a good illustration of the difficulties the French have had coming to grips with this new reality. *Francophone* was coined by a French geographer, Onésime Reclus, in 1880, while he was writing a linguistic geography of the world. (Reclus also invented terms like *anglophone, arabophone, germanophone, hispanophone,* and, for Portuguese speakers, *lusophone.*) *Francophone* was then forgotten until the 1930s, when it was revived to describe colonial subjects who had renounced their culture to become French. In the 1960s, as the former African colonies had become independent, the Senegalese president Léopold Sédar Senghor resuscitated the term and restored its original meaning of "anyone who speaks French." The term then slowly spread throughout the postcolonial French-speaking world. The result was that the French came to think of a Francophone as anyone from *outside* of France who speaks French. Thus, the French consider themselves "French," not francophone.[5] Few French identified themselves as Francophones the way Quebeckers or Belgians more or less automatically would.

The issue was further complicated by French politics. The French Right has always been more open to the French-speaking world, although many see it as the perpetuation of the old empire. But traditionally, it's the attitude of the Left that dominates public discourse on immigration. The French Left sees the *francophonie* as the product of French colonialism and therefore nothing to celebrate. The closer you get to Paris's power circles, particularly on the left, the more pronounced this attitude gets. Even the fact that both Quebeckers and postindependence Africans identify themselves as Francophones—a phenomenon that should normally appeal to the Left—has not been enough to completely change French views of the term. For the same, essentially political, reasons, language protection became, and has remained, a right-wing cause in France. The French Left is suspicious about it. It evokes nationalism to them, and they associate nationalism with fascism. Many French today would prefer to see English invade their country than stoop to what they consider chauvinistic patriotism or, worse, *nationalisme*. Because of this stance, the French have traditionally underestimated the number of French speakers in the world in a kind of self-imposed blindness.

The French also have some less honorable reasons for refusing to embrace the *francophonie*: namely, if they admit they are part of a larger French-speaking world, that means France isn't the center of that world anymore. Of the 275 million French speakers in the world, only 66 million live in France. A large block of the French intelligentsia clearly opposed the implications of considering themselves part of a larger whole. In a recent interview, the philosopher Alain Finkielkraut actually scolded journalists and editors for writing "Victor Hugo, *poet*" and "Léon Blum, *former prime minister*" because in his mind, neither Hugo nor Blum needs a title.[6] Finkielkraut, one of the main grouches of Parisian intellectual circles, was completely ignoring the fact that for some Francophones outside of France, such cultural references— especially Léon Blum—really do need explanation. In the mind of certain French intellectuals, like Finkielkraut's, Paris is not just the center of the world, Paris is the world.

But things are changing. It's getting common to hear young Parisians or people from the regions refer to themselves as Francophones, and to acknowledge, sometimes even embrace, the idea that French-speaking civilization is more than just a satellite, or a big fan club of France. This is partly because young French are growing up in a more cosmopolitan society. People from France's regions play up their *francophonie* ties, particularly with Quebec, to get the edge over Parisians by bypassing Paris to access the growing international networks of French speakers in science, business, or culture directly. Younger generations of French (and those from classes that don't benefit from the Paris-centered culture) are exposed to much more French-language culture from outside France today. One reason Quebec culture is gaining popularity in France is precisely because of its popular, non-elitist, and accessible side. And many French welcome the idea that

French-language civilization has, or will have, more than one center someday.

Like the new admiration for Quebec, this attitude has also been coming on slowly for decades. French culture has been in a process of *brassage* (stirring, intermingling) since the 1960s. Since the Tunisian writer Tahar Ben Jelloun won France's prestigious Goncourt Prize in 1987, one laureate out of six not only has been foreign born, but did not have French as a mother tongue—including the American writer Jonathan Littell (2006) and the Afghan writer Atiq Rahimi (2008). In 2007, the French chose a president, Nicolas Sarkozy, who is of Hungarian and Greek Jewish origins. France's current prime minister, Manuel Valls, was born in Barcelona and is of Catalan origin. And the mayor of Paris, Anne Hidalgo, is from Cádiz in the south of Spain. One minister in the government, Axelle Lemaire, was born and spent her childhood in Quebec. In effect, what is happening is that the French-speaking world, the *francophonie,* is beginning to work just like the English-speaking, or the Spanish-speaking, worlds, with circulation between many cultural (and economic) centers. Yet France's official public discourse only recently started to reflect this reality.

Just eleven days after we arrived in Paris in September 2013, two financial analysts at the French investment bank Natixis, Jérôme Bodin and Pavel Govciyan, published a study on the financial prospects of the French media. Bodin and Govciyan had looked at statistics about the number of French speakers in the world and proceeded to draw the obvious conclusion that France's media should wake up and look beyond France's border, to the global French-speaking market, the same way English-language and even Hispanic media have.[7] To our knowledge, this was the first time French financial analysts took such a bold stance in favor of internationalizing the French media. The idea was revolutionary in Paris. Incredible as it sounds, nobody in Parisian business circles had ever argued for an international strategy for the media.

Bodin and Govciyan were back in the news the following spring when *Forbes* quoted them regarding the potential for expansion in the francophone world.[8] The fact that this was news in France shows how adamantly Paris had been ignoring the economic potential of the *francophonie,* or at least has until now. This time, the story had a discernable impact. In the fall of 2014, fifty French-speaking CEOs of media companies from eighteen different countries met in Montreal to discuss the future of francophone media. Two months later, the Summit of the International Organization of the Francophonie (the French-speaking version of the British Commonwealth) in Dakar got more media coverage than the biennial event had garnered before.

The French can see it's time to update their worldview, including their view of the *francophonie.* Half the countries in Africa have French as one of their official languages, and many francophone countries have had economic growth rates of 5, 6, and even 10 percent in the last fifteen years. Major African capitals like Kinshasa, Abidjan, and Dakar all have the potential to become important francophone centers. As African populations explode, and as their economies grow, the potential for francophone media and business to develop ties beyond national territories will grow, too. The French could miss out on some tremendous opportunities—when all they have to do to take advantage of them is start looking a little differently at the outside world.[9]

~ 14 ~

Economy of Speech

Fifteen years ago, it was regarded as a highly specialized field of study. Most French barely had an opinion about it, and even if they did, they systematically avoided it in conversations. It was practically a taboo.

We're talking about economics. The year we arrived in France, we discovered that economics had gained a new respectability, if not outright popularity, among conversation topics. For the first time, we heard people in polite society quoting national debt figures, taxation rates, unemployment figures, and interest rates, and even mention esoteric concepts like derivatives. At first, we thought we were hallucinating. We weren't. Economic coverage in the French press, we discovered, had almost doubled in the decade prior to our stay. A study by the Institut pour le développement de l'information économique et sociale (Institute for the Development of Social and Economic Information) found that the percentage of airtime French media devoted to economics had jumped from 6.5 percent in 2007 to 11 percent in 2008. Economic journalists, like François Lenglet on France 2 and Nicolas Bouzou on iTélé, had become household names in France.[1] The change in attitude about money was so disconcerting we had to constantly remind ourselves it was okay to talk about it.

The European Union was one of the big factors that explained France's new openness to economics. The European Union began as the Common Market in 1958, and it morphed into the more political European Union in 1993, but it's still mostly about business. Many of its policies have to do with economics, trade laws, currency (the euro), the removal of borders, and budget rules for member countries. The financial crisis of 2008 also contributed to the change. It got the French to look at how heavily they were being taxed in comparison to their neighbor countries (taxes make up 57 percent of France's GDP). In a survey by Ipsos-Steria published in the French daily *Le Monde* in January 2014, 56 percent of the French said they were worried about unemployment and 43 percent about high taxation. The proportion worried about taxes had increased from 27 percent the previous year.[2]

During our stay it was common to hear people say quite confidently that "something had to be done about" taxes, or the economy. This was not the France we had lived in fifteen years earlier, when a good friend who was a high-placed functionary in France's Ministry of the Interior actually told us the economy "didn't exist."

In a period shorter than a generation, the topic of money has gone from being "touchy" to "acceptable." Yet money is still, roughly speaking, a taboo in French conversation. Even at business meals, the French typically only get around to the topic *entre le fromage et le dessert* (between cheese and dessert)—meaning late in the evening, if ever. Talking openly about money is considered a little vulgar in France. It's a confounding cultural difference for Anglo-Americans, who talk about any kind of money, anywhere, pretty much anytime.

But there are now a number of avenues available to broach the topic.

The key to talking about money in France is in understanding the different ways the French talk about it, which are all arranged on a sort of gradient of acceptability. There is impersonal money (the economy), money that you want to make (business), then personal money (your own). The only really acceptable way to talk about personal money, still today, is to talk about what you don't have. That's why the French spend so much time talking about *les bons plans* (the best deals). Discussions about where and how to save money are almost universal. Rich or poor, the French constantly exchange tips about where to get deals. The summer before we moved to Paris, the head of media relations at the International Organization of the Francophonie, whom we had just met, insisted we check out a Web site called leboncoin.fr, where we could find used goods in Paris by neighborhood. (She wasn't exactly the type of person you'd think needed to buy used furniture, but she gushed about the site, so we assumed she used it.) We subsequently discovered there were a remarkable number of Web sites and ads that pushed *le bon plan* in France: lebonplan.fr, le-bon-plan.com, le-bon-plan-immo.com (for real estate), plusdebon splans.com (even more *bons plans*), bonplanlocal.com (for local deals), lebonplanmotard.fr (for motorcyclists), and the list went on.

The French also love talking about how expensive life is. The code for this is: *la vie chère*. Techniques for saving money are sort of an ideal conversation topic, not to mention the fact that it flatters French fatalism. The French talk a lot about *le Système D,* the D-system, with *D* referring to *débrouillardise* (resourcefulness, or the ability to improvise to get something done, though the term also refers to the underground economy). In short, whatever socioeconomic milieu you find yourself in, you are bound to hear the expressions *Système D* and *le bon plan* pop up in conversations.

French attitudes about the third category of money, "impersonal" money—economics and the business world—have changed the most dramatically. A decade ago, French business news was practically nonexistent. This always struck us as odd, France being the world's fifth economy. France has as many Fortune 500 companies as Germany does, with a smaller population,[3] and French entrepreneurs regularly win awards for their innovations. Even in the middle of a recession, when we were there, France was creating more businesses than anywhere else in Europe, including Germany and the UK.[4] Foreign investment in France has had its ups and downs, but France's workforce has long ranked as one of the most productive in the world. Yet no one even talked about France's economic strengths, probably because traditionally, the French have always thought about business principally as a source of tax revenue. In French minds, the state makes the world turn. Business just supplies the funds.

But today, even left-wing publications in France have started covering business news. French unions, which traditionally garnered a lot of sympathy, have borne the brunt of this change in attitude. Labor relations are now seen in a completely different light. Unions are viewed with increasing skepticism, even a degree of resentment. While we were in France, there were plenty of protests but few calls for strikes, and—to our amazement—the ones that did happen failed to garner much popular support. In June 2014, railway workers voted to strike to protest a reorganization of the national railway system. But instead of sympathizing, popular opinion turned against them. Since 2007, France has required striking transport workers to provide "minimum" services, perhaps a sign of the times, but even this wasn't enough to stave off public frustration. After two weeks, the strike petered out and normal service returned.[5]

When an Ipsos survey in the fall of 2013 asked the French what "institution" they trusted the most, an amazing 84 percent of respondents said it was *la PME* (small and medium-size businesses), followed by the army (79 percent), the police (73 percent), schools (68 percent), mayors (63 percent), the justice system (46 percent), and finally big business (38 percent). Unions, politicians, and the media got scores in the 20 to 30 percent range. Only 8 percent of French claim to trust political parties. The results surprised us, particularly since business, properly speaking, is not an institution like education or justice is. Not to mention the fact that twenty years ago, "small and medium-size business" and "big business" would have ranked at the very bottom of the list of favorite French institutions, had they even been on it.[6]

The radical shift in French thinking about economics has been one of the many problems Socialist president François Hollande had to grapple with since his election in 2012. When we arrived in France less than a year and a half after the presidential elections, Hollande's support rate had fallen to a record-breaking 12 percent, the lowest rate a French president had registered in sixty-five years. The change in thinking about economics didn't help. Hollande's electoral base would normally have embraced a classic socialist doctrine of high taxation and heavy state intervention in the economy. With the combined realities of the recession and the European Union, large segments of the French population, including Socialist Party supporters, had become interested in the prospects of French business.

To his credit, Hollande read this change correctly. The problem was, Hollande's government constantly blurred the lines between doing something and not doing anything about the economy. He led a policy of doublespeak and moved ahead on issues lobster style (backward). Old-style socialists felt betrayed and the new pro-business socialists didn't take him seriously. In late 2013, Hollande's economic leadership disintegrated into chaos. In August, when all French receive their *avis d'imposition* (tax notice), several million French families woke up to the news that they would have to pay a couple of hundred euros in taxes for the first time in their lives. France's finance minister, Pierre Moscovici, tried to assuage them by inventing a new catchphrase to describe their frustration: *ras-le-bol fiscal* (fiscal fed up-ness) and Hollande announced he would reduce taxes. But his prime minister contradicted him the next day. Popular discontent quickly snowballed into outright rebellion. In mid-October, after a series of unrelated business closures in Brittany, tens of thousands of protesters joined the *révolte des bonnets rouges* (the Red Cap Revolt, named for their head-wear), which lasted until the end of November.

In January 2014, Hollande threw himself into the fire by audaciously declaring himself a *social-démocrate* (though as we mentioned in a previous chapter, this was done partly to deflect media attention from his recently revealed affair with an actress). "Socialism" in France stands for "revolution," while "social democracy" stands for "reform." But the difference between a socialist and a social democrat in France is loaded with historical significance. Although most of what France's Socialist Party has ever done since it first took power in 1983 could be described as "social democratic," the party has explicitly refused the label since World War II. Hollande was the first socialist leader to embrace it. Public opinion was not impressed. Hollande then tried to salvage the situation and boost his popularity by appointing a new prime minister, Manuel Valls, a very popular political figure.

But the Hollande-Valls duet then came out and declared they were *réformistes,* which did nothing to stop Hollande's plummeting popularity. Much of Hollande's tenure as president has been about redefining France's coded terms. This is not an easy thing to do in a highly coded society like France. But if anyone could do it, it should have been Hollande. He was the first French president with an economics background since Valéry Giscard d'Estaing was elected in 1974. Hollande studied at France's preeminent business school, the École des hautes études commerciales de Paris (HEC), and later taught economics at the prestigious Institut d'études politiques de Paris (Sciences Po).[7]

Unfortunately, the task of changing mentalities in France is riddled with semantic booby traps and Hollande fell into many of them. For instance, right-leaning French call France's mandatory social security contribution *charges sociales* (social charges), to stress how much they cost businesses and employees. Left-leaning French, meanwhile, use the term *cotisations* (contributions) for the same thing, implicitly suggesting that the French like sharing their wealth, or at least do so willingly. Sticking to their policy of economic doublespeak, Hollande and Valls tried to erase the cleavage by adopting the right-wing term *charges sociales*.[8] When that didn't work, the duo rebounded by coming up with yet another new expression: they said they were conducting *socialisme de l'offre* (supply-side socialism, ostensibly to encourage business), as opposed to *socialisme de la demande,* which responds to demand. That one didn't fly either, and Hollande's popularity continued to sag.[9]

But while the French are talking more about economics and business now, casual conversation about money is about as sparse as it always has been. The old taboo rears its head the second the topic of money becomes even vaguely personal. Near the end of our stay we met Olivier Poivre d'Arvor, the director of France's public radio channel, France Culture, to talk about doing a radio show on the French language. We spent the first hour comparing notes about international adoption (he had adopted his daughter in Africa), then the next forty minutes or so discussing language issues, which made sense since that was the topic of our show. The actual logistics of the show—like which director we would be working with and how the whole process would unfold—was concluded in twenty minutes. But we didn't manage to get the topic of pay onto the table until we were halfway out the door. All Poivre d'Arvor would tell us was that France Culture had hired Canadians in the past, and we could get paid. We never got anything close to a euro figure out of him.

After writing, recording, and editing the radio show—the whole process took about two months—we still didn't know how much we were going to be paid for it. We kept asking everyone we met along the way, and all they did was send us to ask someone else. After we finished the final edit of the show, our producer finally sent us to France Culture's human resources director, who was supposed to clarify the matter of pay. Instead, she showed us pictures of her daughters on holiday. That discussion was followed by a long one about the importance of learning foreign languages, and another one about Quebec. In the end, we didn't get a euro figure out of her either. She just told us where to go next. The French are normally quite guarded about discussing family with strangers, but in professional situations, we noticed, they are more likely to wax on about their children or their holidays than talk dollars and cents. Every North American we have ever met who does business in France has said the same thing.

One of the only places people seem to be comfortable talking about money is at trade shows. France is something of a capital of trade shows. The reason they have so many is, without doubt, because trade shows are a convenient way for French businesspeople to get around the taboo and talk about money. They have to do it somewhere. It's as if the French have so many rules and customs that complicate business discussions, they had to create these *zone franches* (free zones) where people could skip the preliminaries and get straight to business. But even there one has to be careful. The second you leave the trade show bubble, the normal rules of conversation kick back in and you have to wait until the main course is over before you can broach the topic of money.

Though it sounds a bit breezy, part of the explanation for the French uneasiness with business is probably nothing more, nor less, than "culture." All societies have their disconnects. Why not money? Anglo-American societies, at least from a French perspective, are completely disconnected when it comes to food, and in particular, meat. Though big meat eaters, British, Americans, and Germans tend to prefer to dine in complete denial of the process by which flesh travels to plates: no one wants to hear about how to make sausage, or how much a particular cheese smells like an animal (the French *love* that).

In the same vein, while the French love what money can buy, they can't stomach thinking about where it comes from. Some commentators pin the blame for this attitude on France's Catholic culture, cupidity having a top spot among the capital sins. But while Protestant culture, indeed, places a certain value on acquisitiveness—prosperity is supposed to be a manifestation of divine Providence—there is a limit to the argument. Catholic Italian merchants, after all, put the building blocks of modern capitalism in place, and Catholic Portuguese ushered in global maritime trade.

Some explain the French aversion to money talk by invoking the legacy of French aristocrats, who were notoriously idle compared to their peers elsewhere. French nobles did indeed consider everything related to money, production, or trade to be far below their concerns. And while noble families have no particular sway in modern France, their attitudes still linger in French culture. Political leaders are allowed, even expected, to enjoy a certain level of gilded luxury, which the French assume goes hand in hand with power.

Aristocrats aside, there is also a mundane historical reason average French citizens tend to steer clear of the topic of money—at least their own. Prior to the French Revolution, the French were taxed on apparent wealth, not real wealth. Tax collectors literally looked at people's homes and drew up the bill. So even moderately prosperous French learned to avoid showing off their wealth in order to escape the notice of tax collectors.[10] From a fiscal perspective, it has always been considered safer to pretend you are poor in France. We read an article in the popular Parisian daily *Le Parisien* written by a French lawyer who specialized in tax law warning readers against using tax shelters, *despite* the fact that they are perfectly legal, *because* they attract attention. Tax shelters aren't worth the risk, he argued, because they'll pique the interest of les Finances publiques (France's Internal Revenue Service), which might end up auditing you. In short, the French think tax shelters are a trap: the inspectors in Finances publiques assume anyone using them has something to hide.[11]

No matter what party is in power, traditionally, France's national politics have always steered clear of the topic of finance, either public or private, and more specifically, about how much governments spend. Power in France is concentrated in Paris, and Paris still manages to cast money discussions as being "in bad taste." France's regional leaders (mayors, or presidents of regions or departments) often talk more openly about money. Even socialist politicians in France's regions openly promote business and defend local business interests. But there's a problem: most regional leaders are also, simultaneously, members of the National Assembly. So when they go from their region to Paris to sit in Parliament, they often fall back into their role and clam up about business.[12]

Typically, French economic thinkers get better press and attract bigger followings outside of France, like in Washington and London.

The French economist Thomas Piketty's seven-hundred-page book *Capital in the Twenty-First Century* was a bestseller in the United States, but he is not the darling of university circles in France. Nor is the French economist Esther Duflo, one of President Obama's economic advisers and a professor at MIT. Jean Tirole, winner of the 2014 Nobel Prize in Economics, started a school in Toulouse in 1992 after twelve years at MIT. He certainly chose Toulouse for a reason. Paris is too supercilious about money.

The French aversion to discussing money may also owe to four centuries of life under a strong, central state. The state made France a two-tiered society where members of the business class (owners, financiers, entrepreneurs, and management), no matter how successful, always play second fiddle to politicians and members of France's intelligentsia (journalists and intellectuals). The worst French intellectual is more highly regarded than the richest and most successful French entrepreneur. France's large, powerful market economy has evolved in a parallel universe, hidden from public discourse like a messy basement or a smelly stable.

However, in the long wait to get the French talking about money, foreigners might be listening too narrowly. The protracted French prelude to talking about business does have its own logic. It's during this preamble that the French figure out if they want to do business with you or not. Good conversation is paramount to the French, and all things considered, they would rather do business with an opportunist with whom they can have a proper conversation than with an opportunist who is inarticulate.

Foreigners should not try to push things along too precipitously. Talk is never cheap in France.

~ 15 ~

Silent Labor

The last thing a French person will tell a stranger is that she loves her job. It just sounds naïve. At best, if she actually does love her work, she'll tell a close friend, because liking work is a private, almost intimate sentiment in France. It's definitely not something you advertise to the world.

We always suspected there was some posturing behind this attitude. The French can't possibly hate their jobs as much as they say they do. In 2013, a French job site, monster.fr, confirmed our doubts. The site had commissioned a study to compare French attitudes about work to those in six other countries. The French daily *Le Parisien* published the results with the headline "Almost 10% of Employees Hate Their Jobs." Old habits seem hard to break. The negative title was misleading because the study actually showed a positive: that nine out of ten French actually *don't* hate their jobs. Only 8.8 percent of French respondents said they didn't like their work. That was less than the proportion of Germans (10.1 percent) or British (12.3 percent) who claimed to dislike their jobs. What's more, the survey asked respondents if they *liked* their jobs. Here, the French ranked relatively high: 42.7 percent said yes, slightly fewer than the British, at 46 percent, but considerably more than the Germans, at 34.5 percent.[1]

One might argue, tongue in cheek, that with their long lunch breaks, thirty-five-hour workweeks, and five weeks of paid holidays per year, the French work less than the Germans or the British, so they have less reason to hate their jobs. But according to the OECD, the short French workweek is something of a myth. The French actually work as much as industrious British and German employees do, and four more hours per week than the Dutch.[2]

None of this makes a dent in the negative spin the French habitually put on their working lives. Unlike North Americans, the French rarely boast about being "busy" at work. It's just not something you brag about in France. On the contrary, portraying yourself as a tad idle shows you are in control and not concerned about what is expected of you. To French ears, that sounds way better than being productive.

Yet more than anything, when it comes to what they do for a living, the French are simply evasive, even, as Julie saw, when the context begs the question. Julie was researching France's language-protection movement when she discovered that most of the "defenders" of the French language were actually volunteers, many retired. At one of the larger associations she visited, one volunteer literally squirmed in his seat when she asked him, out of mere curiosity, what he used to do for a living. The gentleman wouldn't disclose his job title until Julie pressed him to. It turned out he had been a journalist who wrote publicity for a French bank, nothing to be ashamed of. But even in professional situations, it is normal for the French to be tight-lipped about their working lives.

Curiously, once the French feel assured they are in the company of friends, the floodgates open. That's when you find out that behind the hedonistic image, the French are as obsessed with work as North Americans are. But they aren't concerned about the same issues in their working lives.

The French actually work long days, even with the official thirty-five-hour workweek. A typical workday in France is not nine to five, but nine to seven, mostly because the French are encouraged to take long lunches. Of course, longer workdays mean longer school days. The elementary school days are not the same every day, but most days start at 8:30 A.M. and end at 4:30 P.M. (with a two-hour lunch break), and many kids stay at school until 6:00 P.M. thanks to a gamut of reasonably priced after-school day care activities offered in schools.

But the French workplace is quite a different universe than what North Americans are used to. When we returned to North America in 2001 and again in 2014, one of the main cultural countershocks we experienced was finding ourselves in the face of unapologetically incompetent employees. In New York or Phoenix, Montreal or Toronto, unless you are eating in an upscale restaurant, it's not uncommon to be served by someone who doesn't actually know that much about food. That's rare in France where waitering is considered a profession with standards. In North America, taxi drivers who aren't fluent in English (or French in our case) are not rare. Even in specialized retail outlets like bookstores, and especially in the large chains, it's common for clerks to know relatively little about literature. The reason is simple. There are a lot of part-time employees in North America. Customers anticipate this and lower their expectations accordingly. There is simply much less part-time work in France. Service employees usually work full weeks and are generally well trained.

The French have a lot of respect for *métiers* (a word that can refer to trade, occupation, or profession). One reason is that getting a *métier* in France requires a lot of effort and investment.

Access to the French job market in any domain comes at a high price. Because the goal of French family education is to *se placer* (find a situation), as we saw in chapter 5, most French have invested heavily in the preparations. French families do whatever they can to help their children secure the best jobs possible. In many, if not most, cases, jobs are the result of a family investment geared to maximize a child's performance in the system. Even bakers go to specialized schools to learn their *métiers*. Taxi drivers pay the equivalent of $300,000 for a taxi license.

Part of the issue is that nothing about getting a job in France is simple. The French job market is more rigid and less mobile than anything a North American would experience. If you don't like your job, switching careers or getting a different type of job is difficult. And if you started your career at the lower echelon of a business, there are few chances you'll ever rise above midlevel: stories of people "working their way up from the bottom" are pretty rare in the French business world. Those who get to the top usually begin at least at midlevel because they attended one of the right specialized schools, *les grandes écoles*. The French job market is like the army: not many rank-and-file soldiers rise to general. Promotions come late, and people in positions of authority make sure the odds work against any new contenders.

The only really surefire way to get ahead in France is by excelling in school. Luckily, the French school system is geared to mobility, at least more than systems elsewhere in Europe. In Germany, for instance, children are funneled into a specific educational track at the age of twelve. Before they start the equivalent of junior high, German kids have been identified either as university, trade school, or technical school material, and once they are categorized, there is hardly any turning back. In France, the determining factor in a young adult's future doesn't come until the famous *bac* exam students take at age eighteen. Because it's the gateway to future careers, the *bac* is big. One reason teenagers rarely work summer or part-time jobs in France is that they are preparing for the *bac*. Families keep teenagers out of the job market so they can spend as much time as possible studying. If students aren't spending their summers preparing for the next school year, parents expect them to "rest" so they can start the next year on the right foot.

The family investment doesn't stop there. Education in France is theoretically free, but at the end of high school, families generally spend between 1,200 and 1,500 euros for their children to take a dozen, if not two dozen, exams to win a much coveted spot in one of France's *grandes écoles*. To take those exams, you need to study an additional two years in an extracurricular preparatory school, for which parents fork out another 5,000 euros per year for private ones. For the most prestigious public preparatory schools, which are free to those admitted, the government spends over 15,000 euros per year per student, or 4,000 more than it spends on students at public universities and double what it spends on average every year per student during the twelve years of schooling prior to university.[3]

Whether they study at the highest level or just train for a trade, all French students must do a *stage* (internship) or a *compagnonnage* (apprenticeship), often for hundreds of hours, for no pay. It is a surprisingly exploitative system, especially considering that the labor market has so many protection measures for workers built into it, but for millions of French people, this is just how the working world works.[4]

And even when you have grown up, finished school, and are working in a profession—whether you are a nurse, teacher, accountant, soldier, or have any position in the public sector—you still have to take exams to get promoted to a new position. Jean-Benoît was riding the train from the suburbs back to Paris after a hike with friends one Sunday when the train stopped in Arcueil. Across the street, Jean-Benoît noticed an eight-story building with a slightly frightening name: La Maison des Examens (The House of Exams), written in very large blue letters from roof to ground. Half a dozen members of the group exclaimed in an irruption of nostalgia: *"Ah! La Maison des examens!"* As it turned out, they, or one of their close relatives, all had come to this very establishment to take at least one *concours* (contest) or *épreuve* (test) to get a job or promotion, or to take a school exam. Many French spend a large chunk of their professional lives studying for tests. It's one of the few ways you can climb the ladder in France or change tracks once you have chosen your educational path.

So if the French work so hard to get into the job market, why are they so loath to express affection for their jobs? Whether garbage collectors or well-educated midlevel managers, French employees rarely have anything good to say because even employees higher up in the workplace hierarchy believe they only work because they have no choice, not because they want to. It's unusual to hear even people at the top echelons of a profession say that they love their work. Most pretend that they work because they have no choice.

Like many cultural traits in France, this attitude also has historical roots. The French word for business, *les affaires,* comes from the expression *à faire,* meaning "what is to be done"—the term dates to the twelfth century. The English word "business," dating from the sixteenth century, comes from busy-ness—or the state of being busy, probably because industriousness was established as a key virtue in post-Reformation England. The French word *affaires* emphasizes how external demands force people to work, against their will.

We met a specialist in labor relations, Professor Jean-Pierre Lebrun, of Laval University in Quebec City, who does consulting work both in Canada and in France. He told Jean-Benoît that the most striking feature of the way French people talk about their jobs is the recurrence of the word "mission." In English, the term simply suggests one must go somewhere to accomplish a task. But in French, *mission* carries the meaning of having been dispatched to some task with the additional connotation of a moral responsibility of the person *missionnée*, "mission-ed," to achieve the task. Even two executive managers in France will ask one another, "What's your mission?" meaning, what orders have you been given? A mid- or upper-level manager with seven years of university studies will claim to be at least somewhat powerless in virtue of the fact that she has been *missionnée*.

French business owners and shopkeepers of course find themselves in a conundrum because they can't blame a boss for making them work—and can't really pretend they didn't choose their *situation* (position), unless they inherited it, of course. But owners and shopkeepers find other ways to project the distinctly passive posture the French assume whenever they talk about work. French shop owners, for instance, are amazingly forthcoming about the various problems they have serving the public, like troubles with their suppliers. The news seller in our neighborhood was a textbook case of this. He never told us his name, despite the fact that we chatted with him almost every day of the week for a year. Instead, he complained like clockwork about problems with his distributor, and about capricious clients—all with a smile.

What the French will discuss with complete strangers is how hard work is, and what they enjoy doing when they are *not* working. The French openly embrace long lunches and long holidays—even if they can barely afford to take them—at least partly because it's a way of showing how much they dislike working. They are also comfortable talking about wanting to retire as early as possible because it emphasizes how little work interests them. Gilles Davidas, a radio director we worked with at France Culture, was sixty-four at the time. In our first meeting he told us he would be retiring right after our show went on air. But it took him a month to admit he had mixed feelings about it. Although he was retiring voluntarily, he was having second thoughts. It was obvious to us that he still felt he had a lot to offer professionally and would miss his coworkers. Still, it was fascinating to watch an effective and committed director actually avoid saying he liked his job.

The French of course love talking about holidays, but again, it's often an indirect way of showing how little they like working. The French do take a lot of holidays. To some extent, the system forces them on people. French children get two weeks off around Halloween, two more weeks at Christmas, two weeks for a midwinter "ski break," and then finally two weeks at Easter. That's a total of eight weeks of holidays *before* the summer. Out of curiosity, we added up the number of days French kids spend at school (the school year is two weeks longer) and the number of hours they spend in class, and the total worked out to be roughly the same as the time they spent at elementary school back in Montreal. The difference is just that the French organize the school year to make a lot of two-week holidays.

As if eight weeks of holidays aren't enough, in May, just when we thought we were free from school holidays, the French drain the month of work days with a suite of statutory holidays, starting—somewhat ironically—with Workers' Day (the Fête du Travail, on May 1), followed by V-day (May 8), and the Catholic Ascension Day holiday (forty days after Easter). Whenever these holidays fall on a Tuesday, Wednesday, or Thursday, the French just go ahead and *font le pont* (make the bridge)—take an extra one or two days off to make a long weekend. So the month of May ends up being a series of four-day weekends combined with three-day workweeks.

Even merchants take long holidays in France, closing shop sometimes for a month or more. In August, which the French don't call August, but just *les vacances,* even one of the hotels in our neighborhood closed for the month. All the nearby butchers closed, including one for an impressive six weeks. (It was no wonder his stuff was so expensive, we realized, we were paying for his holidays.) Stores rarely closed just for a week (why bother?). More often they closed for between two and six weeks. When you spend the summer in Paris, you essentially walk around the city reading signs in store windows to figure out where you can get a hair cut or buy a light bulb. And the signs never include the words *nous sommes désolés* (we're sorry), because of course, no one in France is going to apologize for not working.

The question, of course, is how everyone can afford to take so much time off. Holidays are considered a basic necessity, like hot water, and the French refer to their holidays as an "expense," not a "splurge." Throughout the year, as each vacation approached, we noticed parents started complaining like clockwork about how "tired" their kids were and how much they needed to "rest" (although curiously, teachers always assigned homework for the holidays). Even people who can barely afford holidays still find a way to take them. One cost-cutting technique is to squat at a parents' or in-laws' country home, or even just their regular home. It's also very common for couples to send children *chez mami et papi* (to grandma and grandpa's house) for long stretches of the summer. (We never really heard how grandparents felt about this, but it sounded like they never got much say in the matter.) And not everyone actually goes away. One of the ritual once-a-year stories in the French press is the *vacances-des-pauvres* (holidays for the poor), or *les exclus des vacances* (the holiday underclass), on how poor people manage to take holidays.[5]

But as much—or perhaps even more—than holidays and benefits, when the French talk about work, it's all about "contracts." Even street artists and buskers have job contracts in France. As we discovered, you can't work in France without one, even if you are a foreigner, and a freelancer. When we produced our radio show at France Culture, we had to sign two contracts, one about copyright, another specifically for *intermittents du spectacle* (casual entertainment workers and artists). In the latter, we agreed to make a mandatory contribution to unemployment insurance and vacation pay. That even gave us the right to strike. Among the few strikes that did take place the year we were in France, one was by the *intermittents du spectacle:* in principle, we should have been out on the streets protesting, too.

Sophie Maura, a friend who works as a labor lawyer, informed us there are no fewer than forty-eight different types of work contracts in France. They are divided into *CDI* and *CDD: CDI* stands for *contrat à durée indéterminée,* and that's a permanent job. A *CDD* is a *contrat à durée déterminée,* meaning temporary work. The *CDI* is the basic work contract, which 85 percent of French workers have: it provides remarkable protection, including mandatory compensation in case your position is eliminated (including unemployment insurance and health coverage, which go without saying).[6] Of course, not all businesses can afford to give people permanent positions, especially with all the perks this entails—not even the French government can. So the French have created a byzantine labor system that is a maze of contracts. For French workers who do not have a *CDI* (15 percent of the workforce), there are forty-seven different types of *CDD,* ranging from one-month job contracts to contracts for probation periods. The rare youngsters who do work summer jobs, for instance, sign a *CDD.* The *CDD* for employees on probation automatically becomes a *CDI* after the *CDD* has been renewed once or twice. Other *CDDs* are not renewable. The nuances of France's many *CDDs* still elude us.[7]

It's easy to see why the French are obsessed with work contracts. The first thing landlords, moneylenders, or insurance salespersons— and occasionally even people in sales—want to know from you is not just how much you earn, but what kind of work contract you have. That tells them everything they need to know about your financial security. Getting a loan without a permanent work contract is next to impossible, as is taking out a mortgage or even renting an apartment. The first time we rented in France, we had to call Jean-Benoît's father back home and ask him to sign as a guarantor, even though back in Montreal, we had already owned (and sold) our first home.

The French know perfectly well that the rigidities of their labor market, specifically the contract system, form huge obstacles to hiring. But our attempts to discuss this topic usually ran into a brick wall. When we argued that getting rid of the contract system would free the labor market, people were incredulous. Most French people simply just can't contemplate a job market without contracts. Back in 2005, then prime minister Dominique de Villepin tried to simplify the job-contract maze. The move sparked huge protests as people pointed out the obvious: without permanent job contracts, no one would be able to get insurance or sign a lease.[8] And that was the end of that.

Job contracts are also a product of the ingrained French belief that work must be rationed. The French, like all Europeans to some extent, embrace this very Malthusian idea. They know there is growth and that growth creates jobs, but they cannot help but think that there is only so much work to go around. Perhaps once you have your piece of the cake, the French think it's just better to keep the news to yourself.

To be fair, the French are also fixated on job contracts because of a legitimate fear that without them, business owners will necessarily exploit laborers. It's a mentality more suited to the era before the industrial revolution, but it's understandable. Prior to World War II, French capitalism was harsh. Much of the contract system and social protection in France was subsequently designed to protect workers from being exploited. To this day, business owners in France can show themselves to be pretty remorseless in their decision making. One of the big scandals of 2013 was the discovery that a loophole in European labor regulations allowed businesses to hire workers from other countries and avoid paying benefits. But there was an even bigger scandal behind it: among the 144,000 "foreign" workers hired in France, the second largest group were French (after Polish). French companies had somehow found a way to hire French workers outside of the country and avoid paying them benefits back in France.[9] When we arrived in France, we tried to open a bank account, but since we came from abroad and had no job contract (being self-employed), three banking institutions told us they "could not" open an account for us. Their claim was not only false. It was also illegal. We thought our problem was an isolated incident, then learned that Bank of France had intervened 51,000 times in 2013 (up 20 percent from the previous year) to force French banks to follow the law. One bank, the Société générale, had been fined \$2.5 million (2 million euros) for discrimination.[10]

By the same token, while France's social benefits system protects people from a wide range of problems and issues, it can be surprisingly harsh. The social security and retirement benefits the French collect are almost always tied to the type of job they have and depend on how many years they worked. Retirement benefits in France are universal, but not generous. For health, the state refunds a maximum of two-thirds of costs, often less, so people cannot get by without a costly private insurance scheme—1 percent of households end up paying over \$6,000 of medical expenses per year.[11] It's no wonder that French households save 16 percent of their income—three times the savings rate of the United States, according to the OECD. Given the nature of the job market, not to mention all those holidays, they need a lot of savings just to get by.

~ 16 ~

Boys and Girls

It was a miserable winter day in Paris, cold, gray, and rainy, and our bus was packed with wet passengers. The windows were so steamed up all we could see outside were shadows of multicolored umbrellas clustered around the doors. At each stop, the bus driver tried to coax passengers to the back of the bus with the same mechanical appeal: *"Avancez vers l'arrière s'il vous plaît"* (Please move to the rear of the bus). No one was listening, so the driver attempted some dry humor: "Don't worry, the people at the back of the bus won't eat you." That triggered a few smiles, but still no action, so the driver tried another tack: "It's okay to touch each other, as long as you don't have naughty thoughts." That got chuckles all the way to the back of the bus, not to mention results.

If a public employee in North America were to make a suggestive joke like that, he or she would quickly be staring at a disciplinary committee. In France, naughty little jokes are the salt of daily life. When we visited the Immigration Office to obtain work visas, the nurse who did Jean-Benoît's medical exam mistakenly checked the "female" box on his form. At the X-ray stage, Jean-Benoît mentioned the oversight to the two female technicians, who proceeded to laugh out loud. Jean-Benoît quipped, "I can prove I'm a man, you know," and one of the women shot back: "Oh, that's no proof. They make excellent implants these days." The joke had made the rounds of the office by the time we got to the front counter to pay. The clerks who handled signing visas were chuckling as they changed Jean-Benoît's official sex back to male.

One of our friends, Marie-Dominique, who regularly hosts American university students in her apartment in Paris's eighteenth arrondissement, can't believe how easily offended Americans are by jokes she makes about sex, or about relations between the sexes, and especially about women. North American–style political correctness just escapes her. But of course the French do joke about sex, and about the relations between the sexes, in ways that make North Americans shudder.

Julie visited a doctor in Paris to have some wax removed from her ear. The doctor was a trim, high-spirited man who she guessed was in his midseventies. He led her into a cramped consultation room in the back of his office, where he pulled a hand pump and basin out of a cupboard. Then, while he was filling the pump with water, he instructed Julie to remove her shirt. "This is going to be wet," he explained. Julie reeled. She'd had this procedure before, and no one ever asked her to strip half naked for it. As if to prove his point, he immediately removed his own shirt. To lighten things up, or perhaps to make fun of her prudishness, he leaned over and whispered in her ear: "We'll have to be careful not to get caught." Again, a North American doctor who casually joked about sexual scenarios with patients would be asking for trouble.

It's one of the most striking features of French conversation: they don't hold back from making jokes about sex, even in professional situations, and even when children are present. The French willingness to joke about sex in public never goes as far as discussing one's actual sex life—that topic is as private in France as it is in Anglo-American societies. And the French do have strange hang-ups when it comes to sexuality. They refer to toilets as *les garçons et les filles* (the boys' and girls' rooms), rather than *les messieurs et les dames* (gentlemen and ladies) or even *les hommes et les femmes* (men and women), as if they are trying to avoid thinking of grown-ups from the waist down. Yet the French are incredibly creative when it comes to coining new words for sex: since 1978, when the linguist Pierre Guiraud paved the way by publishing his *Dictionnaire érotique* (Erotic dictionary) that featured seven thousand words and expressions, including six hundred for the male sex, as many for the female sex, and thirteen hundred for coitus, not a year goes by in France without a new *dictionnaire coquin* (naughty dictionary).[1]

This ease in making sex jokes, even with people they hardly know, is a good gauge of French attitudes about gender relations in general. When it comes to the French and relations between the sexes, foreigners are prone to launch into superlatives, and opinions are almost always polarized. Depending on whom you ask, France is either very progressive or entirely regressive. The truth is, France is both. On the one hand, French women play an important role in politics and intellectual life. Successive French governments have put in place incredibly progressive social measures, notably to get more women into the workplace. But then the French turn around and openly express sexist ideas. They don't particularly like questioning gender stereotypes and cling to ideas that sound traditional to North Americans, like the idea that the sexes are "complementary."

In short, the French are masters of the art of uniting opposites.

In what other country but France could two liberated thirtysomething twin sisters publish a book with the title *La femme parfaite est une connasse* (The perfect woman is a stupid bitch)? This 160-page booklet, authored by thirty-three-year-old Anne-Sophie and Marie-Aldine Girard, was the surprise literary hit in France in 2013 (six hundred thousand copies sold). A humorous guidebook for the modern young French woman, it ridicules the French woman's effort to incarnate an unattainable ideal: stay thin, be superorganized, and personify the perfect hostess, all at once. In a similar spirit to the British author Helen Fielding's fictional Bridget Jones series, the French authors offer raucous advice on how to deal with being dumped, having dreadful holidays, and showing up in an unflattering photo (and even how to face the new French stigma of not being able to speak English). The book has been translated into eight languages but curiously, English wasn't one of them. In an interview, the authors commented, "English-speaking journalists are so convinced the French woman is perfect, they actually peg us as the stereotypes we are trying to defeat in our book! We're telling women to stop feeling guilty about not being perfect."

Gender relations in France are like two documentary films with two versions of the same story, playing simultaneously.

Sex and gender relations are not the same thing, but they are linked. In Anglo-American cultures, the French have the reputation of being liberal if not libertine about sex, partly because they speak more freely and often creatively. Whether they are actually more active in bed is entirely hypothetical. Consider the high-profile case of a libertine like Dominique Strauss-Kahn, the former French economy minister and the former head of the International Monetary Fund, who was accused, briefly, of the rape of a chambermaid at the Hotel Novotel in New York City and was charged with pimping in France in relation to orgies that took place in the North of France.[2] There is nothing particularly French about Strauss-Kahn's behavior. What was uniquely French was the degree to which his behavior had been hushed up by the press for most of his political career and the manner in which French intellectuals and politicians tried to excuse his behavior when he was formally accused of rape in New York City. This speaks of a double standard in law for celebrities but also of a particularly high tolerance for questionable sexual behavior.[3]

There is no question that French politicians, even at the national level, can be atrociously sexist, particularly when it concerns female opponents. Female reporters in France complained of politicians stroking their hair, telling them they were "prostitutes waiting for clients," complaining about them wearing turtlenecks instead of low-cut blouses, groping them in their offices, and worse.[4] The blatant sexism is astonishing given how widely represented women are in French politics, and in the Fench job market. Then again, North American journalists are subjected to this kind of harassment, too. The real difference in France is probably just how blatant it is.

At any rate, wherever the two societies place in the sordid ranking of sexist behavior, it's probably fair to say the state of affairs in France is not helped by the fact that there are very few taboos in talking about sex or gender relations. One reason, as the historian Theodore Zeldin argues, might be that the sexes started mingling—and conversing—in France earlier than elsewhere. In his book, *Conversation,* he argues that women and men in France engaged together in the art of conversation long before this became the norm in the United States. In Zeldin's opinion, it was this mixing of the sexes, not French men's reputed gallantry, that gave the French tongue its reputation as "the language of love." Women were also present in the workforce in France much earlier than in Britain or the United States, and in much larger numbers. So the sexes mingled outside homes.

The Quebec author Louis-Bernard Robitaille, an astute commentator on French society for the last thirty years, points out in his book *Les Parisiens* that French women have for centuries enjoyed a degree of freedom of speech, and behavior, that would have been considered provocative in American or British circles (the tourists from these countries were the first to reprehend French women's conduct). Before the mid-twentieth century, the list of outstandingly influential French women was virtually unmatched in most European societies: from the seventeenth-century trailblazers of salon culture like the marquise de Rambouillet (who founded one of the most influential early French salons) or Madame de Pompadour (mistress, but also aide and adviser to King Louis XV), or, as we have seen, Madame de Staël, to writers and creators like George Sand, Colette, Simone de Beauvoir, Marguerite Duras, Coco Chanel, and Sarah Bernhardt, not to mention Nobel Prize–winning scientist Marie Curie, who discovered radium.[5]

On the other hand, French women were slow to gain legal rights: women obtained the right to vote only in 1944, or twenty-four years after American women did. We witnessed one case of historical sexism that was almost comical in scale. In 2013, the French government finally repealed a two-hundred-year-old French law that made it illegal for women to wear pants. The law was originally passed in 1800 to prevent women from cross-dressing in order to practice a male vocation. A French senator and member of Parliament finally proposed repealing the law because it contradicted the principle of equality between men and women inscribed in the French constitution since 1946. The question was, why had it taken almost seventy years?[6]

One reason the French talk so freely about gender is that the French love of conversation generally trumps ideology. There's less taboo about expressing sexist attitudes publicly in France, even when everyone knows they are sexist—up to a point of course. The French just like to feel free to say what they think even when attitudes are outdated. In July 2014, the French government introduced a new law that would oblige employers to extend parental leave. The legislation had been a subject of debate all year. The catch was that in order for a couple to benefit from extended leave, the father had to share the *congé* (leave) and spend some time at home with the kids. The idea was popular on the whole, and the law passed despite men's hesitations.[7] But when it was announced, men reacted in a way that struck us as way too blunt. One French man told a journalist, "I'd be happy to spend more time with my kids if it didn't have negative repercussions on my career, or affect my salary."[8] That kind of public comment would get women's groups up in arms in North America, where it sounds like a declaration of male entitlement. To the French, such a remark is not necessarily viewed as sexist but realist: men who approve of the extension of parental leave to men, and who avail themselves of the benefit, could indeed see their careers stalled by other men who disapprove of it. (Just ask a woman.)

In a French study on sexism in the workplace, carried out in nine of France's largest companies among a total of fifteen thousand employees, 80 percent of women and 56 percent of men claimed to have witnessed sexism at work. Some 90 percent of female employees said it was "easier for men to pursue a career" because of sexism, and 62 percent of men agreed. Again, to the French, these men don't come across as entitled or complacent. They sound like they are telling the truth.

But the French do occasionally draw the line. During the Sochi Olympics in 2014, a duo of commentators on France Télévision, Philippe Candeloro and Nelson Monfort, commented not just on performances, but on the physical attributes of female athletes, in particular, figure skaters. They made a notoriously sexist comment about the skater Valentina Marchei: "[She] has a lot of charm, a bit like Monica Bellucci, just a little smaller in the chest, but what can you do?" They had commented on skaters' "pretty little bottoms" in the past. France's media regulatory agency, the Conseil supérieur de l'audiovisuel (French Broadcasting Authority), got hundreds of complaints about the pair during the games (many more complaints than it ever gets about English words), and they issued a warning.

Closer to home, we witnessed French people promoting women's rights and sexist attitudes at the same time. Brigitte, the divorced engineer who was our friend and neighbor, and a midlevel executive at a computer engineering firm, told us about the challenges she faces after jumping the gender barrier first into engineering, then into management in an engineering firm. "You can't give men orders. So I have to use other methods to get the message across," she explained. "Like humor." Then she explained one of her favorite techniques. "I do a helpless woman routine," she said, tossing her hair over her shoulder, rolling her eyes, and fluttering her eyelashes like a silent-movie star in distress. "It just works."

When we were exchanging notes on our perception of feminism in France, we realized something that we had never thought about before. Julie thought there were a lot of feminists in France and Jean-Benoît thought there were few. The reason was that French women declared themselves as feminists willingly to Julie, but not to Jean-Benoît.

There are a number of factors that explain why, when it comes to gender relations, the French can seem one thing and the opposite. In the first place, the French don't tend to be very ideological about the relations between the sexes. French feminists historically rejected "radical feminism." Until the 1960s, the feminist movement everywhere was mainly focused on the issue of women's rights. Then, in the middle of the 1960s, when women in most developed countries had obtained equal rights, feminism switched its focus to attacking sexism (which of course hadn't disappeared). French feminists agreed with the principle, but refused to take the approach Anglo-American feminism adopted, which to some extent meant rejecting femininity and the principle of complementarity between the genders. The famous French intellectual Élisabeth Badinter got flack from American feminists in the 1980s when she declared that women and men were "collaborators, not adversaries" in seduction, as in life.[9]

But Badinter's posture, contradictory as it might seem, is representative of how most French women think. Few French women, even feminists, see any merit, or any interest, in eschewing the accoutrements of femininity. This is pretty obvious to anyone walking around Paris, or any other French city for that matter. We were strolling in Paris's Jardins des plantes when we saw a woman in overalls and clogs walking with her daughter. We could tell from one hundred meters away she wasn't French, and sure enough, when we got close enough, we heard her American accent. One sporadically sees French women dressed for work in running shoes, but more often than not, they are wearing them because the outfit calls for them (sneakers, which the

French call *les runnings, les baskets,* or even now, *les sneakers,* were very trendy the year we were in France). On one of our first excursions in Paris's moneyed sixteenth arrondissement, we stared in amazement as a young woman pedaled by us on a Vélibre, one of Paris's rental bikes, in stiletto heels. Only two weeks after school started our daughters asked us to take them shopping for scarves. "Even men here wear pretty scarves," they reported after spotting a man in the metro in a pinstripe suit with a white cotton scarf looped elegantly around his neck. And so they do.

Generally speaking, the French also respect tradition for its own sake. In 2002, France had passed a law that would allow French parents to legally give their offspring either parent's surname, not necessarily the father's. Ten years later, 82.6 percent of children had still taken their father's name and only 8.5 percent had taken both parents' names. At the immigration office, while Jean-Benoît was busy transforming his official sex from female back to male, Julie noticed that her papers designated her as "Barlow *épouse* Nadeau" (Barlow wife Nadeau). It was strange because Julie's Canadian passport had no mention of Jean-Benoît's surname—in Quebec, women legally keep their maiden name after marriage unless they specifically ask to change it to their husband's. As we discovered, France has almost the same law: since 1794, French women's legal name is the one they had at birth; they are allowed to assume their husband's name after marriage, even if their legal name remains their maiden name. But most French people we spoke to had never heard of the law, including, strangely, the immigration office at the Paris Préfecture de police. No matter how hard Julie tried to remove the "*épouse* Nadeau" from her French visa, the clerk insisted it couldn't be done. "*C'est d'usage,*" she proclaimed. That's how it's done.

The French are not prone to talking about whether gender differences are the result of biology or social conditioning—the famous "nature versus nurture" debate. They take difference as a given; the reasons don't matter and the topic rarely comes up. In France's most conservative circles, as we saw, even questioning the principle of gender difference can become an explosive issue. In 2014, the French minister of education, Vincent Peillon, along with France's minister of women's rights, Najat Vallaud-Belkacem, launched a series of workshops in six hundred classes in ten of France's twenty-six school districts to break social stereotypes, which are very present in French society, and also to deflate gender prejudices that influence career choices down the road. The program was called the "ABCDs of Equality." The idea was to supply training, resources, and materials to primary schools to help fight prejudices and clichés, and teach children about the equality of the sexes. The work was based on academic "gender" studies that examined the question of how sexual identity is acquired.

But the use of the word "gender" was enough to push right-wing conservatives and religious groups—Catholic and Muslim alike—into the streets. Initially, a few hundred parents showed up at school and pulled their children out of school for a day. They claimed to be protesting "Gender Theory," which they claimed the government was using to "deny biological differences between the sexes," and "encourage masturbation."[10] When that argument started to run out of steam, the movement pounced on a book, reportedly endorsed and distributed by France's National Education system, called *Tous à poil!* (Everyone in the nude!). It turned out the book was not, in fact, part of any program of the National Education system, but France's Catholic Church had joined the clamor by then, and the controversy dragged on for months.

Again, it's as if there are two entirely different documentaries play-ing simultaneously everywhere in France on the place of women.

Conservative groups can actually find much to complain about in France. The French have done a lot of social engineering to offset sex-ism and its effects. For one, the French government has put in place many measures to encourage women to stay in the job market after they have kids. As in many traditional societies, French grandparents are expected to pitch in when it comes to taking care of grandchildren. So there is a nifty combination of traditional values and progressive gov-ernment measures that together make France a working mother's paradise. The state fills the gaps where grandparents are absent. France has great services for "families" that are clearly geared at keeping mothers on the job market. Children can start preschool as early as age three. Schools in France have inexpensive school cafeterias and after-school activities that can keep kids occupied until 6:00 P.M.——and the price is adjusted according to family income. Throughout the school year, which runs from September to July, French schoolchildren stop for holidays roughly every six weeks, which sounds like a nightmare to working parents who don't get the same holidays, but the whole system is remarkably well organized to provide day camp for children who don't go on their vacations in the Alps or whose parents don't have country homes.

Moreover, France's social programs and education system are struc-tured in a way that help make it possible for women to work like men. Aside from religious and national holidays, there are no surprise days off in the middle of the week, like parent-teacher conference days. During scheduled school holidays, children can go to affordable day camps in schools—and, again, the price is adjusted to income. This is very different from Germany, where school days end at noon. And French working mothers are not stigmatized the way they still are in Germany, where there's an expression for working mothers, *Rabenmutter* (literally, "mother crow," meaning uncaring, unnatural, unfeeling, or just plain bad mother).

The French government has been promoting women's rights explicitly since the 1970s, and today affirmative action is a fact of life in French politics (which of course doesn't mean that life for female politicians is necessarily easy). The first president to set the example was Valéry Giscard d'Estaing. His first prime minister, Jacques Chirac, appointed four female ministers in 1974 and two more two years later. When Chirac became president in 1995, his prime minister, Alain Juppé, appointed twelve female ministers. Since Prime Minister Lionel Jospin in 1997, gender parity among ministers has been the norm. But President François Mitterrand's government (in power from 1981 to 1995) was the first to pass antisexist laws, starting in 1983, at the initiative of Yvette Roudy, minister of women's rights, who created laws on abortion and job parity. These laws have been progressively improved over the years. In 2012, France's prime minister went as far as banning the title *Mademoiselle* (the equivalent of Miss) from all government correspondence and writing, the logic being that nothing in the male title *Monsieur* implies the married status of men. Forms have also replaced the expression *nom de jeune fille* (maiden name) with *nom de famille* (family name).

France has had laws requiring political parties to propose an equal number of male and female candidates since 2000. Loopholes have been progressively eliminated, and women now make up a quarter of all *députés* (elected representatives) and senators. In François Hollande's first government, almost half of the thirty-nine ministers were women.

Women represent only 16 percent of France's mayors but make up nearly half of city and regional councilors, which typically function as a farm to recruit candidates for the upper echelons of French politics.[11]

That's not to say the French job market is especially egalitarian. A recent study showed that half of French women work in just ten sectors, including social services, health, and education. The same study showed that women occupy 97.7 percent of the jobs in housekeeping, child care, and domestic services. In some professions, gender segregation appears to be increasing: thirty years ago, 56 percent of teachers were women. In 2014, that number had risen to 66 percent, and 82 percent in primary schools.[12] But the famous glass ceiling that prevents women from rising to top executive positions appears to be falling faster in France than in other industrialized countries: in 1960 16 percent of French executives were women. Today it's around 40 percent (compared to about 20 percent in the United States).

And some deeply ingrained traditions are ceding to the forces of change, like job titles. In classic French the proper title for either a man or a woman holding the function of minister is *le ministre,* a masculine noun, with the masculine article. *La ministre,* with the feminine article, has traditionally been the title of the *wife* of the minister. Even in the 1920s, when French women were first granted the right to graduate from high school (by taking the final *baccalauréat* exam introduced by Napoleon in 1800), the word *étudiante* denoted the *wife* of a (male) student, not a female student. The same logic has applied to *président.* Until quite recently, a female president (say, of a company, or a board) who introduced herself "*la présidente,*" with the feminine pronoun *la* and the final *e,* caused confusion because some French still assumed she was the "wife of" the president.[13]

But things are changing. The example is coming from Quebec. In the late 1970s, Quebec's government displayed strong sympathies to the feminist movement. In 1977, the government created a commission to produce feminine versions of titles. By 1979, it had come up with feminine versions of titles for some five thousand jobs, sometimes with a mere change of article (*le* or *la ministre*), sometimes by adding an *e* at the end, as in *la professeure* (the professor, the masculine version being *le professeur*). Sometimes this required more elaborate changes in suffixes, as for *le directeur,* which became *la directrice* (the director).[14] Belgium adopted this revolution wholesale in 1993, and Switzerland followed in 2002.

The French are following the example haltingly, but they are following it. The French government tried to pass similar laws to feminize titles in the 1980s but met the resistance of the ultraconservative French Academy—among others—whose members made the ludicrous claim that feminizing titles would "debase the French language," or, even more absurdly, create "segregation." But those attitudes are fading. In France today, if you say *madame la juge,* you may get corrected, but you will not be laughed at. Most newspapers and media in France use *la juge* or *la ministre,* though some do so only if the woman in question expresses the wish to (many French women avoid feminizing job titles to dispel any suspicion of benefitting from affirmative action). In 1995, Prime Minister Alain Juppé was ridiculed for agreeing to have his female ministers called *la ministre.* But the designation is now common. The French media refer to a female minister as *la ministre,* and, more and more, female members of Parliament as *la députée.*

Unfortunately, as we would see, whether it's Madame *le député* or Madame *la députée,* nothing changes the growing contempt the French public has toward politics, and specifically, its traditional political parties.

~ 17 ~

The Poetry of Politics

Julie got involved in school politics just a few weeks after our arrival when she rather naively inquired about the possibility of joining a parents' committee. Our school principal's first answer was a flat *non*. By the end of the morning, Julie understood why. Parents don't volunteer in France; they run for office.

Every fall, two French associations present parent-candidates in school elections across the country. After being directed to a parent meeting taking place at a café down the street from our school, Julie found herself running for La liste indépendante (the independent slate), which was looking for a parent available at the last minute to complete their slate of fourteen candidates. After a brief discussion, one father took a head shot of Julie, posted the list of candidates in the display cabinet on the front wall of the school, and voilà, Julie was running in a French election.

Luckily she didn't win. The day after the election a parent from the opposing party, the FCPE (Fédération des conseils de parents d'élèves), informed her that La liste indépendante was "right wing and religious," definitely not Julie's crowd.

Before learning that there are political parties, and that parents choose camps according to political ideology, the thing that amazed us most about school politics in France was the voting process itself. If anyone needed proof that the French take voting seriously, this is where it is. The school election process is governed by the French state. School votes take place simultaneously across the country. Nothing is improvised: there are voters' lists, voting booths, and real ballot boxes. Of the 600-odd parents at our school, some 188 voted, an impressive turnout in a country where beyond helping children with their homework, parents aren't supposed to stick their noses into school business.

Of course the fact that school elections actually had institutionalized, ideologically opposed parties shouldn't have surprised us. The French did invent the political "Right" and "Left," after all. The concepts arose from how members of France's National Assembly were seated at the beginning of the French Revolution—those in favor of the royal veto (the aristocracy and the clergy) sat on the right side of the king, while those who opposed it sat on the left. The cleavage became more entrenched when the Right went on to unite ultraroyalists and counterrevolutionaries, and the Left brought together revolutionaries, liberals, and those defending individual liberties.[1]

In addition to the left-right distinction, the French coined dozens of new words during the French Revolution, some of which went on to lead successful international careers in other political systems: like "revolutionary," "vandalism," and even the term "terrorism." Others, like the term Jacobinisme (from the Jacobin Club, a revolutionary movement), referring to proponents of extreme centralization, remain part of political vocabulary in France and are still commonly used even though they sprouted from a phenomenon that took place over two centuries ago. Yet whether at school, municipal, or national levels, politics is a radically different art in France, and talking about it requires mastering completely novel concepts and an entirely new class of vocabulary, much of which doesn't translate. You can't even begin to understand what's going on until you know the nomenclature.

Strangely, when it comes to devising new political terminology, the French ignore the language purism that bridles them in other areas of life (like education or publishing, as we saw). During our stay in France, French socialists were trying to cope with France's burgeoning conservative movement, which was leading the protest against same-sex marriage and assisted reproductive technology. In the process, French conservatives invented a term that became their rallying cry, *familiphobie* (family-phobia), which they used to implicitly accuse socialists of destroying family life by changing its definition. Progressive politicians, meanwhile, shot back with a new expression to discredit the influence of conservatives on the right: *la tea-partisation* (the Tea Party-ization) of French politics. While that was going on, the proponents of a growing antitax rebellion in France repopularized the medieval protest terms *jacquerie* (peasant revolt) and *fronde* (seditious revolt). And with both the French Right and Left in an identity crisis, a term coined by the late singer Serge Gainsbourg in 1977 came back into style: *aquoiboniste* (from *à quoi bon?*, what's the use?), for proponents of "what's-the-use-ism" (fatalism). It certainly captured the mood of many French the year we were there.

And then there are all the parties themselves. Under France's Fifth Republic (the name of the regime after France's constitution was rewritten in 1958), there have been 789 registered political parties so far. Even for Quebeckers, like us, accustomed to a political environment with half a dozen parties spread over two levels of government, it's hard to grasp why the French could possibly need so many political parties. Between them, France's two traditional political family trees have about five separate trunks: right, center-right, communist, socialist, and ecologist, each of which has a dozen national parties. Innumerable parties then sprout from these like different-sized branches, or sometimes just twigs, each embodying a subtle ideological distinction. Part of the plethora of parties can be explained by the fact that some exist at only one level of government, like the famous Parti Chasse, pêche, nature, et traditions (Hunting, Fishing, Nature, and Traditions Party), which won 7 percent of the vote in the European elections of 1999, and only operates at the European level. There are also a number of parties that present candidates only in France's regional elections, notably in Brittany.[2]

And if this isn't complicated enough, some political parties in France are essentially nothing more than organized followings of a single charismatic politician, who for some reason decided to stick to the same platform but gather his or her admirers under a different party banner. For instance, the only difference between the Socialist Party and the Mouvement Républicain et Citoyen (Citizen and Republican Movement) is the latter's founder, Jean-Pierre Chevènement. The same is true of the Communist Party and the Parti de gauche (Left Party), whose members are followers of Jean-Luc Mélenchon, a brilliant orator but notorious loose canon who can't seem to function inside the bounds of an established party. On the right, one can see how the strong personalization of French politics endures beyond the grave with the chronic debate over who is Gaullist (follower of General de Gaulle, who passed away nearly five decades ago) and who isn't. The cult of leadership even spawns subparties within parties. When the media speculate over whether something is Hollandais or Aubryen, they sound like they are talking about cheese or sauce (au brie, Hollandaise), but in fact they are pondering distinctions between the policies of President François Hollande and those of his socialist nemesis, Martine Aubry.

The extrapoliticized French media are the trailblazers in this endless political branding exercise. French journalists love using one popular device in particular to inject drama into political stories: they label political figures by their initials, like DSK, for Dominique Strauss-Kahn, the former socialist minister and director of the IMF. Using their initials somehow endows them with larger-than-life status, whether good or bad. During most of 2014, France's left-leaning weekly magazine *Le Nouvel Observateur* was hard at work rebaptizing France's new generation of political leaders by their initials, starting with Prime Minister Manuel Valls who became "MV," and Education Minister Najat Vallaud-Belkacem, who became "NVB."[3]

The French press also scrambles to report on the latest *petite phrase* (sound bite) from a politician's mouth, and by doing so, sanctions new expressions as mainstream political vocabulary. Politicians' crafty—or clumsy—words can keep them in the news for months. When we arrived in September 2013, political commentators were still having a ball with a blooper the former prime minister François Fillon had committed—four months earlier. Fillon was talking about the upcoming municipal elections and tweeted: "*J'appellerai à voter pour le moins sectaire des candidats*" (I'm asking voters to choose the least partisan among the candidates). The intended message was that he wasn't going to support the National Front, but the phrase was meaningless, verging on silly (it's pretty hard to imagine a nonpartisan candidate in party politics) and consequently sparked a wave of ridicule. The media continued to badger Fillon about the comment for months.

Politicians' televised New Year's wishes, *les vœux,* is another topic the media love to dwell on, often for the whole month of January. French politicians are expected to start off the year by eloquently expressing good wishes to their constituency in televised speeches. The press spends the weeks leading up to the speeches anticipating what politicians might say and editorializing about what they should say. To be fair, the speeches are substantive. President Nicolas Sarkozy told the French one year that he "understood their frustration"; François Hollande promised to "fight unemployment." But *les vœux* are above all an important ritual in French democracy. The French actually write back to politicians, even to the president himself, to tell them what they thought about their speeches and present their own *vœux.* The media then continue to dissect the speeches for a few more weeks.

One term coming out of politicians' mouths while we were in France turned out to be more serious than it initially sounded to us: *le ni-ni,* meaning "neither-nor." (The term has no relation to the English "ninny" despite the similarities.) The *ni-ni* had quite a history, we learned. It was originally an anarchist expression, taken from the title of the nineteenth-century socialist libertarian journal *Ni Dieu ni Maître* (Neither God nor Master). François Mitterrand repopularized it in the 1980s when he defined his policy as one of "neither nationalizations, nor privatizations." In the next decades, the *ni-ni* served politicians as a popular *pirouette* (clever evasive reply) to legitimize indecisiveness: it's a way of saying what you won't do by not saying what you will.

But *ni-ni* took on a whole new significance when France's National Front Party appropriated it, starting in 1995. The rapidly growing support for this party was *the* political topic during our year in France, and a baffling phenomenon, even for the French. Everybody (except those who voted for it) wondered how an extreme-right party was managing to take center stage in French politics. Part of that had to do with the *ni-ni*.

It would be a mistake to try to explain the success of the National Front as a strictly French phenomenon. France does not float in a political void. In the European elections in May 2014, extreme-right parties fared well all over Europe, from the United Kingdom to Denmark and Austria. In the U.S., the Tea Party was part of the same trend. In Europe, new political blocs and coalitions were emerging everywhere, possibly because the fear of communism no longer cemented right-leaning parties in Europe, and the rejection of capitalism was no longer binding the Left. There is no reason this wouldn't happen in France, too, all the more so since the National Front, which was founded in 1972, was a well-structured populist party well before the Berlin Wall collapsed. It's now poised to cash in on the shifting political mood across Europe.

The National Front's rise in popularity has not been steady or regular. Since its creation, and until recently, electoral results have swung between 3 percent and 15 percent of the vote. The ups and downs had a lot to do with Jean-Marie Le Pen's success, or failure, in attracting populist electors from either the Right or the Left. That was the reason he pounced on the *ni-ni* concept. Le Pen originally used it in the slogan *Ni droite, ni gauche* (Neither right, nor left), a slogan designed to convince voters the National Front was the anti-system party, fighting the established "system" of French elites and political parties. In the same vein, Le Pen coined and popularized the acronym UMPS, a clever linguistic twist that presents his principal opponents, the Gaullist, right-wing Party Union pour un movement populaire (Union for a popular movement, known by its initials, UMP), as one and the same as the PS (Parti socialiste, Socialist Party), even though they are ideological opposites. Le Pen's message was that France's traditional parties are stagnant and that only the National Front can really change anything.[4]

Since his daughter Marine Le Pen took over the party leadership in 2011, National Front scores have been steadily climbing. In 2013 and 2014, we watched two French elections: municipal elections in March and European elections in May. In both cases, the National Front scored alarmingly high, well above the 25 percent line. The French were even wondering (though not for the first time) if the party could win more than one seat in the National Assembly or maybe even the French presidency.

Part of Marine Le Pen's success owes to how she cashed in on the *ni-ni* slogan by actually adopting a centrist platform (including many features of the Socialist program). She has also worked steadily to rid the National Front of the stigmatization that long hampered its growth—her father's anti-Semitic outbursts in particular. To do that, she coined and popularized yet another new term, *dédiabolisation* (de-demonization), which essentially chastises the French for "demonizing" the far right in the past. To prove that the National Front was turning a page, Le Pen demoted her father from president to honorary chairman of the party. In 2015 she actually kicked him out of the party. The stratagem worked: Marine Le Pen has been steadily luring voters from outside the National Front's traditional far-right support base, from moderate right-wing parties, and even from the French Left. It would be an exaggeration to say that 25 percent of the French population (the National Front's current level of support) actually holds fascist-leaning, far-right beliefs. But Marine Le Pen's "far-right light" façade has been potent enough to garner support from France's lower classes, whether left or right leaning. In the fall of 2015, a survey credited her with as much as 31 precent of voter intent. During the regional elections of December 2015, the National Front won an overall 27.7 percent of the vote. In two regions, in the north and in the southeast, it got about 40 percent of the vote and was in the lead in four more regions out of a total of thirteen in continental France. The four overseas regions are definitely not leaning toward the National Front.

The fact that Marine Le Pen is rallying people who would have voted for the Communist Party fifteen years ago is one of the most fascinating and harrowing developments in French politics in years. Unfortunately, her success owes to more than clever branding. She is supplying many French with something no other party has ever dared give them. As the former prime minister Laurent Fabius (now the minister of foreign affairs under Hollande) put it in the 1980s, the National Front "asks good questions even if they yield bad answers" (*pose de bonnes questions, mais apporte de mauvaises réponses*). The "good questions" to which Fabius was referring are ones about the European Union, the euro, the economy, immigration, French identity, and, broadly speaking, the "system," or France's static political establishment. As the French writer and journalist François de Closets argued, in the old days of the National Front, Jean-Marie Le Pen made these issues taboo among France's Left just by talking about them.[5] In effect, for the last thirty years, the French Left has played Le Pen's game by leaving the field open to him—and now to his daughter—when it comes to talking about sensitive issues in the country. Laurent Fabius was harshly criticized within the Socialist Party for even broaching the topics, let alone suggesting they represented valid concerns among the French.

Though it's hardly what you would expect from a country of conversationalists who value their *liberté d'expression,* the French can be amazingly punctilious about certain issues from their past, and about the question of national identity. These two topics push the French to get as close as they ever will to being "politically correct." France's colorful record in capital punishment is a good example. Before we visited Paris's Conciergerie, the former tribunal cum prison where Marie Antoinette was imprisoned before she was guillotined in 1793, today a museum, we had heard that the actual guillotine used to kill the queen would be on display. As it turned out, the museum only had a sample guillotine blade—not even *the* blade. When we asked an employee where the actual guillotine was, he replied that French museums have not been allowed to display guillotines since 1981, the year France abolished the death penalty. We thought it odd that the French would disavow one of the key symbols of the revolution of 1789. The French state is officially secular but that has never prevented museums from displaying crucifixes or other religious symbols. Yet it turns out the French are more adamant about ignoring some aspects of their past than we had imagined. On one of the rare occasions when the guillotine was brought out of mothballs, in 2010, for an exhibition called *Crime and Punishment* at Paris's Musée d'Orsay, the museum published a disclaimer warning visitors that "certain works" in the exhibition might *heurter la sensibilité* (offend the sensitivities) of visitors.[6]

It's completely paradoxical, but in France, the world capital of conversation, the *inability* to discuss a number of politically sensitive topics is fueling the rise of the Far Right. No other political party in France will go near two issues in particular: patriotism and Europe. Much of Marine Le Pen's success comes from the fact that, where those taboos are concerned, the National Front is the only drinker at an open bar.

Though we'd seen France's Bastille Day (fourteenth of July) parade on the Champs-Élysées before, we thought it was only natural to take our daughters to see it when we were there. For the occasion, Jean-Benoît fashioned a periscope out of cardboard and mirrors so we could see over the crowds—we knew there would be a million other people in Paris trying to see the parade with us. We even carted a stepladder and a climbing stool to the parade, both useful when we found ourselves at the corner of the Champs-Élysées and avenue Montaigne, craning to see the parade from behind twenty rows of spectators. For an hour we watched as ninety planes and helicopters swept across a patch of Paris sky above our heads, and hundreds of vehicles and thousands of soldiers marched down Paris's most famous avenue. Yet one of the most striking sights of the day was the complete absence of flags. City authorities had decorated the area with red, white, and blue ribbons and *cocardes* (cockades). But there wasn't a soul in the crowds actually waving a flag. This was a sharp contrast to any parade we had seen in North America, particularly the Martin Luther King Day Parade we attended in Mesa, Arizona, in 2010, where our daughters bought their first American flags and waved them for the rest of the evening, imitating paraders. Generally speaking, the only people who dare wave flags in France are tourists or members of the Far Right (or soccer fans, but even then, it's often other countries' flags). The French do not raise flags on their front lawns. They will brag about the French republic, or more specifically about republican "values," but rarely about their country, per se. In moments of collective emotion, like sports events, they sing France's national anthem, "The Marseillaise." But a substantial part of the crowd will abstain. During the 2007 presidential elections, Socialist candidate Ségolène Royal was viewed with suspicion by many voters on the Left who did not appreciate her demonstrations of patriotism, like flag-waving and singing "The

Marseillaise" at political rallies. Five days after the *Charlie Hebdo* massacre, following a particularly moving speech by Prime Minister Manuel Valls, French members of parliament broke out into a spontaneous Marseillaise. It was the first time members of parliament sang the national anthem at the National Assembly since the armistice of 1918.[7]

Flag-waving began in earnest in January 2015 following the massacres at *Charlie Hebdo* and the Hyper Cacher grocery. It was regarded as an excusable oddity. But in the minutes that followed the news of the November 13 attacks, French citizens of all political stripes began waving the *tricolore* (nickname for France's three-colored flag) and posting it on social media. For the state funeral of the victims, President Hollande actually asked citizens to display the flag everywhere they could, to the extent that companies selling flags ran out of stock. Such flag-waving had not been seen in France since World War II, and will certainly liberate the expression of patriotism in France, which was previously limited to far-right circles.

The French allergy to expressing overt nationalist sentiment has owed mostly to France's experience during World War II, when the country was partly occupied by, and collaborated with, Nazi Germany. The French had their own fascists, and like Germany and Italy, fascism was closely linked to nationalism. At the end of the war, after France was liberated from the Germans, the French threw the nationalist baby out with the fascist bathwater and, until the terrorist attacks of 2015, most French intuitively equated displays of nationalism with fascism.

And that's where the National Front comes in. The French still love their country. But the National Front was the only political party that expressed that love openly and gave the French the opportunity to feel good about saying they love their country, too. This is one of the main keys to explaining its growing support. A party willing to ignore the taboo of nationalism appealed to many French who don't necessarily have far-right sympathies.

There is no doubt that President Hollande's willingness to use the flag as a rallying symbol was a first attempt, by the Socialists, to steal some of Marine Le Pen's thunder. And indeed, his personal popularity ratings, which had been abysmal until then, have more than doubled to reach 50 percent. In the regional elections of December 2015, which everyone had expected to be a Socialist rout, it was actually Nicolas Sarkozy's party, Les Républicains, who suffered. Hollande's Socialists made a stronger show than predicted.

Europe is the other taboo that Marine Le Pen has slyly turned to her advantage. Paradoxically, Marine Le Pen's only electoral seat for most of her political career has been as a member of the European Parliament, a strange quirk in French politics since the National Front is profoundly anti-European. But the irony doesn't seem to bother National Front supporters. The rest of France's political class, whether Right or Left—the National Front dismisses both as "the system"—has almost universally supported the creation of Europe's institutions, including the euro, which were built as a rejection of European nationalism on the whole. However, the French population's attitudes about the EU are mixed, leaning toward negative. When President Jacques Chirac held a referendum on whether to ratify the European Constitution in 2005, 55 percent of the French voted no (a ratified treaty was voted by the European Parliament in 2007).

Once again, the National Front is happy to step in as the only political party in France that dares reject the European Union outright. And as in the case of nationalism, that stance has won it support from both the Left and the Right. On the right, many French resent how the European Union has supplanted national sovereignty in areas like immigration. But even on the left, people feel that France's membership in the EU has cost it control over social and economic policies. Tough economic times usually make the French more hostile to the European Union.

A lot of Marine Le Pen's populist support comes from disenfranchised socialists and communists who feel that the traditional Left no longer promises them protection. Many of France's anti-Europe sentiment is the by-product of the political class's own cowardice. French politicians have been using the European Union as an excuse for every unpopular economic decision they've ever made in the last forty years. Even in cases where there has been a good rationale for budget cutting or eliminating programs, French politicians have tended to dump the blame on Europe. And when the investigation over the November 13 attacks in Paris showed that the attackers had used Brussels as a rear base, and that some of them were non-Europeans who had circulated freely within the European Union, Marine Le Pen simply announced, "I told you so," and let the continuing police investigation speak for her.

The National Front has also built support by capitalizing on the resentment many French feel toward Paris. Repressed defiance toward Paris and toward other elites has always simmered throughout France. As we saw earlier, France itself was built as a virtual colony of Paris. In 1983, the French state attempted to appease generalized resentment toward Paris by creating regions, a new level of local administration, but that had little effect on negative attitudes toward Paris. France's regions don't have much power—much less than a German Land or a U.S. state. And worse, whenever regions actually do question Paris's authority, political operators in Paris strike back by arguing that "doing things locally" somehow violates the principles of the French

Republic. In 2014, President François Hollande unilaterally decided to reduce the number of regions from twenty-six to seventeen without consultation. To the French population beyond the walls of Paris, this was just proof that the establishment is deaf to local sensibilities. And that, in turn, means more votes for the National Front.

The National Front is also cashing in on the growing defiance the French have toward their own elites, whether in Paris or elsewhere. Fifty years ago, when only 10 percent of the French population had more than a grade 11 education, it made sense to train political and managerial elites in special schools and grant them certain privileges in exchange for taking on the responsibility of managing France (and the elites did prove to be quite efficient). Producing this elite was the exclusive prerogative of France's famous highbrow universities, *les grandes écoles*. But things in France have changed. Today nearly 75 percent of the population has the equivalent of a grade 13 education and 42 percent of twenty-five- to thirty-four-years-olds have a university degree, 7 percentage points above the European average. High unemployment is endemic in France, around 11 percent when we were there. Together, this makes it hard to justify a two-tiered education system where the most expensive and exclusive schools are specifically designed to select and confer privileges on an elite. It's also hard to see what France still has to gain from this system. Stories of ridiculous decisions by France's elites have become a staple of the French media, as in 2014, when France's national train company ordered 341 trains for regional transport. The wagons turned out to be too wide for the railway platforms in some thirteen hundred stations outside of Paris, which consequently had to be widened by a few inches, at a total cost of 50 million euros ($65 million). Apparently no one at France's state-owned railway company thought to check with local train stations to see how wide they were, before ordering new trains. The story was actually leaked to the press when the national train company tried to get the regional governments to foot the bill. Stories like this just feed the growing dissatisfaction of the French populace with their Parisian leaders, who they regard as utterly out of touch with reality.

Education is actually part of the problem with France's leadership. When we were in France, the OECD published a study comparing the education systems of its thirty-four member countries. France did not shine particularly brightly. More important, the study pointed out that France's educational model no longer performed the role it did a century ago, which was to provide equal opportunities to all and promote the best candidates on the basis of merit alone. Instead, it was just helping the country's higher socioeconomic classes hang on to their advantages. This was eye-opening news to those French who still believe that their education system operates as a social equalizer. Anyone can see that is no longer the case. Our neighborhood in Paris, the Latin Quarter, is considered one of the most prestigious spots to live in the country (although it's not the wealthiest). Some families we knew were living in minute apartments they could barely afford just to secure a place for their offspring in one of the quarter's elementary schools, which operate as feeder schools for prestigious secondary schools, the *collèges* and *lycées*. Attending those, in turn, will help you get into a prestigious university. Everyone knows you get ahead in France by attending these schools.

In an influential study on why France's popular classes choose the National Front over the Communist or Socialist Parties (who historically defended them against the rich), the renowned French demographer Hervé Le Bras blamed France's elites for hijacking France's education system to perpetuate themselves, a syndrome that has become more pronounced over the decades, he argues. According to Le Bras, even thirty years ago, a large proportion of France's political elite came from the popular classes. Today, only half do. A high proportion of those who get elite educations—the only ticket to the high management jobs—are the children of people who already had them, the lucky ones who made the cut a generation ago.[8]

The self-perpetuating reflexes of this class are remarkable. France's elites are alarmingly conservative in their attitudes about anyone who doesn't completely fit the established pattern of a future French leader. Typically, elites qualify these people as *hors des cadres* (outside of the usual processes and frameworks), but in France this is not a compliment. France's famous pro-market think tank, the Institut Choiseul, made the news in 2014 when it published a ranking that identified the one hundred *leaders économiques de demain* (economic leaders of tomorrow). The group included many young French who were not graduates of the main *grandes écoles,* and many of them had worked, or were working, abroad. After the study was published, one of the members of the group indulged in a bit of *provoc* by creating a Facebook page characterizing the one hundred young leaders as *les Barbares* (the Barbarians). It is a great commentary on the entrenched elitist mentality that still reigns in France: the French actually call people with high potential, who think out of the box, "barbarians."[9]

Local or informal initiatives are still considered strange things in France. For that matter, the French administration has always looked at local initiatives with a suspicious eye. The celebrated French writer Alexandre Jardin also founded a movement to promote initiative among citizens, businesses, employees, and associations, which he dubbed Les Zèbres (the zebras), in reference to his most famous novel *Le Zèbre,* but also to the expression *drôle de zèbre* (oddball). Throughout the

1990s and 2000s, when the French political class discussed the role of local administrations, they characterized them as debates over *le droit à l'expérimentation* (the right to experiment), implying that the notion of giving local administrations power was, itself, risky.

Such political taboos about the nation, Europe, "the system," and individual initiatives have created a climate in France that just provides more fodder to the only political party that dares discuss them (though badly): the National Front.

Like nationalism and patriotism, another set of French taboos—religion, immigration, and national identity—are also feeding support for the Far Right, too. And once again, the main problem is that the French can't figure out how to address them directly.

~ 18 ~

Proof of Identity

When we lived in Arizona in 2010, three pieces of information seemed to define us: our name, our gender, and our race. Whether we were registering our daughters at school, signing up for an online language Meetup group, or filling out doctors' questionnaires, every form we handled asked us for our race. This always made us uncomfortable, and not just because as a family, we didn't fit a single category. We just couldn't believe how comfortable Americans were using the term "race."

It took us a while to understand what was really going on. To Americans, race is not just about skin color. "Race" evokes membership in a community. People we met in the United States reflexively referred to our daughters—born in Haiti but Canadian citizens—as "African Americans," because they saw them as members of a familiar community. Our daughters, of course, weren't part of that community, but no one knew which one they did belong to and no one seemed to be able to just call them "black" (the term was rarely used in conversation, we found). Although Canadians seldom use the word "race" in casual conversation, like Americans we organize our world into ethnic and language "communities." The fact that the actual categories are often problematic doesn't matter. The point is: North Americans see their societies as made up of "communities," not just citizens.

This North American cultural trait might never have struck us had we not lived in France. The very idea of communities is alien to the French, and if you ask them, they'll say they don't have any. Forms in France ask for name, gender, and citizenship. In France you are either a citizen or you are not. That's not to say the French have avoided categorizing people with awkward labels. While North Americans talk about language groups and ethnic communities, the French bat the term *étranger* (foreigner, the opposite of citizen) around in a way that also felt strangely casual to us. We tried not to take it personally. To the French, the idea of "belonging" has nothing to do with communities, but simply who is officially "in" and who is not.

We would never suggest France is some sort of racially blind utopia. Tensions exist between France's white, primarily Catholic majority and everyone else. But what Americans call "race" is virtually absent from France's public forums. And it's not just a question of vocabulary. Partly because of their very aversion to "communities," the French don't collect statistics on ethnicity or religion. It's a kind of willful blindness that runs very deep in French culture. One demographer Jean-Benoît interviewed told him how difficult it is for researchers to get information about ethnic origins even by questioning people directly. "Whenever we try to ask about race, people answer, 'pink,' 'vanilla,' 'tanned,' and the like. It's useless. As researchers, we can't try to study people using social categories they don't identify with."

The French, of course, think and talk about race. They just don't call it race. When the French talk informally about other people's color, or race relations in general, they use euphemisms like *les jeunes* (youth), *insécurité* (insecurity), and *les 93* (alluding to the immigrant-dominated areas in France where there were violent riots in 2005). The less principled among the French use terms like *les bronzés* (tanned people, or "darkies") but even when you hear someone refer to *les noirs* or les Blacks, it's generally a signal of racial intolerance, as it is when anyone refers to les Arabes, les Beurs, or les Rebeus ("Arabs").[1] The French simply don't have any acceptable, "official" terminology that can be used to talk about race in a neutral manner. Perhaps more significant, they don't have a positive notion like "community" that cushions the subject by making it about more than skin color.

We sometimes wondered why the French didn't simply insert the concept of communities into the political landscape. Wouldn't that allow them to lift the taboo on the term "race" and talk about it constructively? But that will never happen in France and for one simple reason: the French think communities are scary. In North American minds, communities are built, grow, and achieve things through collective effort. Which isn't to say the French don't believe communities are powerful: they know from experience that communities can tear their society apart. In French minds, communities can pit citizens against one another.

Like many things in France, the roots of that mentality go back centuries. In their history, the French have fought many wars over religion and ethnicity. The French started building their state, beginning in the seventeenth century, by actually bulldozing all the "communities" spread throughout the kingdom (the Basque, Breton, Provençal, Picard, and dozens of other populations that once populated what is France today). France only recognized these "communities" (under pressure by the European Union) in the 1960s. By then—conveniently—most of their different languages and cultures had been wiped out, so language communities no longer posed a threat to French unity. Religious communities still exist in France, but the state tolerates them. It doesn't encourage them. They are allowed to exist only if they conform to strict rules and an organizational structure dictated by the state: Protestants, Jews, and Muslims all have official spokespersons who interact with the French state. In short, religious communities are structured in a way that gives the French government the option to say *non* to them if it feels it needs to.

For the French, the notion of communities also flies in the face of a pillar of their political culture: the concept of *assimilation*. As we explained in an earlier chapter, *l'assimilation républicaine* (republican assimilation) is considered a desirable objective in France, an ideal to be attained. The assimilation credo has spawned an attitude where the French have come to feel that "blending in" is a civic duty. In France, citizens who are not white and Catholic want to be considered French first, even if they have another identity that is dear to them. It's the main reason why, as we explained in chapter 9, if you bluntly ask someone in France, "Where are you from?" the person will take it as a slight. The question insinuates that the person you are talking to is not entirely French.

French immigrants were not even allowed to create their own associations until 1981. The French feared such organization might foster *communautarisme ethnique,* ethnic communitarianism. The term does not have positive connotations as it does in English, where it refers to the idea that some collective rights have precedence over individual rights. Coined by political theorists in the 1990s, it only entered popular usage in France after the terrorist attacks on the World Trade Center. It popped up again during the 2005 rioting in Paris's suburbs. Its meaning remains negative and pejorative: in French minds, *le communautarisme* signifies deliberate attempts by ethnic or religious minorities to contravene "the principles of the Republic" by differentiating themselves, either by helping one another exclusively, or by distancing themselves from the rest of French society.[2]

Our point here is not to offer an assessment of how racist French society is, or isn't, but to show how different the terms of discussions of race are. You can't talk to the French about anything related to immigration without understanding the vocabulary the French use to discuss the issue, not to mention the reasoning behind the words.

One reason the French embrace assimilation as a value is that it has served some noble goals in the past, and arguably still does. France was a brutal colonial power in Africa, and the French have a well-deserved guilty conscience, particularly among centrists and the Left, about their participation in the slave trade and their colonial history. But the French never practiced systematic segregation, partly because of the assimilation ideal. Caribbean writers and thinkers became influential in France as early as the eighteenth century, like the composer Chevalier de Saint-Georges, and then in the nineteenth century, like the writer Alexandre Dumas (whose father was from Saint-Domingue, today's Haiti), who authored some of the most famous French novels of all time, including *The Three Musketeers* and *The Count of Monte Cristo*. (At the same time in history, the United States was fighting a civil war over slavery.) In the early twentieth century, poets like Aimé Césaire (from Martinique) and thinkers like the psychiatrist Frantz Fanon (also born in Martinique) made major contributions to Western culture. African American artists flocked to Paris in the 1920s to escape racism. A small town of the Loire valley called Sablé-sur-Sarthe elected France's first black mayor in 1929, a veterinarian named Raphaël Élizé, born in

Martinique, who remained in office until he was conscripted in 1939. (In 1940, German authorities refused to reinstate him as mayor on the basis that blacks could not be mayors. Élizé joined the resistance and died in Buchenwald in February 1945.) During the 1940s and 1950s, a number of Caribbeans and Africans became prominent members of France's National Assembly and ministers in French governments.[3]

Unfortunately, believing in assimilation itself has not allowed the French to tackle the systemic and cultural discrimination that is widespread in their country. One problem is, like nationalism, race and religion are taboos in France. Everyone is afraid of broaching the topics. This is especially true of the French Left, who would normally be sympathetic to the idea of eliminating racism. French taboos about race and religion are incredibly strong. You can end up being accused of racism for merely raising the issue of France's integration problems. The topics of identity, religion, and immigration are so stigmatized that anyone broaching them is instantly suspected of far-right sympathies. Not only socialists, but even conservative Gaullists in France tread carefully when discussing the issues, and usually start by professing their faith in the principles of the French Republic first. We even learned to do that ourselves.

The taboos about race and religion spawn some surreal exchanges in France. In the winter of 2014, Jean-Benoît was stuck covering an extremely boring visit by a prominent Canadian politician in Paris. Jean-Benoît was standing around with a pack of journalists in the interior court of Matignon Palace, the house of France's prime minister, where everyone was waiting for the guest to arrive and go through the obligatory greetings. It was freezing outside, so to pass the time, Jean-Benoît struck up a conversation with the *gendarmerie* (military police) officer who was in command of the detachment of Garde républicaine (Republican Guards) in full parade uniform for the occasion. The officer had just returned from a four-year stint in Africa and welcomed the distraction of chatting with a foreign journalist. The conversation then veered toward "France's problems," a regular subject of small talk in France. After a few minutes the officer seemed to remember he was talking to a journalist and abruptly put an end to the exchange, explaining: "I can't talk to you about France's real problems. People who do that can end up losing their jobs." The comment was strange enough on its own, but a few seconds later, things got even stranger. A French journalist whom Jean-Benoît knew personally, who had been listening in on his conversation with the *gendarme*, turned to Jean-Benoît and whispered, "He's an extreme-right racist." Jean understood that by merely alluding to the problem of integration in France, the officer made himself look morally suspicious—even before he actually uttered an opinion on the subject.

The few French officials who have tried to address the issues—or at least those who have done so in the spirit of improving things—have quickly found themselves in a political land mine. Following the *Charlie Hebdo* massacre of January 2015, the French prime minister Manuel Valls made the daring move of qualifying the immigrant ghettos around Paris as a situation of "apartheid" (the killers, born in France, were sons of Algerian immigrants). France's Left was in shock. What Valls was referring to is more the result of France's neglect and oversight than actual policy. Yet Valls was nevertheless the first politician of stature (outside of the National Front) who had dared to break the taboo about race by openly speculating about how France's failure to integrate immigrants contributed to the rise of extremism that led to the January killings.

Yet one of the most ominous developments in France today is how quickly this racial taboo is disappearing—and unfortunately, for the wrong reasons, and with the absolute worst results. Fifteen years ago it was only common to hear racist remarks in private or small groups. Now people are making racists comments, and even arguments, in public. And the racist rhetoric is not exactly coming from the fringes. It was the debate on national identity launched in 2010 by Nicolas Sarkozy that actually opened the floodgates. Sarkozy had set the bar for discussing race very low. During a visit to Dakar in 2007, he made a fifty-minute speech in which he declared that "the African man has not yet come into History." Sarkozy went on to declare that "the problem of Africa is that it lives the present with the nostalgia of the lost paradise of childhood. [. . .] In this mindset whereby everything always starts afresh, there is neither room for the human adventure nor for the idea of progress."[4]

After France's head of state set the example in racial slander, France's next government, fortunately, announced it would put a stop to it. Yet the race taboo proved to be a stubborn obstacle to the government's good intentions. In the fall of 2013, France's minister of justice, Christiane Taubira, who was born in French Guiana, stepped up to tackle the issue directly. Taubira complained publicly about the racist slander she'd encountered. In 2013, while she was traveling the country defending a new law in favor of gay marriage, protesters frequently called Taubira a gorilla, a *guenon* (female chimp), and a macaque (monkey). Yet while many members of the government expressed sympathy and support to her in private, no one stepped up to defend her in public. Taubira decided to speak out against her own government's apathy. Her outburst shocked France's political class into action and led to one former National Front candidate being sued for *injure raciste* (racist insult) for a remark made about Taubira.[5]

But as we discovered, conversations about integration and racial tensions in France can be tense even when you are talking with friends. That's because the topics are at the nexus of many other touchy issues, namely French national identity (feelings about which are not expressed easily in France, as we saw in the previous chapter), postcolonial prejudices, France's guilty postcolonial conscience, and just ordinary xenophobia. These topics, already heated ones, enter into discussions about race quickly and blur the lines of conversation to the point that it's hard to follow what people are actually talking about.

Discussions of race, of course, are touchy in any society, but the topic is even harder to tackle in France because of an interesting blindspot. First, the French can't discuss race relations with anything more than unfounded opinion, because they don't have any facts to back them up. The French constitution forbids questioning anyone on the basis of skin color or religion and forbids the state from keeping information on this matter. The motivation for this ban was noble: during World War II, the French used information collected in the country's national census to identify Jews. But seventy years later, France is struggling with the unintended consequence of a generous principle combined with a generous immigration policy (forty years ago, there were very few obstacles to gaining citizenship in France). Officials are forbidden from asking questions about race and religion, so it's impossible for anyone to factually assess any situation related to race and religion in any objective manner. More important, it's impossible for anyone to disprove the inflammatory rhetoric of the National Front Party with numbers. There are none. The National Front can—and does—say whatever it wants about immigration, and no one can prove the party wrong. What's more, the National Front knows, because of the taboo about race and immigration, that no one will ever contradict it openly anyway.

Jean-Benoît interviewed a statistician at France's Institut national de la statistique et des études économiques (National Institute of Statistics and Economic Studies) about the challenges specialists face researching the question of race in France. One way they circumvent the limitation is by asking people their country of origin or that of their parents. By doing so, French demographers have established that there are roughly 5 million *immigrés* (foreign born) in France and 6.7 million children of immigrants (half from Spain, Portugal, and Italy). That's almost 20 percent of France's population. However, researchers can only infer religion and ethnicity from a respondent's country of origin. This has obvious limitations.

French specialists have been debating the need for reliable statistics on the matter for twenty years now. The debate resurfaced in March 2015 when Prime Minister Manuel Valls openly declared that France's integration problems would not go away if the French continued to ignore them. He pointed out that the problem of sexism in France was being addressed successfully because there were statistics available that leaders could use to create policies.[6]

We were in France for a book launch in 2005 when a massive wave of riots erupted in the suburbs of Paris. To grasp what happened, it is necessary to understand that the "geography of poverty" in France is the opposite of what it is in North America. When you hear about riots in French suburbs, these are not what Americans think of as suburbs. In France, it's the cities and downtowns that are affluent and middle class. The suburbs are where the poor and disenfranchised populations live because they are cheaper. The French reaction to the 2005 riots was not to investigate the matter in depth (because they are singularly ill-equipped to do so for lack of statistical information). Instead, they invested nearly 20 billion euros in new buildings and infrastructure and in affirmative action programs for the people who lived in the suburbs, regardless of their ethnicity.[7]

Despite the taboo about race, and the lack of statistics it has engendered, the French have found ways to fight racism and facilitate integration of immigrants. Freedom of expression may be a cherished value in France, but when it is used to foment discrimination or racism, the French have shown they are willing to curb it. Six months before the events at the French magazine *Charlie Hebdo* in early January 2015, when terrorists broke in and murdered twelve people, French authorities forbade a stand-up comic, Dieudonné—a brilliant black actor whose humor stooped to anti-Semitic slander—from performing. Three days after the massacres, he was arrested again for *apologie du terrorisme* (praising terrorism). In 2014, the former National Front candidate Anne-Sophie Leclère, who had compared Minister of Justice Christiane Taubira to a monkey, was sentenced to nine months in jail and a $30,000 (22,500-euro) fine.[8] (The French state has no clear policy of affirmative action on race, but French leaders in the last decades have been deliberately promoting members of France's minorities in their own governments. The first government of Nicolas Sarkozy had a number of high-profile ministers from minorities, particularly minority women. France's socialist prime minister Manuel Valls, himself of Catalan origin, appointed six ministers from visible minorities: two Moroccan, three Caribbean, and one Korean.)[9]

When it comes to religions, foreigners and French often end up in a dialogue of the deaf because, once again, the terms of the discussion are so different. Like "communities," the French consider religion to be potentially divisive.[10] To understand what the French are saying when they talk about religion, you need to grasp the sense of a curious concept, almost untranslatable to North Americans: *laïcité* (pronounced lah-hee-see-tay). The word translates as "secularism" but *laïcité* means much more: it is a government policy that excludes religion from anything related to the state and institutions. You will never hear a French minister say, "God bless France," or "In God we trust," or see one pray in public. The concept of *laïcité* was formulated in the nineteenth century with the principal objective of fighting Catholic extremists in France who were opposed to democratic institutions. Julie interviewed a French expert on religion, the sociologist and philosopher Raphaël Liogier, about the origins of the concept of *laïcité*. As Liogier explained, the original idea was not to guarantee freedom *of* religion, but freedom *from* religion. Religion has frequently posed a threat to democracy in France. Catholic radicals continued to reject the basic principles of democracy well into the twentieth century. In 1940, they used the pretext of the lost battle against Germany to impose a fascist regime on France, the Vichy government (named after the spa town where the new capital was established).

The French consider the enforcement of *laïcité* as a perpetual struggle, and ongoing project, something like teaching French. While the principle of *laïcité* applies to all state institutions—including hospitals and even cemeteries—France's schools have always been the most sensitive arena for the struggle to enforce it. The role of schools is crucial: they have been the main battleground in favor of secularism since the French government took over education from the clergy in 1880. As Liogier explained, in the French perception, "Schools are where you create the civic values, the citizens, the political parties of tomorrow, and this had to be done completely independently of Catholicism." The view of schools as the battleground of *laïcité* explains some of the sensitivity the French have about the presence of the Islamic veil in public schools.[11] Indeed, in September 2013, the government required all secondary schools to post a new *charte de la laïcité* (statement of secularism), which, among other things, states that students are forbidden from wearing ostentatious symbols of religious affiliation, like Islamic veils.[12]

Parents at any school in France are almost certain to witness some type of squabble about the application of *laïcité* there. In our case, the squabble spiraled into outright conflict. The story began at one of the parent-teacher meetings at the beginning of the school year. When Jean-Benoît walked into the class of Monsieur Laouni a few minutes after the meeting had started, the teacher, who was born in Morocco, had already locked horns with a parent. The mother was arguing that the principle of *laïcité* should be applied to the letter. Monsieur Laouni told her that her version of *laïcité* was strictly Christian. He had a point. Among the thirteen official holidays in France, only four are not religious (Workers' Day on May 1, Victory Day on May 8, the Fourteenth of July, and the Armistice of November 11). And that's not counting the fact that the school cafeteria didn't serve meat on Fridays, in line with Catholic custom. (To the credit of the system, the cafeteria in our school was discreetly accommodating to other religions. Whenever there was pork on the menu, the school cafeteria offered halal and kosher alternatives without advertising them as such.)

Things got off to a bad start for Monsieur Laouni, who we suspect had alienated parents by inelegantly flaunting his *culture générale* (which really was vastly superior to the norm, even at our school). Whatever the initial motivation, one group of parents decided he had to go. Throughout the fall, they hovered like hawks waiting for him to make a wrong move so they could denounce him. Julie—who, after the elections, continued to attend occasional meetings of the right-wing parents' political party—heard all the complaints as they unfolded. One morning, the parents were particularly agitated: Monsieur Laouni had crossed the line. While discussing world religion with his students, he had asked if there was a Jewish student in the class who could fill him in on some Jewish customs. "*Ça ne se fait pas!*" the parents at the café shrieked. They immediately filed a complaint about him to the "Inspectrice," the education inspector who manages teachers.

With all this lofty rhetoric about *laïcité* shooting around, we were a bit taken aback when, in late November, a Christmas tree popped up inside the front door of our school. We wondered how *laïc* (secular) this five-foot-tall blinking symbol of the ultimate Christian holiday could really be? "Ah, that's different," the café parents reported. "It's cultural." Monsieur Laouni didn't buy the culture argument and decided to rub parents' noses in their own *laïcité:* he told his students not to bring him Christmas gifts, and he didn't so much as acknowledge the holiday in the weeks leading up to it. His message was clear enough to us: this is what *laïcité* looks like to a non-Catholic. (But it just stiffened the café parents' resolve. After months of accusations and counteraccusations, Monsieur Laouni finally gave in and went on sick leave, leaving the school before the end of the year.)

There are several reasons the French embrace *laïcité* so wholeheartedly, or even, as we saw, blindly. First, it doesn't really hurt the Catholic majority, or Christians at all for that matter. That's because *laïcité* was, at its origins, a gigantic political barter: the state, which is officially neutral, got the clergy out of schools but left the Christian holidays more or less intact, including pretty obscure ones like la Toussaint (All Saints' Day, November 1), The Feast of Ascension (forty days after Easter), Pentecost (fifty days after Easter), and the Assumption of Mary (August 15), all statutory holidays in France. In addition to the two weeks of holiday for Christmas and New Year's Day, kids get two weeks of holidays at Easter and All Saints' Day.

We had never heard the French talk as much about *laïcité* as they did the year we were there. That's certainly because in the twelve years between our first and second stays in France, discussions about race relations went from being mainly about skin color and ethnic origins to being about mores and religion. As Raphaël Liogier explained to Julie, and as we could see for ourselves, Catholicism is no longer the sole target of *laïcité;* Islam is, too.[13]

Broadly speaking, the global phenomenon of mounting Islamist extremism is colliding with a set of homegrown factors in France that intensify reactions to it. An estimated 7.5 percent of France's population is believed to be Muslim (though the numbers cannot be confirmed, since no one declares his or her religious affiliation in official documents). To the French, this large population raises the specter of *communautarisme,* not just because the French see communites as a threat in themselves, but because they fear Islamic groups or associations could potentially be radicalized and/or used by Islamic extremists. The result has been the growth of *islamophobie* (Islamophobia), a word that appeared in France about fifteen years ago but is now a daily topic of discussion in the French media.

Once again, France's National Front is the only political party willing to openly address the issue, so the floor is open to it to say pretty much whatever it wants, and the National Front does say terrible things. One of Marine Le Pen's most skillful political moves has been to target Islamism and Islam in France by invoking the values of the French Republic, specifically *laïcité*. As she did with Europe, and other sacred cows of France's political culture, Le Pen legitimizes prejudice by going where no other party will go, broaching political taboos they won't touch. This political exploitation of principles by a far-right party, in turn, makes it that much harder for the rest of the French to neutrally discuss either racial tensions or the integration of immigrants in France. If they bring it up, they have to talk about the National Front, too. (To steal some of Marine Le Pen's thunder, former president Nicolas Sarkozy, who has returned to politics, renamed his party Les Républicains, though by presenting his party as the unique defender of the values of the French Republic, he of course infuriated French socialists as well.)

Given all these factors, will mounting Islamophobia turn out to be insurmountable in France? Curiously, shortly after the *Charlie Hebdo* massacre of January 2015, two French sociologists, Céline Goffette and Jean-François Mignot, set out to examine just how anti-Islam the satirical magazine actually was. They reviewed 523 cover images of *Charlie Hebdo* from 2005 to 2015 and discovered that the vast majority, 336, were devoted to politics and politicians (mostly to Nicolas Sarkozy and Marine Le Pen); another 85 covers were about economics or social issues; and 42 were about sports and entertainment (the other 22 were multitargeted). Only 38 *Charlie Hebdo* covers (6 percent) actually made fun of religion, and of those, only 7 took issue with Islam. The other 21 were about Catholicism.[14]

Could the aftermath of the *Charlie Hebdo* massacre and the November 13 attacks somehow shake the French out of the current stalemate caused by the taboos around racial tensions and integration? Much in the way that the French invented *laïcité* to get themselves out of a nineteenth-century conundrum, we're certain there's a French thinker out there who is already hammering out some new words and expressions for new concepts that will help the French state overcome its present challenges.

You can always count on the French to talk their way out of things.

Epilogue

❧

Our original idea for this book was a kind of learners' guide called "How to Speak to the French in Twelve Easy Chapters." We wanted to explain how to communicate with the French in a progressive step-by-step approach, starting with "beginner" topics like *bonjour,* moving to intermediate subjects like language, and concluding with advanced themes, like politics. We decided against that when we sat down to write. We simply hadn't predicted how eye-opening it would be to spend a year watching our daughters as French school literally configured them for conversation. We were awestruck hearing the results at the end of every school day and understood how important this "formatting" is in the way the French communicate. We ended up devoting an entire chapter to it, but it informs the whole book. (There was another reason we steered away from the *faux* guidebook approach: we met fascinating people, had surprising experiences, and ended up with a lot of stories to tell.)

In the end, we divided the chapters of this book into two sections that cover roughly how the French are formatted to speak ("Form") and what they like and don't like to talk about ("Content"). At the same time, we didn't entirely dispense with our original idea. The chapters in each section still roughly progress in difficulty, from simple lessons to complex subjects.

Nor did we forget our original goal, which was to provide readers with guiding principles they could use right away to improve communications with the French. So we decided to conclude the book with a list of tips we divided into five categories: Twelve Guiding Principles of French Conversation, Dos, Don'ts, Topics You Can Discuss Anywhere in France, and Topics You Should Broach with Care.

Although we researched this book in Paris's Latin Quarter, in some ways a microcosm of French society that runs on *its* own rules, we have, to date, lived in France for four years and traveled widely throughout the country. So we are confident these rules apply pretty much everywhere in France.

Twelve Guiding Principles of French Conversation

1. The French don't communicate. They *converse*.
2. The French correct others all the time. It's normal public behavior.
3. The French say no even when they mean yes.
4. The French hate saying, "I don't know." They will do anything to avoid it.
5. The French are terrified of making mistakes—*des fautes*—and avoid looking like they've made them at all costs.
6. The French think being negative is good. It makes you sound smart.

7. If a French person talks to you, it's a sign he or she wants some kind of relationship. So talk back.

8. When the French don't want to talk to you, they don't open their mouths. So take the hint.

9. The point of talking in France is to show you are interesting, not merely to convey information.

10. The French don't look for consensus in conversation.

11. Disagreement among couples is acceptable public behavior. It's considered a sign that a relationship is strong.

12. The French are comfortable making jokes about sex, even in professional situations, even when children are listening.

Dos

- Say *bonjour* like you mean it and say it a lot. If it feels like you're saying it too much, that's just enough.

- Be provocative. It's better to say something outrageous than agree politely.

- Never take *non* for an answer. Keep talking until you get a *oui*.

Don'ts

- Don't ask for people's first names. It's invasive in France.

- Don't make jokes about yourself. In France, self-deprecating humor makes you sound stupid.

- Don't ask, "Where are you from?" It's insinuating. Ask, "What region are you from?"

Topics You Can Discuss Anywhere in France

- Language. The French love talking about words.
- Geography or history. The French are well versed in both topics.
- Food. Always easy, but better when you know a bit about French geography and history.
- Art, cinema, or literature. The French always have an opinion about culture.
- Finding deals. This is the only way the French talk about money.
- Holidays. This is how the French prove they don't like their jobs.

Topics You Should Broach with Care

- Family. It's private in France, something you only talk about with close friends.
- Work. Don't ask what someone does for a living. The French consider it either boring or nosy.
- Money. No one thinks it's interesting.
- National identity, immigration, race relations, and politics are tricky. Stick to asking questions.

On that final note, we wish you a bon voyage in the land of French conversation.

Acknowledgments

We are extremely grateful to our agent Roger Williams for going to bat for us with the idea for this book, and to Michael Flamini, our editor at St. Martin's Press, for liking the idea, and loving the final product.

During our year in France many French friends helped us by hosting us, feeding us, questioning our impressions, and sharing their reflections. Among our "old" friends, we'd like to thank: the hikers Daniel Roux, Alain and Liliane Forcade, and Jeannine Coin; Valerie Lehmann and Jean-François Nantel for hosting us in Les Vosges; Miranda de Toulouse Lautrec, who gave us food, board, and incomparable conversation at her farm in the Limousin; Mireille and Jean-Louis de Keiser who welcomed us in the Landes. We were lucky to have had warm and welcoming neighbors and, in particular, would like to thank Robert and Isabel Trésor, Julien, and Angélique for the *apéros* and many other favors. A special thanks as well to Edith Roux, a French teacher in New Jersey, for her careful read of the manuscript.

A number of professionals in diplomacy and the media gave us access to invaluable insight, including Michel Robitaille, head of the Quebec Delegation in Paris, and Norman Smith, spokesperson of the Canadian Embassy in Paris. We would like to extend special thanks to Olivier Poivre d'Arvor, executive director of France Culture; Gilles Davidas, director at France Culture; and Franck Chabasseur, director of international relations at CAVILAM-Vichy. The professional opportunities they gave us were also fantastic windows on French society.

Many parents at our daughters' school welcomed us into their homes, sharing meals, advice, and insight with us, and helping our daughters feel at home. We changed their names, as well as the teachers', to protect their privacy. We thank them all but particularly "Brigitte" for her energy, her insight, and her own special brand of nonconformism, which just warmed our hearts. We would like to thank our daughters' school friends, who were articulate, openminded, welcoming, and just lovely company for our daughters and for us—and congratulations to their parents for raising such *bien élévés* children.

And from the bottom of our hearts, we'd like to thank our friend Marie-Dominique Bédouet, her husband Carol, and their whole family for being our spiritual home base in Paris. It would not have been the same experience without their help. And of course, our friends Anne Dupont, François Digonnet, and their daughter Ambre for their spirited conversation and unconditional support.

Finally, we'd like to thank our beautiful daughters, Nathalie and Erika, for being such good sports after we ripped them from their universe and pitched them into an unknown world against their will. They allowed us to see a side of France we couldn't have glimpsed without their help, and their good-natured curiosity never ceased to amaze us.

Notes

❧

1. I Greet Therefore I Am

1: Expressions like *bon courage* (hang in there), *bonne journée* (have a good day), and *bonne soirée* (have a good evening) are actually variations on *au revoir* and serve the same phatic purpose. They're just more specific to the context.

2: Pamela Druckerman also used the expression in her book *Bringing Up Bébé*.

2. Privacy Rules

1: Simon Kuper, "When a Man Is Tired of Paris," *Financial Times,* January 25, 2013.

2: Since this book is mostly about talk, we do not dig deeply into the non-verbal. What defines these rings, as well as the acceptable behavior to enter them, varies enormously from one culture to another. In France, kissing on both cheeks is appropriate behavior for people in the social or personal sphere. For English speakers, it's an intimate gesture that provokes discomfort in the wrong context. Americans will give an affectionate bear hug to almost anyone, even virtual strangers, whereas the French find it invasive.

Even knocking at the door shows different ideas about privacy between French and North Americans. When North Americans knock at a door, they are asking permission to enter. When a French person knocks at a door, it's to announce she is coming in. Not that strangers walk into other strangers' homes in

France. But in French minds, entering someone's home is a perk you get from already having established yourself as a *connaissance* (you obviously don't need to be a friend).

3: Comparisons are tricky, but it is possible to imagine how speaking can be used to mark a distance. It's the case in American culture. Take again the subway example where strangers are pushed one against another by the crowd. When forced into intimacy, two Americans will actually talk, even joke very loudly, to signify that this forced intimacy is accidental and means nothing.

4: The French, however, did not invent the idea of specific pronouns to signify formal address. It is common in most languages. It was common even in English until the seventeenth century, when people used "thou" as a familiar greeting, and "you" for the formal form. And it's strange that people think English such a familiar tongue when, in fact, we ended up using the formal form of "you" universally.

5: Shortly after he was elected president in 1981, François Mitterand was asked by a journalist, *On se dit tu, n'est-ce pas?* ("We should address with you *tu*, shouldn't we?"). Mitterand, who was notoriously old school, replied: *Si vous voulez* ("If you want," but using *vous*).

6: France is not a place where the idea of "friendship in bulk" resonates. The notion of a Facebook friend is almost an oxymoron to the French. While it is true that Facebook is popular in France (3.6 million users) and Facebook in French uses the term *ami,* the French recognize that 99 percent of Facebook friends are merely *connaissances* or *relations*.

7: The quote is from an interview by the art critic Dora Vallier, in *Cahiers d'art,* 1954, in an article titled "Braque, la peinture et nous." The original French was: "On s'est dit avec Picasso en ces années-là des choses que personne ne dira plus, des choses que personne ne saurait plus se dire, que personne ne saurait plus comprendre . . . des choses qui seraient incompréhensibles et qui nous ont donné tant de joies. [. . .] Et cela sera fini avec nous. C'était un peu comme la cordée en montagne." The English translation is attributed to Richard Friedenthal, *Letters of the Great Artists from Ghiberti to Gainsborough* (London: Thames and Hudson, 1963).

3. Finding the Yes in *Non*

1: Quebeckers don't share this particular cultural reflex of saying *non* outright and the use of the word *si* is not common.

2: "Patrice Leconte," interview by Maryvonne Ollivry, in *Le Parisien,* April 11, 2014.

4. Schools: The Speech Factory

1: Nine-year-old children in France are also expected to do all their school-work in polished longhand, in ink. The second concern the girls' teachers raised with us (after their mother tongue) was whether they actually knew how to write in cursive. The French press regularly runs articles about the disappearance of handwriting skills in North America, where kids now learn to type at the age of five and penmanship is jettisoned. In France, handwriting is important, not merely for tradition's sake, but because it is recognized that children retain more of what they learn when they have made the effort writing it by hand. Other studies even suggest that cursive is best suited to that end. See Lorraine Millot, "Aux États-Unis, l'écriture sur la touche," *Libération,* September 24, 2013; and Maria Konnikova, "What's Lost as Handwriting Fades," *New York Times,* June 2, 2014.

2: The sixty thousand French schools managed as part of France's National Education are rigorously secular, but there are a relatively large number of private schools in France as well. The 8,800 private schools, which are mostly religious, account for less than 14 percent of all establishments, and about 17 percent of all students. Most of these private schools are Catholic, but 280 are Jewish and 20 are Muslim. But 98 percent of these are not strictly private, but *sous contrat* (under contract), meaning they are for the large part subsidized by the French government and required to meet a certain number of requirements in curriculum and training prerequisites for teachers. For more information see "Repères et références statistiques sur les enseignements, la formation et la recherche," at www.education.gouv.fr. For the breakdown of schools by religion, see "Quel avenir pour les écoles privées musulmanes en France?," published August 18, 2014, http://www.al-kanz.org/2014/08/18/ecole-privee -musulmane/.

5. The Family Factor

1: When it comes to birthrates, Europe is mostly a two-tier system: southern and eastern Europe, including Germany, have birthrates below 1.5 children per woman, and northern and western Europe have slightly higher rates, with 1.7 children per woman.

France's high birthrate is an interesting reversal. Between 1750 and 1945, population growth was actually slower than in the rest of Europe for reasons no one has ever really established. That changed starting in 1945, when the French started making babies with a vengeance, relatively speaking. It was the post–World War II baby boom, so France was not an isolated case, but the boom did last ten years longer in France than it did elsewhere. The result is that since 1945, France's population has increased from 40 to 66 million and is expected to almost double to 72 million by 2045.

It's not all because of babies: immigration and increased life expectancy have contributed to France's sustained population growth, but over the last thirty years, the birthrate has been the main factor. In fact, it was so robust that the French government decided to cut down on immigration. The cuts are often blamed on France's anti-immigrant National Front Party, but the truth is, France doesn't need immigration the same way, say, Germany does.

2: The history of this little document goes back to the Franco-Prussian War of 1870 and the Paris uprising of 1871, during which the Archives of the City of Paris were destroyed. In one day, the records of the civil status of a large segment of the population went up in smoke. It took years of painstaking work to partially reconstruct the records. So to avoid the disaster reoccurring, the French government started distributing standardized booklets of records that individual families have to keep as a backup to the official archives. In the case of a natural disaster or war, it would be relatively simple to reconstitute the État civil.

3: The custom of the family as a tax unit explains why France is one of the last countries in the developed world where employees aren't taxed at the source, with deductions made from paychecks. Instead, French employees receive full salary and have to keep reserves to pay taxes at the end of the year on their own. There is talk of changing this system and taxing at the source, but it's a challenge. For one, the way the system is set up, employers would need information about the rest of an employee's family's income.

4: Quoted by Anaïs Delbarre in *Devenir adulte en Europe,* November 7, 2013, www.nouvelle-europe.edu.

5: Interestingly, according to the *Oxford English Dictionary,* the English word "ridicule" was borrowed from the French in the eighteenth century. The French had borrowed it from the Italians two centuries before that, so there's an argument to be made that the French have just had longer to let the idea sink in.

6: Hélène Haus, "Thomas et Marie, rois des mentions," *Libération,* July 5, 2014.

7: Divorce rates in different countries are calculated differently, making it hard to compare statistics. Some countries count separation from a common law union as a divorce while others don't. These are the most reliable figures we could find.

6. The Art of Conversation

1: Our translation.

2: Our translation, from Fumaroli, ed., *L'art de la conversation.*

3: Even if the French practice their own form of political correctness, as we will see.

4: Fumaroli, ed., *L'art de la conversation.*

5: Unless otherwise indicated, all translations of Godo and Sansot are ours.

6: Salons were immensely popular throughout Europe and spurred offshoots everywhere, including in America, which got *saloons,* though the spirit was somewhat different there, not to mention the spirits.

7: Jean-Didier Wagneur, "Hydropathes et buveurs d'eau," *Libération,* March 13, 2014, quoting Anthony Glinoer and Vincent Laisney, *L'âge des cénacles, confraternities littéraires et artistiques du XIXe siècle* (Paris: Fayard, 2014).

8: Our translation.

7. *Très* Talk

1: Isabelle Hanne, " 'Le monde' perdu de Nathalie Nougayrède" (Nathalie Nougayrède loses *Le Monde*), *Libération,* May 15, 2014.

2: The French love voting and they vote more than anyone else in the world: citizens vote in the presidential, legislative, European, regional, departmental, and municipal elections. And except for the European elections, which are one round, all other elections have two rounds. That means the French vote eleven times in six elections! This excludes the senate elections. French senators are elected by an electoral college composed of elected representatives: mayors, MNAS's, and all elected councillors at the municipal, departmental, and regional levels. But even this election is done with a two-round system.

The principle for the two-round system is simple: if one candidate actually wins a majority in the first round, that candidate wins the election. Otherwise, the lowest-scoring candidates are eliminated according to a formula that varies from one election to the next. And people vote again. During the 2012 presidential elections, there were ten candidates in the first round, and the top five garnered between 28 percent and 11 percent of the vote. Only Nicolas Sarkozy and François Hollande made it to the second round, and Hollande was elected with 51.64 percent of the vote.

One effect of this system is that it makes it possible for a wide variety of parties to present candidates: in any election, electors have the choice of three to four types: left-wing parties, extreme-left parties, right-wing parties, or even far-right parties (though presently the Far Right has been united under the National Front Party). Had we been allowed to vote in the March 2014 municipal elections, we would have had the choice among the Union de gauche, Union de droite, Diverses droites, Europe-Écologie-Les Verts, Parti de gauche, and Front National, to name only the six that garnerered more than 3 percent of the vote.

This extreme spread meant that in 2002, the socialist vote was split between a number of fringe candidates, and the Socialist Party itself was eliminated from the second round—which gave the National Front leader Jean-Marie Le Pen his first serious shot in a presidential election. Fortunately, the horrified left-wing voters all rallied between the incumbent president Jacques Chirac, who won the second round by a resounding 82 percent.

The French simply cannot resist sending messages—whatever the price.

3: Quoted in Leo Damrosch, *Tocqueville's Discovery of America.*

4: Ibid.

5: "Bac 2014: Les sujets et les corrigés de philosophie," *Le Monde,* June 16, 2014.

6: The 2014 options were: Is having choices enough to make you free? (*Suffit-il d'avoir le choix pour être libre?*), why search to know one's self better? (*pourquoi chercher à se connaître soi-même?*), or discuss an excerpt from Hannah Arendt's *The Human Condition.*

7: Véronique Radier, "Écrire, c'est aussi un métier," *Le Nouvel Observateur,* October 3, 2013.

8. Food for Talk

1: Interview with Claude Fischler by Laure Noualhat, "Chacun veut se réapproprier le contenu de son assiette," *Libération,* January 4, 2014.

2: Chrine Nehring, "In Defense of the Notoriously Arrogant French Waiter," *The Wall Street Journal,* February 19, 2015.

3: Jean-Paul Frétillet, "Y a-t-il un chef en cuisine?" *Le Parisien,* April 23, 2013.

4: The study was quoted in Jacqueline de Linarès, "La folie des lunchbox: Salade et ordi," *Le Nouvel Observateur,* November 28, 2013.

5: In the 1990s, theories about the so-called French paradox ran rampant in the North American media. Nutritionists wondered whether some magical ingredient in the French diet explained why the French could eat such rich food and drink more wine than Americans, while staying thinner, living longer, and having fewer heart attacks. By the following decade, the experts had pretty much agreed on the answer, and it had nothing do with red wine or olive oil. It wasn't about *what* the French ate, but *how much* they ate.

In 2005, the American philosophy professor Paul Rozin, who studies food choice, tested portion sizes in French and American restaurants and grocery stores for a study published in *Appetite* magazine. He wandered from McDonald's outlets to Chinese restaurants with his scale and discovered that French portion sizes were consistently smaller. An individual yogurt that weighed 227 grams (8 ounces) in the United States came in a 125-gram (4.4-ounce) format in France. When the calories of a whole day of eating smaller portions were compiled, the difference wasn't enormous—roughly the equivalent of an apple a day. But an apple a day does add up to a pound of fat by the end of the year. In the United States, that single pound eventually makes its mark in national obesity statistics.

9. Know-It-Alls

1: "Le poilu, l'une des figures les plus œcuméniques du XXe siècle," interview with Nicolas Offenstadt, by Véronique Soulé, in *Libération,* January 25, 2014.

2: "Les communards ont suivi par devoir de camaraderie," interview with Robert Tombs, by Dominique Kalifa, in *Libération,* April 10, 2014.

3: Ernst and Young, *Au cœur du rayonnement et de la compétitivité de la France,* November 1, 2013.

4: BOP Consulting and Mayor of London, *World Cities Culture Report 2014.*

5: *Les mondes de Gotlib,* Musée d'art et d'histoire du judaïsme, March 12 to July 27, 2014.

10. Down by Nature

1: Read also Guillaume Duval, Sandrine Foulon, Sandra Moatti, and Laurent Jeanneau, "Cinq idées reçues sur les Français," *Alternatives économiques,* July–August 2015.

2: It's predictable for the Anglo-American press to indulge in French bashing—Francophobia has been a subgenre of English literature since 1066. Anti-French articles, whether written in 1951, 1973, 1998, or 2013, almost all say exactly the same thing, and the ones that will be written in 2029 or 2041 will probably be similar. They focus on familiar themes: "France is in decline"; "The French language is on the decline"; "France is too centralized"; or "The French resist change." In our opinion, they all display the same flawed logic and bad faith (this was the subject of our first book, *Sixty Million Frenchmen Can't Be Wrong*). On the other hand, such criticism is fair game, since the French have produced plenty of anti-British and anti-American writing themselves. For that matter, the link between foreign policy and the international content in the press is ancient and well documented. Even when printers started producing early forms of newspaper in the seventeenth century, kings granted printers charters on the condition that they write strictly about local gossip and foreign affairs.

But a large part of the negative bias in reporting on France is explained by the fact that foreign journalists get their information and opinions from the French themselves. The French are the last ones to put forward a positive assessment of their country: they tend to say France is in a crisis no matter what's actually going on. Curiously, French defeatism then begets even more French defeatism as the French turn around and mirror what has been said about them in the foreign press. In short, French bashing *à la française* gives new meaning to the expression "self-fulfilling prophecy."

3: *The Road to Recovery: Insights from an International Comparative Study of Business "Birth" and "Death" Rates,* RSM International, July 2013.

4: Suicide rates in France (15 suicides per 100,000 inhabitants) are 50 percent higher than the European average, which is just slightly higher than that of the United States. The British reduced their suicide rate from 16 to 6 per 100,000 in the last fifty years partly because they declared it a public health issue in the 1950s and developed programs to fight it. The French regarded it as a personal matter until the 1990s and are still doing very little concretely to prevent it.

5: France's self-help publishing industry dates back a century to a pharmacist named Émile Coué (1857–1926) who created a method of "autosuggestion" (akin to mind-body intervention). His goal was to help people with physical ailments and psychological problems cure themselves. The method became very popular worldwide, particularly in the United States, where it generated a whole school of positive thinking that then, in many ways, went on to conquer the world. Coué's theory fell out of favor in France after his death in 1926 when autosuggestion became identified with right-wing conservatism. Today, the Coué method is a common metaphor the French press use to disparage anything resembling optimism or boosterism.

6: Jamel Debbouze's actual words were "What really gets on my nerves in this country is that you have to sound pessimistic to come across as intelligent," in an article called "Non, la France n'est pas raciste!" (No, France isn't racist), published in *Le Parisien,* November 27, 2013.

7: Rousseau's most famous quote, "Man is born good and society corrupts him," is a summary, not his actual words. The opening words of Rousseau's *Social Contract* are: "Man is born free; and everywhere he is in chains. One thinks himself the master of others, and still remains a greater slave than they." (translation by G.D.H. Cole, 1782).

8: In "Intuitions," 1932, published posthumously in 1976 as part of *Youthful Writings.*

9: It can even be argued that pessimism is structural to French society since its political economy is largely Malthusian. Robert Malthus was a British demographer whose 1798 *Essay on the Principles of Population* theorized that crisis was a permanent feature of humanity since people fought for a limited resource called land, which did not expand at the same rate as the population. Two centuries of industrial and postindustrial growth have proved him wrong, but the French have, curiously, organized all their labor around the idea that jobs are rationed—in other words, there will never be enough. Hence their very complex labor code.

10: Systematic pessimism can be said to answer some deep psychological impulses. This idea has been demonstrated in the twentieth century with the theory of cognitive dissonance. Cognitive dissonance describes the unease a person experiences in the presence of two ideas that cannot be reconciled. Consider these two ideas: "France is the greatest country in the world" and "France is not that great." The more you believe the first idea, the stronger the dissonance—unless you react by developing an adapted discourse, like: "France was never that great anyway," which reduces the dissonance. Negativism in France fills exactly that role.

11: There are many stories in the news about France's Revenue Services cracking down on tax shelters. In a fascinating interview on such shelters, the tax specialist Paul Devaux explains that the main risk in using them lies in "attracting the attention of France's Revenue Service inspectors." See "Les conditions pour bénéficier de ces dispositifs sont souvent complexes," *Le Parisien,* November 4, 2013.

12: The famous prelude to the French Revolution, known as the episode of the *cahiers de doléances* (registers of grievances), sheds an interesting light on how negativity operates where money is concerned. The grievances were compiled over the months of March and April 1789, a few months before the French Revolution began. There were sixty thousand of them coming from as many towns and parishes, and much of their content is about the harshness of life. As Graham Robb puts it in *The Discovery of France,* they are not completely reliable because they could be used to avoid taxes in a time when people were taxed on apparent wealth. There is no doubt that harvests had been bad since 1784 and particularly bad in 1788, but the uniformity of the language in the *cahiers de doléances* also suggests a willful if not sly posture. It can be argued that this posture endures.

13: Many extreme expressions of negativism have their roots in repressed ideas, like nationalism, and their function is very similar to those of a geyser: they're like a natural steam valve. The historian and psychoanalyst Élisabeth Roudinesco, author of *La famille en désordre* (The family in disorder), argues that the very strong opposition to the same-sex marriage law in France expressed deep-seated convictions but also fear of the loss of the nation and the loss of sovereignty (mirrored by the refusal to change the parent-child relation). "There is a great fear, the fear of the future, the fear of being reduced to nothing," she said. Quoted in "Notre identité est bien triple: biologique, psychique, sociale," in *Libération,* February 10, 2014.

11. Fixation on French

1: Quebeckers have a radically different culture of the language. This is partly because of their exposure to English, but the main reason has to do with history. Two centuries ago, the vast majority of the French still did not speak French as a mother tongue but only learned it at school. This was not the case in Quebec. Quebeckers all spoke French and learned it from their families. So Quebeckers have a much older, and much less elitist, relationship with their language. Part of what makes Quebec French sound so strange to the French is not the accent, which is not particularly unusual, but the Quebec culture of language, that is, what Quebeckers consider good and bad in language. Quebeckers cultivate a strong populism and nonelitism that the French find unsettling. They do not aspire to speak as they write. Many assume these cultural traits are borrowed from the surrounding English culture. In fact, it simply comes from the fact that Quebeckers' language culture does not come exclusively from school.

2: Eric Liblot, "Guillaume Gallienne: Singulier, pluriel," *L'Express,* November 20, 2013.

3: We explain the history of purism in detail in our book *The Story of French.*

4: Contrary to the stereotype, the French norm developed mainly outside of institutions like the French Academy by a number of enterprising lexicographers, including Antoine Furetière and César Richelet. Both wrote the first true French dictionaries in the seventeenth century. In the nineteenth century, companies like Larousse were founded and became very successful businesses. Richelet, Larousse, and Littré are the equivalents of Johnson and Webster in English, and equally influential.

5: The one thing that escapes most French purists when they discuss the decadence of their language is how much it echoes the discourse on the decadence of Spanish from Hispanic purists or the decadence of English from British or American purists. And it's the same as the one held by German or Arabic purists about their own languages. In a way, its lack of originality speaks of a larger truth.

Since World War II, three things have happened to most international languages: a lot more people speak them; a lot more people are schooled in them; and a lot more people write and publish owing to new technologies based on writing. No generation has written and published more than the present one. Consequently, people now publish writing very spontaneously in a variety of registers. And the fact that these writings can reach so many people so quickly creates a natural tension between standards and actual language. How speakers of a language react to this tension varies depending on the culture of the language. There are purists in English who complain about falling standards in writing, but English has a strong culture of simplicity so purism remains marginal. Spanish speakers are more purist, but since the language has twenty-two academies, the idea that there are competing standards is a fact of life. French has the same evolution with the difference that errors are qualified as *fautes,* not to be tolerated, but since they occur nonetheless, the discourse on the decline of French is equally great. People will blame the young or foreigners, but standards change because the French are just keeping up with the times.

12. English Envy

1: We explain this at length in our book *The Story of French.*

2: The linguist Henriette Walter, in *L'aventure des mots français venus d'ailleurs,* examined the thirty-five thousand most current words in French dictionaries and found that four thousand come from other languages, including one thousand from English. There are a lot more English words being used in spoken French, but it is impossible to count them. The spoken language shifts constantly, and most borrowings in speech never make it into the dictionary.

3: The debate on anglicisms is complicated by the fact that some so-called anglicisms are not anglicisms at all. *Obsolète,* for instance, became common in French in the 1960s as a result of the influence of the English word "obsolete." But it was originally a French term, derived from Latin, which fell out of usage during the eighteenth century and was repopularized through English, but with new meaning. So how much of a borrowing is it, exactly? Since its English derivatives, "obsolescence" and "obsolescent," have Latin roots to begin with, they don't require any adaptation to be used in French.

Words that are labeled anglicisms are often the results of the normal process of the evolution of languages. The verb *réaliser* (to realize) has half a dozen definitions in French, much like in English. In fact, the English word itself and most English senses of the term come from French. But one of the meanings of *réaliser* (to understand clearly, to be fully aware) only entered the French language in 1850, under the influence of the poet Charles Baudelaire, who was translating Edgar Allan Poe. Writers adopted the new sense of the word, introduced by Baudelaire, and used it in italics for two or three generations before it was accepted in their language.

French purists often pounce on the influence of English in French word order or sentence structure, but their conclusions are often debatable. The French singer Lorie marked generations with her song called "La positive attitude" and purists claimed it violated the nature of French (the proper French would be *l'attitude positive*). In fact, there are many cases of adjectives that acquire new meaning depending on whether they are placed before or after nouns in French. For example, a *simple soldat* (a private) is not a *soldat simple* (a stupid soldier). Another case of English syntax in French is the use of the English genitive in *'s,* as in "my mother's mother." However, the only case of a Frenchified English genitive is the officially accepted *la pin's* (a pin), which was introduced in the 1990s. This constitutes absolutely faulty English (it's supposed to be plural, not possessive) and cannot be regarded as an anglicism of syntax, but rather as faux English.

4: To French-speaking Quebeckers, Madinier's assessment makes it sound like she is downplaying, or even rationalizing, the threat of English. French-speaking Quebeckers are much more adamant about protecting French from English than the French are, and with reason. The risk of French disappearing in Quebec, where 7 million French speakers are surrounded by a sea of English, is very real. To offer an illustration of how much more serious Quebeckers are about language protection: Quebec's Office of the French Language has *ten times more employees* than France's DGLFLF.

5: See the fascinating study *L'anglais hors la loi? Enquête sur les langues de recherché et d'enseignement en France,* by François Héran, in *Population et Sociétés,* INED, May 21, 2013.

6: For readers interested in the finer details of this, the French administration often requires that official documents in a foreign language be translated into French. This requirement doesn't come from the Loi Toubon, but from the 1539 Ordinance of Villers-Cotterêts, which still has the force of law in France. This edict was about the management of institutions, particularly those concerning the administration of law and justice. Two clauses state that French is the official language of French administration (as opposed to Latin, Italian, or any of the regional languages). Even if this law is nearly five centuries old, French tribunals regularly cite it in their decisions—concerning not just English but any of the two dozen national languages of the European Union.

7: The importance of the French Academy is mostly symbolic. As a matter of fact, the French Academy doesn't really "do" much at all. Its original purpose, when it was founded in 1635, was to produce a French dictionary. It is notoriously slow in doing this (the last edition appeared in 1935), and the dictionary itself is notoriously incomplete (and has been rarely used by the French public). It sells very little, and nowhere near the sales of Larousse, or the dictionary of the Spanish equivalent, the Real Academia Española in Madrid.

8: Few know that the original version of the show was not American, but Dutch, although it had an English title: *The Voice of Holland*. The Americans were the first to buy it, and called it *The Voice*.

9: In typical French negativist spirit, the symposium's title was *Quel avenir pour la langue française dans les médias audiovisuels?* (Is there a future for French in the audio-visual media?), December 9, 2013.

10: There are plenty of legitimate reasons to protect one's language, but in France, the defenders of French often weaken their arguments in two ways. First, they base many of their arguments on aesthetic judgments. They will say that English borrowings "disfigure" French. That, of course, flies in the face of the etymology of most French words, which come from foreign sources. Secondly, French defenders tend to pepper their arguments with gratuitous, chauvinistic, and sometimes quasi-racist comments that might have flown a century ago but sound ridiculous today. A typical author along this line is Alain Borer, who wrote a book titled *De quel amour blessée?*, essentially a collection of pointless aesthetic pronouncements and chauvinist clichés. The French language defenders would be better off without such bad advocates.

For that matter, discussions of language are often complicated by the fact that people confuse the science of language, that is, linguistics, with a set of values that they ascribe to a language—which is inherently political and sociological. The common assumption that English is simpler or more precise actually has nothing to do with English itself. It's about the culture that surrounds English and shaped the language. The case of English influence and anglicisms is compounded by notions of foreign policy and anti-American (or pro-American, as the case may be) feelings. Opinions about English are shaped by external values that have nothing to do with the language.

11: Many studies conclude that the French are less bilingual than other Europeans, but there's a catch. The surveys are based on voluntary declaration, and the French often claim not to speak a language when they actually do. The issue, again, is purism and their idea of language. They transpose this purism onto other languages, assuming other cultures feel the same way about their language as the French do. The result? The French won't say they speak German unless they speak *very good* German.

13. Looking Out for France

1: From the study *Enquête sur l'expatriation des Français,* by the Direction des Français à l'étranger et de l'administration consulaire, Ministère des affaires étrangères, May 2013.

2: Because of its official policy of language protection, the Quebec government puts a lot of effort into coming up with French terminology. It monitors two hundred sectors to identify new specialized terms and novel technical jargon, then defines and translates the terms if it deems this necessary. The Quebec Office for the French Language (OQLF) has created a huge online database called *Le grand dictionnaire terminologique* (The great terminological dictionary), which has millions of entries. Each year, it receives 50 million information requests. That is twenty-five times more requests than the French Academy gets—what's more, half the requests come from Europe. The University of Sherbrooke, in Quebec, spent twenty years developing an online dictionary called *Usito.* This is the first case, in the history of French, of a general standard dictionary being produced outside of France.

3: See *La visite du général De Gaulle au Québec,* directed by Jean-Claude Labrecque, 35 min., 1967.

4: See Alexandre Wolff, ed., *La langue française dans le monde 2014* (Paris: Nathan, 2014).

5: The Paris-centered worldview doesn't mean that France was closed to outsiders. It has always been an important country of immigration. Many personalities and artists that the French regard as French were foreigners. Frédéric Chopin and Marie Curie were Polish. Picasso was Spanish. Le Corbusier was Swiss. Samuel Beckett was Irish. The singer Charles Aznavour is Armenian. The actor Yves Montand was Italian. In fact, one remarkable feature of French colonialism was that the French made their colonies part of France. African leaders like Léopold Sédar Senghor of Senegal and Félix Houphouët-Boigny of Ivory Coast were part of the French government in the 1950s before they became presidents of their respective countries. For more on this, see Pascal Ory, ed., *Dictionnaire des étrangers qui ont fait la France* (Paris: Robert Laffont, 2013).

6: "Le 'J'accuse' de Finkielkraut," interview by Alexis Lacroix, in *Le Point,* March 6, 2014.

7: Read Jérôme Bodin and Pavel Govciyan, "La Francophonie, une opportunité de marché majeure," *Natixis,* September 11, 2013.

8: Pascal-Emmanuel Gobry, "Want to Know the Language of the Future? The Data Suggests It Could Be . . . French," *Forbes,* March 21, 2014.

9: This was the warning in *La Francophonie et la francophilie, moteurs de croissance durable,* a report by Jacques Attali presented to the president of the republic, August 2014.

14. Economy of Speech

1: See Christine Monin, "L'économie, nouvelle star de la télé" and "Les prévisions des télé-experts pour 2014," *Le Parisien,* January 24, 2014.

2: "L'extrême défiance de la société française," *Le Monde,* January 22, 2014.

3: Claude Bébéar and Philippe d'Ornano, "Pour un Mittelstand à la française: Favoriser la transmission des entreprises," *Le Monde,* October 8, 2013. This short but excellent article explains that where France really lags is in mid-size businesses. France has 4,600, less than half the number in Britain (10,000) and a bit more than a third of Germany's (12,500). This category mostly consists of family-run businesses. France's problem, according to the authors, is a series of regulations that complicate the transfer of family businesses.

4: *The Road to Recovery: Insights from an International Comparative Study of Business "Birth" and "Death" Rates,* RSM International, July 2013. For more on this, read the excellent "Qu'est-ce qu'un écosystème entrepreneurial?" by Nicolas Colin in *The Family,* August 31, 2015, https://medium.com/welcome-to-thefamily/qu-est-ce-qu-un-écosystème-entrepreneurial-86e7644147f3#.pz8d8krxo.

5: Daniel Schneidermann, "Le lynchage des cheminots," *Libération,* June 23, 2014; "Pourquoi les appels à la grève ne font plus recette aujourd'hui," *Le Figaro,* February 7, 2014; "Les conflits sociaux ouverts se font plus rares," interview with Dominique Simonpoli, by Christophe Alix, in *Libération,* June 16, 2014.

6: "L'extrême défiance de la société française," *Le Monde,* January 22, 2014.

7: Benoît Floc'h, "A HEC, il 'exprimait des idées de gauche,'" *Le Monde,* May 5, 2012 ; Régis Soubrouillard, "Hollande, pur produit HEC ou Sciences-Po?," *Marianne,* May 13, 2012.

8: Jonathan Bouchet-Petersen, "Hollande defend sa ligne bec et ongle," *Libération,* January 2, 2014.

9: Even the ideas that the market can be a factor of progress or that the poor can benefit from it are anathema to orthodox French socialists. See "Le marché peut être progressiste, les pauvres doivent en profiter," interview with Laurence Fontaine, by Anastasia Vécrin, in *Libération,* February 22, 2014.

10: French history is full of stories of famous people who lost everything because they conspicuously displayed their wealth, like Jacques Cœur (c. 1395–1456), a character that Jean-Benoît discovered when he visited the city of Bourges in central France. By the time he was forty-five, Jacques Cœur had founded a trade empire throughout the Mediterranean. He had twelve ships and his own silver mine to pay people in real money. He even had a Turkish bath built in his personal castle at the center of Bourges. His motto *À Vaillans coeurs riens impossible* (To a valiant heart nothing is impossible) seemed particularly apt. At forty-five, he became treasurer for King Charles VII of France. He was also a natural choice for nobles who needed to borrow money from him. But in the end, too many nobles, including the king, owed him money, and he ended up being tried under a false accusation and jailed. He did not die in jail, but as a fugitive. His ordeal was indicative of the kind of risk money entailed.

11: See interview with the tax specialist Paul Devaux, "Les conditions pour bénéficier de ces dispositifs sont souvent complexes," *Le Parisien,* November 4, 2013.

12: See Christine Kerdellant, "Mon maire, ce Ayrault?," *L'Express,* October 9, 2013.

15. Silent Labor

1: Marck Lomazzi, "Près d'un salarié sur dix déteste son job," *Le Parisien,* November 18, 2013.

2: Average usual weekly hours worked, OECD iLibrary, www.oecd-ilibrary .org/employment/data/hours-worked_lfs-hw-data-en;jsessionid=1jtbckm fchsve.x-oecd-live-01.

3: *L'effort de la collectivité nationale par niveau d'enseignement et par élève,* Observatoire des inégalités sociales, April 30, 2014.

4: See Véronique Soulié, "Les apprentis laissent béton," *Libération,* September 5, 2013.

5: See Juliette Pousson, "Les vacances prennent congé des pauvres," *Libération,* August 20, 2014.

6: Alexandre Léchenet and Jonathan Parienté, "Qui sont les salariés en France?" Le Monde.fr, December 20, 2012.

7: For a good starting list, see the Ministère du Travail, de l'Emploi, de la Formation professionnelle et du Dialogue social (Department of Work, Training, and Labor Relations), http://travail-emploi.gouv.fr/informations-pratiques,89 /les-fiches-pratiques-du-droit-du,91/contrats,109/.

8: In a very perceptive article published in the *Financial Times,* the journalist Simon Kuper remarked that "France's high unemployment is, in part, a choice. Most workers here would rather remain unsackable than countenance a looser labour market that helps young people find work. The French know there's loads wrong with France, but they have long holidays, good healthcare, early pensions, high longevity and 70 years of peace." "France—the Way the French See It," *Financial Times,* September 12, 2014.

9: Vincent Vérier, "Quand la France importe sur son sol des salariés . . . français," *Le Parisien,* December 2, 2013.

10: Bruno Mazurier, "Avoir un compte, quelle galère . . . ," *Le Parisien,* April 17, 2014.

11: "Les tarifs de santé ne sont plus maîtrisés," interview with Brigitte Daumont, by Eric Favereau, in *Libération,* March 14, 2014.

16. Boys and Girls

1: Anne-Claire Genthialon, "La langue autour du sexe," *Libération,* September 30, 2013; Vincent Montgaillard, "C'est la pro des préliminaires," *Le Parisien,* July 15, 2014.

2: Dominique Strauss-Kahn was discharged in both cases.

3: The case of the soap opera at the Élysée Palace, in December 2013, when President François Hollande was caught by paparazzi on his way to his mistress's apartment while his official spouse, Valérie Trierweiler, was at the Élysée Palace is yet another story. What really disappointed people was that he got caught.

4: See letter signed by seventeen female journalists, "Nous, femmes journalistes politiques et victimes de sexisme . . . ," *Libération*, May 4, 2015.

5: Until 2014, Marie Curie was the only woman buried in the Panthéon based on her own merit. The other two women were wives of men buried there. In 2015, two women, Resistance fighter Geneviève de Gaulle-Anthoniuz and ethnologist Germaine Tillion, entered the Panthéon.

6: "Le pantalon n'est plus interdit pour les parisiennes," *Libération,* February 4, 2013.

7: Catherine Mallaval, "Parité et égalité sur la voie de la réalité," *Libération,* July 24, 2014.

8: "Les pères pas emballés par un congé parental obligée," *Le Parisien,* September 13, 2013.

9: Jane Kramer, "Against Nature," *New Yorker,* July 25, 2011. Elisabeth Badinter has been at odds with French feminists since 2000, when Badinter took a very principled and spirited stand against *parité* (positive discrimination).

10: "Souligner ce qui construit la différence," interview with Frédérique Matonti, by Sylvain Bourmeau, in *Libération,* January 31, 2014; Alain Auffray, "L'UMP s'engouffre dans la brèche sas complexe," *Libération,* January 31, 2014; and V. M.-F., "Ce qui se passé dans 600 écoles," *Le Parisien,* January 31, 2014.

11: "La représentation des femmes à l'Assemblée et au Sénat," *Observatoire des inégalités,* Octobre 21, 2014; "La représentation des femmes en politique au niveau local," *Observatoire des inégalités,* October 21, 2014.

12: "Une répartition déséquilibrée des professions entre les hommes et les femmes," *Observatoire des inégalités,* December 11, 2014.

13: It is a strange custom, having wives take a feminized version of their husbands' titles. In France, it was traditionally assumed that if the husband became *maire* (mayor), the wife automatically became the *mairesse*. In a way, it's just recognition of her status. But of course it is an achingly outdated idea about how to balance sexism: the husband gets the title and the wife shares in name and rank, but has no de facto power.

14: Monique Biron, ed., *Au féminin, guide de féminisation des titres de fonctions et des textes* (Publications du Québec, 1991). For more up-to-date information, please refer to the Web site of the Quebec office of the French language: http://www.oqlf.gouv.qc.ca.

17. The Poetry of Politics

1: Their position was a measure of the degree of their fervor: the Far Right was the farthest to the king's right and the Far Left was farthest to his left.

2: "Les 10 grands partis politiques," *Participer à la vie démocratique,* http://democratie.cidem.org.

3: Marie Guichoux and Julie Martin, "NVB Derrière le sourire . . . L'énigme Najat Vallaud-Belkacem," *Le Nouvel Observateur,* November 6, 2014; "MV: Un entretien avec Manuel Valls," *Le Nouvel Observateur,* October 23, 2014.

4: Even though Nicolas Sarkozy rebranded the UMP as Les Républicains, in May 2015, the UMPS joke is still common among followers of the National Front.

5: "François de Closets critique le FN . . . et ceux qui ont favorisé son ascension, " interview in *L'Opinion,* March 2, 2015.

6: In fact, just locating the last guillotine in the mothballs turned out to be a saga. Pascale Mollard-Chenebois, "Robert Badinter envoie sa 'vieille ennemie,' la guillotine, au musée," *Le Point,* March 12, 2010.

7: Mark Lilla, "France on Fire," *The New York Review of Books,* March 5, 2015.

8: Hervé Le Bras, "La carte du vote FN ou la France partagée en deux," *Libération,* May 28, 2014. For more background, see Hervé Le Bras and Emmanuel Todd, *Le mystère français* (Paris: Seuil, 2013).

9: Sophie Fay. "Ces 'barbares' qui veulent débloquer la France," *Le Nouvel Observateur,* October 30, 2014.

18. Proof of Identity

1: The latter two terms, slang deformations of the word *arabe,* are controversial. *Les Beurs* (Beurette in the feminine) was used commonly thirty years ago to designate French-born children of North African descent, but it has lost favor since a lot of North Africans have come to consider themselves *berbère* (Berber, meaning indigenous North African) instead. *Rebeu,* a more recent term, is a slang version of the same idea. But today people tend to designate themselves by their original nationality: Algérien, Tunisien, Marocain (Algerian, Tunisian, Moroccan).

2: See "Le communautarisme a-t-il gagné?," an interview with the anthropologist Jean-Loup Amselle and the demographer Michèle Tribalat, in *Le Nouvel Observateur,* November 27, 2014.

3: *Le Métis de la République,* a documentary by Philippe Baron, Pois Chiche Films, 2013; and Pascal Ory, ed., *Dictionnaire des étrangers qui ont fait la France* (Paris: Robert Laffont, 2013).

4: The original quote of Sarkozy's speech in Dakar was: "L'homme africain n'est pas assez entré dans l'Histoire. [. . .] Le problème de l'Afrique, c'est qu'elle vit trop le présent dans la nostalgie du paradis perdu de l'enfance. [. . .] Dans cet imaginaire où tout recommence toujours, il n'y a de place ni pour l'aventure humaine ni pour l'idée de progress."

5: "Des inhibitions disparaissent, des digues tombent," interview in *Libération,* November 6, 2013.

6: Claire Gallen, "L'idée de statistiques ethniques resurgit contre l'apartheid' des banlieues," *Le Point,* March 12, 2015.

7: Christian Rioux, "La France toujours hantée par ses banlieues," *Le Devoir,* October 31, 2015.

8: Vivien Vergnaud, "Injure raciste contre Taubira: Une peine sévère?," le JDD.fr, July 16, 2014.

9: While it is true that the youth living in neighborhoods with large immigrant populations, particularly those with Arab names, suffer from disproportionately high unemployment, the French have their own informal custom of affirmative action. According to a number of statistics compiled by the Institut national de la statistique et des études économiques (INSEE) as well as the Ministry of the Interior, which manages immigration, France has a very high proportion of mixed marriages. While roughly 20 percent of the French are *immigrés* or children of *immigrés,* some 28 percent of unions in France are of mixed origin. For more on this, see Cedric Mathiot, "Mariages mixtes: Et si (pour une fois) Zemmour disait vrai?," *Libération,* October 16, 2014.

10: Lilla, "France on Fire."

11: The French Left was taken by surprise by the intensity of the protest against the gay-marriage law in 2013. One reason the protests were big is that pro-Catholic sentiment in France is on the rise. Specifically, a younger generation of Catholics are proving to be more outspoken than previous generations about their beliefs. This Catholic revival was bound to happen in a society where religion is excluded from public discourse. Alternate media like Facebook and Twitter also play a role in the growth of Catholicism by allowing for nonedited communication and self-published comments to proliferate. France's new class of techno-savvy Catholic youth are playing a large role in raising the profile of social conservatives in France. See Marie Lemonnier, "Un papa, une maman, un curé," *Le Nouvel Observateur,* May 2, 2013; and Estelle Gross, Audrey Salor, and Maël Thierry, "Les nouveaux croisés de l'ordre moral," *Le Nouvel Observateur,* February 13, 2014.

12: Christel Brigaudeau, "La leçon du professeur Peillon," *Le Parisien,* September 9, 2013.

13: Raphaël Liogier, "Ce populisme liquide qui se propage à tout l'échiquier politique," *Libération,* October 14, 2013; "C'est une France maurassienne, même sans le savoir," interview with Danielle Tartakowsky, by Ludovine de la Rochère, in *Libération,* February 5, 2014.

14: Jean-François Mignot and Céline Goffette, "Non, Charlie Hebdo n'est pas obsédé par l'Islam," *Le Monde,* February 25, 2015.

Bibliography

✦

This bibliography lists books. Complete references to articles appear with the notes.

André, Stéphane. *Le secret des orateurs: Politique, media et entreprises.* Issy-les-Moulineaux, France: Éditions Stratégies, 2002.

Baverez, Nicolas. *La France qui tombe.* Paris: Éditions Perrin, 2003.

Bayard, Pierre. *Comment parler des livres que l'on n'a pas lus?* Paris: Les Éditions de Minuit, 2007.

Biron, Monique, ed. *Au féminin, guide de féminisation des titres de fonctions et des textes.* Quebec: Publications du Québec, 1991.

Bloch, Marc. *Strange Defeat: A Statement of Evidence Written in 1940.* New York: W. W. Norton & Company, 1999.

BOP Consulting, ed. *World Cities Culture Report 2014.* London: Mayor of London, 2014.

Borer, Alain. *De quelle amour blessée: Réflexions sur la langue française.* Paris: Gallimard, 2014.

Braconnier, Alain. *Optimiste.* Paris: Odile Jacob, 2013.

Cotis, Jean-Philippe, ed. *France, portrait social.* Paris: Institut national de la statistique et des études économiques, 2011.

Damrosch, Leo. *Tocqueville's Discovery of America*. New York: Farrar, Straus and Giroux, 2011.

Délégation générale à la langue française et aux langues de France, preface Aurélie Filippetti. *Rapport au Parlement sur l'emploi de la langue française, 2013*. Paris: Ministre de la Culture et de la Communication, 2013.

Druckerman, Pamela. *Bringing Up Bébé: One American Mother Discovers the Wisdom of French Parenting*. New York: Penguin Press, 2012.

Dungan, Nicholas. *Companions in Competitiveness: How France and the United States Can Help Each Other Succeed in the Twenty-first Century*. Washington, D.C.: The Atlantic Council of the United States, 2014.

Fischler, Claude, ed. *Les alimentations particulières: Mangerons-nous encore ensemble demain?* Paris: Odile Jacob, 2013.

Fischler, Claude. *L'Homnivore*. Paris: Éditions Odile Jacob, 1993.

Friedenthal, Richard. *Letters of the Great Artists from Ghiberti to Gainsborough*. London: Thames and Hudson, 1963.

Fumaroli, Marc, ed. *L'art de la conversation*. Paris: Garnier, 1997.

Fumaroli, Marc. *La diplomatie de l'esprit: De Montaigne à La Fontaine*. Paris: Gallimard, 2001.

———. *Quand l'Europe parlait français*. Paris: Éditions de Fallois, 2001.

———. *Trois institutions littéraires*. Paris: Gallimard, 1994.

Girard, Anne-Sophie, and Marie-Aldine Girard. *La femme parfait est une connasse: Guide de survie pour les femmes "normales."* Paris: Éditions J'ai Lu, 2013.

Glinoer, Anthony, and Vincent Laisney. *L'âge des cenacles: Confraternités littéraires et artistiques au XIXe siècle*. Paris: Fayard, 2014.

Godo, Emmanuel. *Histoire de la conversation*. Paris: Presse Universitaires de France, 2003.

Guiliano, Mireille. *French Women Don't Get Fat*. New York: Knopf, 2004.

Hazareesingh, Sudhir. *How the French Think: An Affectionate Portrait of an Intellectual People*. New York: Basic Books, 2015.

Jacquet, Nicolas, and Guéric Jacquet. *La France qui gagne*. Paris: Odile Jacob, 2005.

Le Bras, Hervé, and Emmanuel Todd. *Le mystère français*. Paris: Seuil, 2013.

Lhermitte, André. *1er panorama des industries culturelles et créatives: Au cœur du rayonnement et de la compétitivité de la France*. Paris: Ernst and Young Advisory, 2013.

Lilla, Mark. *The Stillborn God: Religions, Politics and the Modern West*. New York: Vintage, 2008.

Ory, Pascal, ed. *Dictionnaire des étrangers qui ont fait la France*. Paris: Robert Laffont, 2013.

Peyrefitte, Alain. *La société de confiance*. Paris: Éditions Odile Jacob, 1995.

Revel, Jean-François. *L'obsession anti-américaine: Son fonctionnement, ses causes, ses consequences*. Paris: Plon, 2002.

Reynaert, François, and Vincent Brocvielle. *Le Kit du 21e siècle: Nouveau manuel de culture générale*. Paris: Éditions Jean-Claude Lattès, 2012.

Robb, Graham. *The Discovery of France: A Historical Geography from the Revolution to the First World War*. New York: W. W. Norton, 2007.

Robitaille, Louis-Bernard. *Les Parisiens sont pires que vous ne le croyez*. Paris: Denoël, 2014.

———. *Le salon des immortels: Une académie très française*. Paris: Denoël, 2002.

Roger, Philippe, and Bowman Sherry (trans). *The American Enemy: The History of French Anti-Americanism*. Chicago: University of Chicago Press, 2006.

Sansot, Pierre. *Le goût de la conversation*. Paris: Desclée de Brouwer, 2003.

Saussez, Thierry. *Les 101 mots de l'optimisme à l'usage de tous*. Paris: Archibooks et Sautereau Éditeur, 2012.

Serres, Michel. *Petite poucette*. Paris: Éditions Le Pommier, 2012.

Tavernier, Jean-Luc, ed. *Immigrés et descendants d'immigrés en France*. Paris: Institut national de la statistique et des études économiques, 2012.

De Tocqueville, Alexis. *La démocratie en Amérique*. Paris: Gallimard, 1986.

Ueltschi, Karin. *Petite histoire de la langue française: Le chagrin du cancre*. Paris: Éditions Imago, 2015.

Van de Velde, Cécile. *Devenir adulte: Sociologie comparée de la jeunesse en Europe*. Paris: Presses Universitaires de France, 2008.

Voltaire. *Candide ou l'optimisme*. Paris: Librairie générale française, 1972.

Winock, Michel. *Madame de Staël*. Paris: Fayard, 2010.

Wolff, Alexandre, ed. *La langue française dans le monde 2014*. Paris: Éditions Nathan, 2014.

Zeldin, Theodore. *Conversation: How Talk Can Change Our Lives*. Hidden Spring, 2000.

Index